THE SECOND WORLD WAR IN CARTOONS

THE SECOND WORLD WAR IN CARTOONS

TIM BENSON

FRONTLINE BOOKS

First published in Great Britain in 2025 by
Frontline Books
An imprint of Pen & Sword Books Limited
Yorkshire – Philadelphia

Copyright © Tim Benson 2025

ISBN 978 1 03610 597 6

The right of Tim Benson to be identified as
Author of this Work has been asserted by him in accordance
with the Copyright, Designs and Patents Act 1988.

A CIP catalogue record for this book is
available from the British Library.

All rights reserved. No part of this book may be reproduced, transmitted, downloaded, decompiled or reverse engineered in any form or by any means, electronic or mechanical including photocopying, recording or by any information storage and retrieval system, without permission from the Publisher in writing. No part of this book may be used or reproduced in any manner for the purpose of training artificial intelligence technologies or systems.

Typeset by Mac Style
Cover Design: Jon Wilkinson
Commissioning Editor: Rob Green

The Publisher's authorised representative in the EU for product
safety is Authorised Rep Compliance Ltd., Ground Floor,
71 Lower Baggot Street, Dublin D02 P593, Ireland.
www.arccompliance.com

For a complete list of Pen & Sword titles please contact

PEN & SWORD BOOKS LIMITED
47 Church Street, Barnsley, South Yorkshire, S70 2AS, England
E-mail: enquiries@pen-and-sword.co.uk
Website: www.pen-and-sword.co.uk
or
PEN AND SWORD BOOKS
1950 Lawrence Road, Havertown, PA 19083, USA
E-mail: uspen-and-sword@casematepublishers.com
Website: www.penandswordbooks.com

Front Cover cartoon: Cecil Orr *Daily Record* 6 September 1940
Back Cover cartoon: Antonio Arias Bernal

Contents

Introduction vii

1 The Road to War 1

2 The Phoney War 27

3 Britain's Finest Hour 57

4 The World at War 111

5 The Tide Turns 161

6 From the Normandy Beaches to Victory in Berlin 211

7 From Hot War to Cold War 255

Although this book is by no means the first cartoon history of the Second World War, the aim was to make it the most comprehensive and informative. In fact, by containing over 700 cartoons, this is by far the largest book of political cartoons ever published on any subject. Previous cartoon anthologies on the war have mainly relied on material from already published collections of cartoons rather than, as I have done here, sourced directly from war-time newspapers both in Britain and abroad. Previous anthologies have therefore tended to show the same well-known images by established names such as David Low, Sidney Strube, Leslie Illingworth and Philip Zec. This book takes a fresh approach to the subject by deliberately avoiding cartoons which have already been seen many times before. It instead focusses on cartoonists many of whom have been unfairly overlooked and whose work has not been seen since it was first published in national and provincial newspapers across war-torn Britain. During my research, and to my added delight, I have even discovered a number of provincial cartoonists who I did not know existed before embarking on this project. Where quotes are taken directly from newspapers, some spelling, grammar and place names have been left as they were printed.

Another important aspect of this book is that it attempts to tell the stories of the cartoonists and their cartoons rather than treating their work as mere illustrations for a narrative history of the war. I have attempted to draw out the news stories behind each cartoon so as to put them into historical context as well as looking at how the war impacted on the lives of these cartoonists. One of them, as we will see, paid the ultimate sacrifice when he left his drawing board to join the Royal Artillery in the battle for North Africa and as a result I have dedicated this book to him.

I wish to thank Warren Bernard and Dr Ulrich Schnakenberg for their help in researching images for this anthology and Steve Bright for colourising the Cecil Orr cartoon on the front cover.

Tim Benson, May 2025

This book is dedicated to cartoonist Percy Lees Walmsley who was killed in action on 11 May 1943 and is buried in the Enfidaville war cemetery in Tunisia.

Introduction

By the end of the First World War, political cartooning in Britain had firmly established itself in both newspapers and humorous magazines, but not in broadsheets, like *The Times* and the *Daily Telegraph*, which considered them too frivolous for a serious newspaper. From the signing of the ill-fated Versailles Treaty, the origins of the Second World War can be visually documented during the interwar period by the daily cartoons that were published in the press. The New Zealander, David Low, arrived from Australia in 1919 to join the London evening *Star*. He would transform and enhance political cartooning in Britain with his acerbic wit and uncomplicated oriental brush style that influenced not only his major rivals, but also generations of cartoonists that came after him. The other significant cartoonist in Britain at the time was the Australian Will Dyson whose graphically dramatic style and radical spirit found a huge audience at the *Daily Herald*. During the First World War, he ridiculed Kaiser Wilhelm II with great unrepentant vigour. H G Wells had observed that Dyson: "perceives in militaristic monarchy and national pride a threat to the world, to civilisation, and all that he holds dear, and straightaway he sets about to slay it with his pencil." Dyson passed away at the beginning of 1938, tragically for political caricature, missing out on the shattering global events of the following years. He was permanently replaced on the *Daily Herald* by George Whitelaw, who as we will see had a major impact on cartooning during the Second World War. According to the Conservative leaning journal *Truth* in January 1942:

> "It is a hard and thankless task to assay the relative values of contemporary cartoonists, but it may be said, without rancour, that in some quarters Low, during the war, has had to compete in popular favour with one or two strong runners-up. Mr. George Whitelaw, of the *Daily Herald*, rarely fails to ring an intellectual bell, even though, as with Low himself, his political point of view may not be very congenial."

The two most popular cartoonists of the interwar period were Sidney Strube and Percy Fearon 'Poy' who drew for the mass circulation *Daily Express* and *Daily Mail* respectively. Compared to Low and Dyson, their

"What an atmosphere"!

Cartoonists found it increasingly difficult to find anything humorous in the events taking place in Europe during the late 1930s.

15 September 1938, Harry Thackray 'Thack', *Leeds Mercury*

output was far gentler in approach, and more embedded in the traditional whimsical humour of the time. Nonetheless, they along with Low and Dyson, continued to remark on the increasing dangers from both the weakness of the League of Nations and the rise of the Dictators in Europe. Hitler and Mussolini's bellicose actions throughout the 1930s led to one diplomatic European crisis after another. Whilst grist to the mill for the serious political cartoonists, those looking for something humorous in the topical events of the times struggled to find anything inherently funny for their readers.

For example, the involvement of German and Italian forces in the Spanish Civil War and the horrors and suffering they inflicted on ordinary Spaniards caused consternation amongst cartoonists in Britain. The *Daily Worker*'s William Desmond Rowney 'Maro' was vitriolic in his cartoons of Franco and the Nationalists. As a committed Communist, he felt so strongly about the conflict that he joined the International Brigade to fight the Nationalist forces. Educated at Sandhurst, Rowney had served in the Indian Army and had held a commission during the First World War. He left England for Spain in January 1937, and was killed a month later at the Battle of Jarama on 13 February. He was one of four *Daily Worker* staff members to die fighting Fascism in Spain.

With the outbreak of war in September 1939, new artists came to swell the ranks of political cartoonists. They were now very much in fashion. Newspapers that had never carried political cartoons began to do so. For example, Philip Zec, who had been an illustrator and never drawn a political cartoon before was employed as the *Daily Mirror's* first political cartoonist. He thought they were mad to employ him, but he proved to be highly adept. Sunday newspapers such as the *Sunday Chronicle, Sunday Pictorial, Sunday Graphic* and the *Sunday Dispatch* also introduced political cartoons for the first time. Those four newspapers promoted their new cartoonists for all it was worth. With the headline 'Our New Cartoonist,' the *Sunday Pictorial* stated: "The greatest cartoonists in the land are Low and Strube. Is 'TAC' our new discovery destined to take his place among them? He Inherits the freedom of the Press; each week he will express his own views — unhampered free to draw what he thinks, whether we agree with him or not. Follow the career of this promising young man." While the competing *Sunday Pictorial* expressed the opinion that: "Our new cartoonist, Pix, gives a vigorous slant to political topics and approaches the subject with a keen sense of humour. Watch out for his amusing and pertinent drawings." In addition to these new appointments, the provincial press moved artists who had covered local and national sporting events – which had been curtailed for the duration of the war — to draw political cartoons. According to one of those affected, Harry Heap of the *Sheffield Star*:

> "As a cartoonist, who for many years has been specialising mainly on sport, the switch from sporting cartoons to the more serious stuff came so completely that I hardly noticed the change sort of like going into church single and coming out married. It took a bit of time to realise the change had taken place. Obviously, with the outbreak of war and the cessation of sporting hostilities something had to be done, if the wolf was to be kept from the door of the old homestead, hence the new departure."

GREATEST NEW CARTOONIST WAR HAS PRODUCED

No newspaper feature has caught the public imagination since the war began like the cartoons of Lees.

His brilliant political cartoons are a great SUNDAY GRAPHIC discovery.

They are sought for eagerly on Sunday mornings — they are week-end topics of conversation in households and clubs.

You must know what Lees has drawn.

Britain is talking about him!

You'll talk about him. Remember! Exclusively in the

SUNDAY GRAPHIC

Illustration for an article by Harry Heap *The Star* (Sheffield), 27 September 1939.

Alongside Heap, Arthur Potts at the *Bristol Evening World*, William Furnival of the *Lancashire Evening Post* and George Butterworth at the *Manchester Daily Dispatch* successfully transitioned from drawing sports cartoons to political ones. However, Butterworth initially found the switch a great strain. He was expected to draw six cartoons a week and occasionally one for the *Sunday Chronicle*. Coming up with the ideas was a challenge. According to Butterworth: "There are plenty of people who can draw. What a cartoonist has got to have is plenty of good ideas." Not only was there no longer employment for sports cartoonists, Leslie Illingworth, who had spent the entire 1930s working successfully as an illustrator, found that the illustration market had also dried up as publishers and advertisers cut back. Illingworth, as he had done in the 1920s for the *Western Mail*, turned to cartooning in order to find employment and also to express his antipathy towards the Nazis. With the apparent success of his work in *Punch*, Illingworth gained employment on the *Daily Mail*, taking over from Percy Fearon 'Poy' who had retired. Most cartoonists were relieved to have found employment fearing the alternative of being called up, as Heap implies here:

> "If anyone had told me a month ago that this September, I should be turning out war cartoons every day I should have said they were "crackers." Still, it just shows how even cartoonists have to adjust themselves to war conditions. Mind you, there are thousands of fellows who have had to adjust themselves to war conditions far more seriously than I have, so I'm not grumbling."

In November 1940, it was announced that cartoonists would no longer be exempt from service in the armed forces. Being over the upper age limit of 41, cartoonists such as Ellison, Furnival, Middleton, Low, Robinson, Walker, Strube and Whitelaw were all too old, in any case, to be conscripted. During the First World War, the editor of the magazine *Passing Show* had asked for an exemption for his cartoonist George Whitelaw, who was now drawing for the *Daily Herald*. Despite the editor telling the London Military Tribunal of "the importance of the cartoon in influencing neutral and other opinion," it refused the application, and Whitelaw was conscripted into the army. He ended up as a sergeant in the Tank Corps' Schools of Instruction at the Bovington Camp in Dorset. The Government did, in practise, make exceptions for cartoonists over 30 if they believed they could serve their country more effectively as a cartoonist rather than as a serviceman. Both Zec and Butterworth, for example, had applied to join the RAF but, in the event, neither served. As Zec recalled: "I was already virtually in the RAF. I'd been passed A1. I waited for my damned ticket, but it never turned up. I didn't get into the RAF. The Government decided I was more useful where I was." Newspapers, such as the *Manchester Evening News*, successfully lobbied to keep their cartoonists at their drawing board. That paper published a spirited defence which read:

> "Cartoonists are henceforth to be unreserved. Why? The number of men thus added to the armed forces will hardly muster a platoon. At the same time the cartoonist has a very vital part to play in the national

effort. No man can do more to keep us sane; no man can more swiftly and more easily create a mood or restore a sense of perspective. Dictatorship, Autocracy, and Bumbledom will flourish the more easily if the cartoonists are stifled."

Even those who regularly bought the *Manchester Evening News* were encouraged to do their bit to keep Hengest at the paper as we see from this example from the readers' page:

"If, as a result of recent modifications in reserved occupations, particularly as affecting cartoonists, your excellent paper should lose the services of Hengest, then indeed is one of the beams that strike our dreary city from the intermittent sun taken away. He ranks with Low — surely praise enough."

'I want you men to imagine the enemy are approaching in large numbers, supported by tanks, flamethrowers, paratroops, etc. etc. . . .'

A Giles cartoon based on his own experience in the Home Guard.
Reynold's News, 12 April 1942

Others like Arthur Potts and Carl Giles were medically unfit to serve. Potts was a chronic asthmatic, who suffered bouts of pneumonia during the war. In March 1940, Giles had received his call-up papers, but was found unfit for military service due to a motorbike accident in his youth where, as a result, he had lost sight in one eye and hearing in one ear. Instead, he volunteered for his local Home Guard unit where his experiences provided him with plenty of material for his cartoons during the war. Like Giles, a number of other cartoonists also joined the Home Guard. Hengest was a rifle instructor and was severely injured in a bomb incident in August 1942. After a short convalescence, he was able to return to his drawing board. J C Walker, who was based in Cardiff, was also a rifle instructor to a Home Guard battalion, which being in South Wales mainly consisted of miners and mining officials. According to Walker: "I spent many happy days in

Carl Giles in his Home Guard uniform being given a guard of honour on his wedding day.

x   THE SECOND WORLD WAR IN CARTOONS

the open air." Leslie Illingworth joined the Home Guard in 1941 and served as a night-time gunner with an anti-aircraft unit in Hyde Park. One evening, Illingworth's old school friend Glyn Daniel, then an R.A.F. Intelligence Officer who would later go on to become a Cambridge professor of Welsh archaeology and find fame on the TV programme 'Going for a Song', met up with Illingworth while on duty at his anti-aircraft unit. On one evening they met, they both looked towards the City of London and saw flames and heard the distant crunching noise of exploding German bombs. In response, Illingworth turned to Daniel and said: "They won't win, they can't win. It's all so evil and evil can't win."

Instead of the Home Guard, Butterworth, Low and Strube volunteered instead to be fire watchers. This meant patrolling the roof of their respective newspaper buildings at night to put out potential fires from incendiaries dropped by the Luftwaffe. This was a particularly dangerous occupation as both London and Manchester were then suffering heavy nightly bombing and they were equipped with only stirrup pumps and sand buckets. Strube was on watch the night Herbert Mason famously photographed St Paul's Cathedral standing majestically amid the flames, smoke and destruction. Strube was also along with Ellison an ARP Warden. This involved responsibility for enforcing the blackout and informing emergency services of any unexploded bombs landing.

Not all cartoonists avoided the call-up. Four promising talents were denied the opportunity of continuing their coverage of the war. The *Daily Worker*'s Jimmy Friell 'Gabriel' was conscripted into the army. The Communist Party offered him a safe job in a factory so he could continue at the *Daily Worker*. He refused the offer stating: "I couldn't do that. I couldn't preach bloody war and go fight and then get myself a safe job." After basic training he was posted to an anti-aircraft battery. However, he was able to continue to draw cartoons when he could for his newspaper until it was closed-down by Home Secretary Herbert Morrison between January and June 1941 for spreading 'defeatist' propaganda at a time when Russia and Germany were nominally friends. In 1944, he was appointed art editor of *Soldier* magazine and promoted to sergeant. Friell followed the British Army into Europe through Brussels to Hamburg. He was discharged on 4 January 1946 with a 'meritorious service' commendation from a Major R. Dibb:

Leslie Illingworth drew himself in his role in the Home Guard as a night-time anti-aircraft gunner.

David Low, stirrup pump in hand in his capacity as a fire-watcher.

"Friell is a cartoonist of considerable merit and a commercial artist and lay-out man of unusually high standard. He is painstaking, reliable and is the type of man who shoulders responsibility willingly. He has never let his officers or the Directorate down and should go far in civilian life."

Bill Baker 'Pix' the *Sunday Pictorial* cartoonist was also called up by the army and joined the 6th Battalion Royal West Kent Regiment. He fought in North Africa, Sicily, Italy (including Monte Cassino) and finished the war in Austria rounding up Russian Cossacks who had been fighting on the side of the Germans. The *Daily Record*'s Cecil Orr was drafted into the RAF. Orr's artistic talents were put to good use. Stationed at Hughenden Manor, Benjamin Disraeli's former home in Buckinghamshire, he drew target maps of Germany for Bomber Command. Although no longer producing political cartoons for the remainder of the war, Orr drew a children's cartoon strip which was serialised while he was in the RAF, as well as working on a mineral water advertising campaign for nearly four years. Orr often used his bayonet as a ruler, owing to lack of proper equipment. He was not the only one suffering from a lack of drawing equipment due to war shortages. According to David Low: "The supply of art materials shortened. I ran out of sable brushes until it occurred to me to make some quite good ones for myself out of my own hair, and then to draw with soft wooden toothpicks, which gave quite a good effect." Finally, Percy Walmsley 'Lees' of the *Sunday Graphic* was called up by the army and joined the Royal Artillery. Lees, who was then showing great promise as a cartoonist, was killed in action in North Africa on 11 May 1943, tragically just two days before the official surrender of all Axis forces in North Africa to the Allies.

Although George Middleton was too old to be conscripted, his son, John Derek Middleton, was a fighter pilot in the RAF. During the Battle of Britain, he was mentioned in dispatches for "gallantry and devotion to duty in the execution of air operations." However, on 19 July 1940, he was reported missing after taking on the Luftwaffe. Despite the tragic loss of his son, Middleton continued to draw his allotted cartoons that July, without any hint in them of what he must have been feeling.

In September 1944, Giles went over to France as a war correspondent with the rank of Captain, with orders to proceed by military aircraft to Brussels to represent the *Daily Express* with the 2nd Army. Just before he left, he witnessed what he thought was the "most glorious sight" of the war, that of the Allied air armada going out over East Anglia towards Arnhem as part of Operation Market Garden. He admitted at that moment to being "a jingoist." Three days later, he was in the battle itself. Giles flew to Belgium in a Dakota, his first ever flight. Once there, he noticed British soldiers grumbling more about the awful weather conditions than about the enemy itself. What he found most disconcerting about his uniform was not the itchy woollen battledress but having to wear WC in white letters on his helmet. "Can you imagine anything so daft?" he remarked. Giles complained about it to his superiors in case others got the wrong impression about what it stood for. Eventually orders came back from London that the 'W' could be removed. "After that", said Giles, "I was required to go round just wearing the letter 'C'. Daft buggers!" Within days of arriving, Giles was driven to the front line near Eindhoven. There he witnessed the fighting for the first time. "The noise was unbelievable," he recalled. "Shattering. At first all you wanted to do was dodge in and out of doorways, like in the Blitz but a bloody sight worse. Bullets seemed to be coming from every direction, which I suppose they were. The last thing that came naturally to mind was to set up an easel, get out the pencils and start drawing amusing cartoons." During the weeks and months that followed, Giles did come up with 'amusing' cartoons that entertained the readers of the *Daily* and *Sunday Express*. In addition, he came up with a new stock of characters for his cartoons after the war, the 'Giles family': "I first conceived the idea and main character when I was a war correspondent, actually, and the whole thing just ballooned from there."

In the Second World War, as in the First, cartoons were important propaganda tools, helping newspapers to keep morale high and remind readers of the principles for which Britain was fighting. In May 1940, the social research organisation Mass Observation found that "almost everybody reads newspapers." At the start of the war, in September 1939, eighty per cent of British families read one of the mass circulation dailies, the *Daily*

Mail, Daily Mirror, Daily Express, News Chronicle or *Daily Herald*, all of which now carried a daily political cartoon. Despite a lot of wishful thinking and their upbeat message, the cartoonists were not able to conceal the long litany of Allied military disasters that dogged the early part of the war. However, they did at least help to underplay or minimise them. According to Lord Lloyd, who became Leader of the House of Lords under Churchill, stated in January 1940:

> "As a nation, we British have always taken a particular delight in the modern art of caricature. We realise it has antiseptic properties, and we applaud it as an effective elimination of humbug."

All cartoonists set out to make it clear that the war was not only an existential threat to democracy but also to the British way of life. "The political cartoonist," Sidney Strube wrote "is a powerful weapon for good or evil and in a righteous cause should be used like a giant." At the same time, cartoonists used ridicule to render the enemy less terrifying. Hitler, Mussolini, Goebbels, Goering, Himmler and later the Japanese Emperor Hirohito and his Prime Minister, Tojo, were the butts of constant jokes and all made to seem absurd, childish and irrational. Winston Churchill, by contrast, who became Prime Minister in May 1940 after the resignation of Neville Chamberlain, was depicted as the epitome of the stoic, never-say-die bulldog spirit that was going to pull Britain through. His magnificent oratory as well as his visual armoury — the cigar, the V-sign, the siren suit, the bow tie — were godsends to cartoonists. Thomas Challen 'Tac', for one, thought although Churchill's predecessor Neville Chamberlain and his Foreign Secretary "good to draw," they lacked the "inspirational qualities" of the new Prime Minister:

Winston Churchill by George Whitelaw, *Daily Herald*, 13 August 1938.

> "Mr Chamberlain, whose aquiline features in photographs might have earned him the title of the Avenging Eagle, is belied by his features. He falls Into lines strongly marked, but sad. Though easily drawn, he Is a static, one-pose man. Lord Halifax, has also only one appearance, but a highly picturesque one. He is the foreigner's ideal, of the horse-faced Englishman come to life."

Interestingly the *Ugandan Herald* picked up on the fact that the cartoonists had for some reason ignored or not noticed Churchill's constant use of his walking stick compared to always highlighting his cigar, hats and V-sign:

> "Mr. Chamberlain's umbrella proved a godsend to the cartoonists. Mr. Churchill is even more devoted to his walking stick than his predecessor was to the famous gamp, but the Prime Minister's foibles which have been caricatured the most are 'his taste in hats and his fondness of cigars. Newspaper photographs of Mr. Churchill invariably show him carrying a cane; and it is nearly always the same one. For most occasions he has used none other since his wedding, when it was given to him by King Edward VII."

Political cartoons proved so popular during the war that exhibitions of the original artwork were regularly organised around the country. One of the first was in 1940 by the Polish cartoonist Arthur Szyk on the subject of Nazi cruelty and barbarity in recently conquered Poland entitled 'War and Kultur in Poland.' It was held at the

Fine Art Society's Galleries in London and then travelled to other regions of the country where long queues preceded to form everywhere it went. Szyk went to the United States that year, where he became famous for his illustrated front covers for *Colliers Magazine*. What followed the Szyk exhibit were numerous other travelling exhibitions, which according to the *Liverpool Evening Express* were of "the finest war cartoons" by the likes of Low, Strube, Illingworth and others. An exhibition consisting of much of this material was later sent over to America where it opened at the American-British art centre in New York. The social cartoonist Leslie Grimes, of the London evening *Star*, had an exhibition on the subject of the Home Guard in Central London. According to the *Westminster & Pimlico News*, "The functions and duties of the Intelligence Section were explained as far as security would allow by Lieutenant G. N. T. Wilson, Intelligence Officer." Early in November 1939, Grimes, whose sketches with the RAF in France were the first to appear in any newspaper, had had the experience of being arrested as a suspected spy. According to Grimes:

Leslie Grimes, *The Star*, 2 December 1939.

"Perhaps there was every reason for it. After all, I was in civilian dress in this land of uniforms, and I was standing on a bomb dump making detail sketches. I don't like to be caught out in my sketches with incorrect detail, and l had been collecting "background," as I call it, to be used as reference. We were in a grim, benighted spot the tall Angus and l. Angus was the Conducting Officer, without one of whom no war correspondent may view the war. Then, out of the wintry trees stepped a Corporal, hand on revolver. Behind him a hairy, tin-hatted sentry, with fixed bayonet. The Corporal asked, "who are you?" in tones that didn't mean "maybe." I explained that I was here in France to make sketches of the R.A.F. at war. None of our talk affected the Corporal, He had been told to look out for spies landing behind the line by parachute, and I looked a likely customer. Had I a permit? I'd show him. His hand kept going to his revolver, so I got him to hold my sketch book while l looked for my permit. And, of course, I hadn't got it with me! So we marched in close formation to the guard post, while I searched every pocket over and over again."

Stalin gave a collection of original cartoons by Boris Efimov, his favourite cartoonist and the Kukryniksy trio to Lord Beaverbrook, when he visited the Soviet Premier in Moscow in September 1941. When he arrived back in Britain, Beaverbrook passed them on to the Ministry of Information, who used them in a travelling exhibition for Aid to Russia week. The show mainly dealt with scenes from the Eastern front. From Belfast to Bristol the exhibition attracted huge crowds. In July 1943, a selling exhibition of original cartoons, caricatures and drawings by Vicky, opened at the Modern Art Gallery in Mayfair, London. All proceeds from the exhibition were donated to the Stalingrad Hospital Fund at Vicky's request. Provincial cartoonists also got in on the

An exhibition in London of Vicky's original war-time cartoons from the *News Chronicle*.

act. The *Manchester Evening News* put on an exhibition of Hengest's original cartoons and sold them for one guinea each in aid of the Lord Mayor of Manchester's Aircraft fund. Meanwhile, Middleton, whose work was published across the Midlands as well as the North of England, helped to stimulate interest in Warship Week by contributing cartoons from the *Yorkshire Observer* to a naval exhibition at Brighouse.

The Ministry of Information and other war-time Ministries found cartoons particularly useful as propaganda tools especially for the purpose of getting campaigns on behalf of the government across to the public. They employed numerous cartoonists who took time out from their normal activities to produce what became iconic posters for the home front. In December 1942 the then Minister of Food, Lord Woolton, enlisted the support of the country's leading cartoonists in both official Ministry projects and through unofficial help in their cartoons to encourage the public to eat more potatoes and to discourage food wastage. Woolton felt that the public was either going to laugh or to cry about food rationing, and that it was better for them that they should laugh — even if it was only a somewhat wry smile — that that they should contemplate too much on the misery of the

Philip Zec's iconic 'Come into the Factories' poster.

position. Philip Zec, recalled half-jokingly that Woolton "wanted us to do cartoons to help save food, to stop people wasting food and to somehow popularise the idea that it was surprising what you could do with an old boot lace and a leather-soled shoe and still make a meal for the kids out of it." A few months after his meeting with the cartoonists, Lord Woolton wrote to Strube conveying his delight with their efforts: "I must let you know how delighted I am

Minister of Food, Lord Woolton, meets the cartoonists.

Introduction xv

with the result of the meeting we had about the Potato Campaign." As well as illustrating posters, political cartoons were also used on propaganda leaflets and booklets which were dropped by the RAF over Germany and occupied Europe.

British cartoonists prided themselves on their sense of humour and made much of the belief that the Axis powers were singularly lacking in an ability to laugh at themselves. Renowned actor Sir Seymour Hicks said of Hitler in a radio broadcast: "This poor man is deficient in the greatest essential needed to achieve victory — a sense of humour. This he can neither manufacture nor buy." In fact, Hitler's inability to understand British humour, led him to actually instruct his propaganda Minister, Josef Goebbels, and his psychiatrists to study Bruce Bairnsfather's famous First World War cartoon of two British soldiers standing in a shell-hole with one saying to the other: "If you know a better 'Ole, go to it" to find out what made the British laugh. Having analysed the cartoon, as it turned out incorrectly, Goebbels told Hitler they had discovered what made them laugh. "The soldier is standing in a big shell-hole," he said, "and what he means is that this is a German shell-hole and that we make the biggest shell-holes in the world." So, neither Hitler nor the Nazis were closer to understanding the British sense of humour. As Strube emphasises:

Bruce Bairnsfather's famous First World War 'better 'ole' cartoon.

> "Neither could they understand our humour. As they goose-stepped along to their downfall, we in this country laughed our way through our difficulties. During these long years of tragedy, juggling with forms and coupons, standing in queues and stumbling in the blackout, humour has been a great relief. What an opportunity Goebbels missed if only he had persuaded Hitler to write and ask for a Low, people would have said, Why, this man Hitler has a sense of humour after all — he can't be so bad! But the Nazis couldn't laugh at themselves."

Many journalists noted that, unlike the British, German cartoonists were instructed by Goebbels not to be amusing but nasty and vengeful. According to one correspondent on the *Sunday Mirror*: "Goebbels encourages anti-British cartoons. They need not be witty or clever. Few Germans have a sense of humour, in any case. To be successful, the Nazi propaganda cartoon must be crudely bitter and vindictive, showing Britain in the worst possible light. For instance, one highly popular cartoon I've seen showed a fat and bloated John Bull sitting on a miniature figure representing India. "This is Britain's humane way of administering colonies," said the caption. Der Sturmer, paper controlled by Jew-baiting Julius Streicher, sinks to unbelievable depths of vulgarity to

Nazi Propaganda Minister Josef Goebbels by Vicky.

throw contempt on the democracies. Some of the anti-British cartoons I have seen in this publication would never be allowed to enter any decent English home; not because of their propaganda sentiments, but simply because they are too foul to be appreciated by anybody of normal tastes." This was supported by an article in the *Cheltenham Chronicle* which stated that the difference between the British and the Germans when it came to the success of cartoons was that the former had a sense of humour: "A German magazine containing several reproductions of cartoons of an English cartoonist, as to which I read that our "ability to laugh off war and to take indiscriminate pokes at friend and foe alike is an English trait. German cartoons are bloodthirsty in their hatred of Britain."

As the Allied war effort came to a victorious conclusion, cartoonists began to turn their attention to domestic issues such as demobilisation, rationing and the General Election set for July. Later in 1945, their attention was drawn to the Nuremberg trials. Within months of the end of the Second World War, relations between those countries that had made up the war-time alliance began to fracture, and cartoonists attempted to grapple with the possibility of yet another global conflict. J C Walker felt it was now more important than ever for cartoonists to do their bit: "And what of the future and the future generations? Here the cartoonist can surely do something of value. Working with my colleagues of the Press in newspapers all over the world, I can do my little bit, by dipping my pen and brush in acid or ridicule, to help to kill, politically, any person or party, political or otherwise, that may attempt to promote or sow the seeds of another conflict."

During the Blitz a bomb had hit the *Evening Standard*'s offices and the shrapnel from it left a hole in one of Low's cartoons. According to the cartoonist: 'The subject was peculiarly appropriate to the circumstance. It represented a British soldier with obstinate jaw defiantly making the thumbs-up sign to a grinning Nazi figure of Death. I wrote around the hole 'Thanks for the compliment — Low' and gave the original to Ernie Pyle, the American war correspondent.'

1
The Road to War

PEACE OR FUTURE CANON FODDER
The Tiger: "Curious! I seem to hear a child weeping!"

After four years of mass slaughter on the Western Front, the First World War came to an end at Versailles. The treaty, which represented peace for some and a diktat to others, sowed the seeds for the Second World War. This prophetic cartoon not only predicted that the Treaty would result in another war, but also the actual year (1940) when hostilities practically began. The cartoon shows the leaders of the victorious Allies, David Lloyd George, Vittorio Orlando, Georges Clemenceau and Woodrow Wilson emerging from the Versailles Conference. As Clement Attlee would later put it: 'That foreboding was justified."

17 May 1919, Will Dyson, *Daily Herald*

THAT "ALL-EMBRACING" LEAGUE!
UNCLE SAM: "Say, Woodrow, what did I tell you about 'Entangling Alliances.' Why don't yer drop the darned thing?"

On 20 November, the United States Senate rejected the Treaty of Versailles primarily because of concerns that becoming a member of the League of Nations would compel America to involve itself in future international military conflicts. This had been exacerbated by President Woodrow Wilson's refusal to take senators' objections to the agreement into consideration.

26 November 1919, Wilmer Lunt, *The Bystander*

THE LORD SLAYER'S BANQUET

According to *John Bull*: 'No amount of argument can override the fact that the civilised world is spending 30% more on armaments today than it did in 1913. It is a startling reflection that could well occupy a place in everyone's thoughts on Armistice Day without in any way detracting from the solemnity of that tragic moment of remembrance. We have long since ceased to talk of "The War to End War." That pregnant phrase, "Never again" has long since fallen into disuse. Year by year, with sincerity and deep-rooted emotion, we pay our tribute to the fallen, but we are sadly in danger of losing sight of the realities of the present beneath the memories of the past. The test of aspirations is still deeds, and swollen armaments still mock the paper promises that are piling up at Geneva.'

9 November 1929, George Whitelaw, *John Bull*

Just in case he goose-steps too much!

On 30 January, in a series of complicated negotiations, Adolf Hitler was appointed chancellor of Germany, with the understanding that ex-chancellor Franz von Papen as vice-chancellor and other non-Nazis in key government positions would contain and temper Hitler's more brutal tendencies. This marked a crucial turning point for Germany. Hitler's plan, embraced by much of the German population, was to do away with politics and make Germany a powerful, unified one-party state.

4 February 1933, Keith Temple, *New Orleans Times-Picayune* (United States)

"This is a God-given signal. If this fire, as I believe, turns out to be the handiwork of Communists, there is nothing that shall stop us now crushing out this murder pest with the Iron Fist." — Hitler at Burning of Reichstag.

On 27 February, the German parliament (Reichstag) building burned down. The Nazi leadership used the fire to claim that Communists were planning a violent uprising. They claimed that emergency legislation was needed to prevent this. The resulting act, commonly known as the Reichstag Fire Decree, abolished a number of constitutional protections and paved the way for Nazi dictatorship.

3 March 1933, William Desmond Rowney 'Maro', *Daily Worker*

RATTLING THE OLIVE BRANCH

The Oxford Union passed a motion that: "This House would not in any circumstances fight for King and Country". It made headline news in the world press. The motion was taken up also by student debating societies all over Britain. The Liberal M.P. Robert Bernays told the House of Commons how he had been asked about the debate later in 1933 by a prominent Nazi youth leader: 'There was an ugly gleam in his eye when he said: "The fact is that you English are soft."'

17 May 1933, Wyndham Robinson, *Morning Post*

PLAYING THE GAME: THE MAN WHO MADE SURE OF WINNING THE SINGLES. (wholesale arrests of Hitler's opponents are being carried out in Germany.)

The first people the Nazis targeted for arrest and imprisonment were political opponents — primarily Communists, trade unionists and Social Democrats. Dachau, the first Nazi concentration camp, was built in March 1933 to imprison political opponents. The Communist Party was banned in March, trade unions were disbanded in May and the Social Democrats abolished in June. Leaders of these parties and unions were arrested or fled into exile. By the end of 1933, there were almost 27,000 people imprisoned in concentration camps, and the majority of these were political prisoners.

27 June 1933, Percy Fearon 'Poy', *Daily Mail*

OUT OF CONTROL

On the day this cartoon was drawn Austrian Nazis under instructions from Hitler attempted to overthrow the Chancellor Engelbert Dollfuss's Government and replace it with one that was pro-Nazi. In the process Dollfuss was murdered in his chancellery, but the putsch failed because the Austrian military intervened to back up the government. The cartoon was not published as news of Dollfuss's assassination came through soon after the cartoon was drawn.

25 July 1934, (Unpublished) Sidney Strube, *Daily Express*

OUT IN THE COLD!

HITLER: "What if I do suffer! He'll lose my custom, anyhow!"

At the World Disarmament Conference, Hitler demanded that Germany be allowed to increase their armaments in the interest of Self-Defence. Some of the delegates felt that Hitler's proposals were reasonable, however, France remained concerned of a German invasion, and refused to consider to disarm or allow the Germans to re-arm. On the 14 October, due to the French refusing to negotiate, Hitler withdrew from the World Disarmament Conference and the League of Nations.

22 October 1933, Wallace J. Coop 'Wal', *News of the World*

Although it might be that at the moment the Far Eastern situation offered the principal threat to peace, yet the threat might be transferred to Europe — Stalin, in the Interview given to an American newspaperman last week.

As an olive branch of peace, Hitler offered France and Britain a 25-year non-aggression pact whilst claiming Germany had no further territorial demands to make in Europe. The Soviet Union, fearing Hitler's demands for Lebensraum would turn his attention to them, took a strong line in denouncing Germany's reoccupation of the Rhineland as a threat to peace.

10 March 1936, James Boswell, 'Buchan' *Daily Worker*

"The Watch on the Rhine."

According to the cartoonist: 'It was on 7 March 1936 that Hitler comprehensively violated the Versailles Treaty by sending troops into the industrial region of the Rhineland, which under Article 180 had been specifically designated a demilitarized zone. Had the German Army been opposed by the French and British forces stationed nearby, it had orders to retire back to base and such a reverse would almost certainly have cost Hitler the chancellorship.'

10 March 1936, Jerry Doyle, *Philadelphia Inquirer* (United States)

"What do I care? The Rhineland isn't on the route to India!"

This French cartoonist captures Britain's indifference to Germany's actions in the Rhineland. Many within the British establishment felt guilty about having imposed what were considered harsh terms on Germany in 1919. "After all," said the Marquis of Lothian, who had been Chancellor of the Duchy of Lancaster in Ramsay MacDonald's National Government, "they are only going into their own back garden." When Hitler assured the Western powers that Germany wished only for peace, Arthur Greenwood, the deputy leader of the Labour Party, told the House of Commons: "Herr Hitler has made a statement . . . holding out the olive branch . . . which ought to be taken at face value . . . It is idle to say that those statements are insincere." That August Germany adopted compulsory two-year military service.

18 March 1936, Rogers Roy, *Le Rire* (France)

GIVING HIM THE JUMPS

Just one thing after another!
Press Baron Lord Rothermere and owner of the *Daily Mail*, was a critic of the Versailles Treaty and believed Britain's obligations to the League of Nations would drag Britain into war with Germany whose leader he admired. Rothermere was an advocate of British rearmament especially in the air and his newspapers were in the words of Reid Gannon "almost obsessional" in their demands for more spending on the RAF.

21 March 1936, Percy Fearon 'Poy', *Daily Mail*

Making his mark.

Parliamentary elections were held in Germany on 29 March. They took the form of a single-question referendum, asking voters whether they approved of the military occupation of the Rhineland and a single party list for the new Reichstag composed exclusively of Nazis.

30 March 1936, Harry Thackray 'Thack', *Leeds Mercury*

Doctor Mandate: "Say ninety-nine!" (Nazis claim a full ninety-nine percent majority for Hitler).

Like previous votes during the Nazi era, the elections were rigged, with a claimed turnout of 99% voting in favour of the Rhineland reoccupation. This was the first German election held after the enactment of the 1935 Nuremberg Laws, which had removed citizenship rights (including the right to vote) from Jews and other ethnic minorities.

31 March 1936, Will Dyson, *Daily Herald*

"The first point on which it is desirable to be clear is whether Germany regards herself as now in a position to conclude genuine treaties." — British questionnaire to Germany.

According to the *Daily Record*: 'The phrase "genuine treaties" in the British questionnaire to Germany may become almost as famous in the annals of diplomacy as Germany's "alsbald." You and I, of course, know what a genuine treaty is, but professional diplomats are already discussing a dozen different interpretations of the phrase. Herr Hitler will have his own interpretation. He has already drawn a distinction between "treaties" and "dictates," and he will realise that by a genuine treaty we mean one which cannot be dismissed at some future time as a "dictate."'

11 May 1936, Bob Rodger, *Daily Record*

The Accused: "Judge at the Bench, have you anything to say before I put on the black cap?"

In October 1935, Italian forces had invaded Abyssinia. Mussolini had continually ignored the League of Nations and fully annexed Abyssinia on 9 May 1936. In July, the League of Nations surrendered to Mussolini's aggression by lifting sanctions on Italy. The Abyssinian Crisis proved that Britain and France prioritised other concerns above the principles of the League. Hitler meanwhile observed the lack of decisive action in response to Italy's aggression.

3 July 1936, Will Dyson, *Daily Herald*

THE SACRIFICE

Prime Minister Neville Chamberlain was determined to recognise Mussolini's conquest of Ethiopia, in return for an Anglo-Italian understanding. Through a secret go-between, he went so far as to negotiate with Italian Ambassador Dino Grandi (seen here in the door way) behind Foreign Secretary Anthony Eden's back. Given previous Italian bad faith, Eden believed such negotiations required demonstrations of good intent. When the Cabinet continued to back Chamberlain, Eden resigned on 20 February and was replaced by Lord Halifax.

22 February 1938, Kimon Marengo 'Kem', *John Bull*

"WELL, THAT'S A FINE START!"

The incorporation of Austria into the German Reich on 13 March left Chamberlain and Halifax bewildered as they failed to comprehend why friendlier moves towards Mussolini had not led to Italian support in Britain's opposition over the Anchluss. Although the union of Austria and Germany was prohibited under the Versailles Treaty, Britain's reaction was negligible. In the House of Commons, Chamberlain said, "The hard fact is that nothing could have arrested what has actually happened [in Austria] unless this country and other countries had been prepared to use force." The reaction to the Anschluss led Hitler to conclude that he could use even more aggressive tactics in his plan to expand the Third Reich.

15 March 1938, Cartoonist unknown, *Daily Herald*

The Road to War

Stable Information

The Nazis organised a referendum, meant to legitimise their absorption of Austria into the Reich. More than 99% of the Austrian population voted in favour of the Anschluss. Despite this, as with previous plebiscites, those who voted were subject to a large amount of pressure from the Nazi authorities to vote this way. As such, the result was highly questionable.

21 March 1938, Harry Thackray 'Thack', *Leeds Mercury*

"Bloodshed was imminent, so I determined to put an end to further oppression in my homeland." — Hitler explaining his Austrian Coup in the Reichstag on 18 March.

Hitler's statement was, of course, a lie. When Austrian chancellor Kurt Schuschnigg had announced that there would be a referendum on a possible union with Germany versus maintaining Austria's sovereignty, Hitler threatened an invasion and secretly pressured Schuschnigg to resign. A day before the planned referendum, the German Army crossed the border into Austria, unopposed by the Austrian military.

22 March 1938, Edward Hynes, *Daily Herald*

"We adhere to non-intervention!"

Neville Chamberlain and French Prime Minister Léon Blum (seen here with hands in the air) were both strong advocates for not intervening in the Spanish Civil War. This was despite the fact that Hitler and Mussolini were providing Franco and the Spanish Nationalist Army with crucial military support. Chamberlain was concerned that had Britain intervened it would have undermined his appeasement of Fascist Italy, which he believed would weaken the Rome–Berlin Axis, and so help constrain Germany.

30 March 1938, Victor Weisz 'Vicky', *Daily Herald*

VALE SELLASIE

Haile Selassie went to the Council of the League of Nations to protest against any move by the League to sanction the recognition of Italy's conquest of Abyssinia. He failed to persuade France and Britain who recognised Italy's control over the country. Mexico was the only country to strongly condemn Italy, and only six other nations, including China, the Soviet Union, and the United States, refused to recognise the Italian occupation. Abyssinia was then merged with the other Italian colonies to become Italian East Africa.

14 May 1938, Will Mahony, *Daily News* (Australia)

CZECH-Or Waiting for the Next Move

Konrad Henlein was leader of the Austrian Nazi Party who agitated for the German annexation of the Czechoslovak Sudetenland to Germany. He demanded autonomy for the Sudeten-German areas. Reports of a German military buildup close to the Czechoslovakian border on 19 May gave rise to fears of an imminent German attack. In response, Czechoslovakia mobilised a number of military reservists on 20 May and strengthened its border defences. Alarmed by the developing situation, the governments of France and Britain warned Germany that they would come to Czechoslovakia's aid in the event of an attack.

24 May 1938, Robert Sherriffs, *Daily Herald*

Musso: "If you get what you want, I must think seriously of protecting the rights of the Italian minority in Soho."

Henlein continued to complain that Sudeten Germans were being mistreated by the Czechs. On the 30 May a directive signed by Hitler declared his unalterable decision to smash Czechoslovakia by military action in the near future.

8 June 1938, David Chilchik, *Daily Herald*

SPORTING OFFER

Hitler threatened the Czech President Edvard Beneš with war unless the whole of the Sudetenland was surrendered to Germany.

21 September 1938, Cecil Orr, *Daily Record*

Neville Chamberlain flew to see Hitler at the Berghof, the Führer's holiday home in the Bavarian Alps near Berchtesgaden and agreed to his demands that Czechoslovakia hand over all areas of the Sudetenland where the population was more than 50% Sudeten German.

21 September 1938, Wyndham Robinson, *Star*

Nobel Peace Prize Winner For 1938 (?)

With the support of the French, Chamberlain proceeded to pressurise Beneš to agree to Hitler's terms. The Czech Government was not consulted and initially rejected the terms. However, politically isolated, Beneš was forced to capitulate on 21 September.

22 September 1938 Jerry Doyle, *Philadelphia Inquirer* (United States)

DOING THE "LAMB"-ETH WALK

Having got the Czechs to agree to Hitler's demands, Chamberlain visited the Führer at Bad Godesberg confident that the crisis was now over. However, Hitler had changed his mind and made further demands, including the breakup of Czechoslovakia and 'the immediate annexation of the whole of Sudetenland'. Chamberlain was taken aback when Hitler then threatened to declare war if these demands were not met.

23 September 1938, George Middleton, *Birmingham Gazette*

Horrible and Fantastic

In a last-minute effort to avoid war, Chamberlain proposed that a four-power conference be held immediately to settle the dispute. The Czechs were not invited. Hitler agreed, and on 29 September Hitler, Chamberlain, Daladier, and Mussolini met in Munich. Like the majority of the British public at the time, Chamberlain felt standing up to Hitler was not worth risking a European war. Chamberlain himself summed up the exhausted mood during a radio address: "How horrible, fantastic, incredible it is that we should be digging trenches and trying on gas masks here because of a quarrel in a faraway country between people of whom we know nothing."

29 September 1938, Jimmy Friell, 'Gabriel' *Daily Worker*

"What a handy article an umbrella is"

At Munich, Chamberlain agreed to Hitler's demand that the German army could complete its occupation of the Sudetenland by 10 October. Czechoslovakia was informed by Britain and France that it could either resist Germany alone or submit to the annexation. The Czech government chose to submit. Before leaving, Chamberlain got Hitler to sign a paper declaring their mutual desire to resolve differences through consultation rather than through war. His umbrella became synonymous with his appeasement of the dictators.

30 September 1938, Vaughn Shoemaker, *Chicago Daily News* **(United States)**

The Road to War 11

VERY BRIGHT THIS MORNING, SIR.

Having signed the Munich agreement with Hitler, Chamberlain triumphantly returned to jubilant welcoming crowds relieved that the threat of war had passed, He claimed to have negotiated, "peace with honour" declaring: "I believe it is peace in our time." His words were immediately challenged by Churchill, who declared, "You were given the choice between war and dishonour. You chose dishonour and you will have war."

1 October 1938, Harold Hodges, *Western Mail*

EXPANDING FRONTIERS

Having swallowed up Austria and the Sudetenland, many wondered which neighbouring country would Hitler turn his attention to next.

1 October 1938, George Aria, *Sun* (Sydney, Australia)

The Man Who Didn't Know the Crisis Was Over

Although the war clouds over Europe were dissipated with the Munich Agreement, workmen in Britain continued to dig trenches in public parks for air raid protection. By the outbreak of war, enough covered trenches were available to shelter half a million people. At the same time, a new form of protection, the Anderson shelter, was issued to the public.

3 October 1938, Cecil Orr, *Daily Record*

"Yes, Bert, all right for a crisis, but it would 'ave to be let out a bit for a war"

According to *The Bystander*: 'During the Great War, Captain Bruce Bairnsfather's "Fragments from France" brought laughter to a grim world. Today, twenty years after, "Ole Bill," like Peter Pan, has grown no older: he never will for he is as much a traditional English figure as Falstaff. If the British Legion should go to Czechoslovakia to see fair play, be sure to send "Ole Bill" will go too. Stoic, wit, optimist and old campaigner — what a grand "policeman" this great Immortal would be!'

3 October, Bruce Bairnsfather, *The Bystander*

WHAT ABOUT IT CHAPS? IS THAT A BETTER 'OLE?

Chamberlain was greeted as a hero when he returned to London from Munich with vast grateful crowds gathering in the pouring rain to greet him. He considered cashing in on his popularity by calling a general election. However, despite the public's euphoria that Britain had avoided war, there was a feeling of growing unease as the Nazis then dismembered Czechoslovakia. By the end of the year, public concerns caused Chamberlain to conclude that "to get rid of this uneasy and disgruntled House of Commons by a general election would be suicidal".

5 October 1938, George Middleton, *Birmingham Gazette*

"War with honour or peace with dishonour" he might have been persuaded to accept, "but war with dishonour — that was too much."

On 3 October, following the Munich Agreement, First Lord of the Admiralty, Duff Cooper, was the only Cabinet Minister to resign. He said that 'War with honour or peace with dishonour' he might have been persuaded to accept, 'but war with dishonour — that was too much'. Fellow appeasement critic and Tory MP Vyvyan Adams described Cooper's actions as "the first step in the road back to national sanity". German propaganda painted Cooper as one of the most dangerous warmongers in Britain.

6 October 1938, Stuart Peterson, *Sun* (Sydney, Australia)

THE PIPES OF PEACE
SAM GOLDWYN STALIN: "You see? They include me out of it!"

The Soviet Union was not consulted or invited to Munich. Stalin saw this as an act of betrayal by the British and French whom he felt preferred a compromise with Hitler than a pact with Moscow. It dealt a mortal blow to the policy of collective security in Europe and would lead to Stalin entering into a separate treaty with Hitler on 23 August 1939.

11 October 1938, George Whitelaw, *Daily Herald*

ANOTHER 'ACCESS TO MOUNTAINS' PROBLEM

Churchill combined a vigorous attack on Chamberlain's Cabinet with a call for a real National Government. "A foreign policy," he said, "should be agreed on which does not divide, but unites the nation. A National Government should be formed, not an outworn sham but a Government embracing all the forces in the country which make for Its strength, Its safety and its survival." However, not only was he ignored, Government whips attempted to crack down on dissent from its own backbenchers including Churchill and Eden.

5 December 1938, Wyndham Robinson, *Star*

14   THE SECOND WORLD WAR IN CARTOONS

They Both Want Peace

On 11 January, Chamberlain travelled to Italy to make one last attempt to bring Mussolini to the side of the Allies. According to Mussolini's son-in-law and foreign minister, Count Galeazzo Ciano: "In substance, the visit was kept on a minor tone, since both the Duce and myself are scarcely convinced of its utility. How far apart we are from these people! It is another world. We were talking about it after dinner with the Duce. These men are not made of the same stuff, he was saying, 'as the Francis Drakes and the other magnificent adventurers who created the Empire. These, after all, are the tired sons of a long line of rich men, and they will lose their Empire. The British do not want to fight. Our conversations with the British have ended. Nothing was accomplished. I have telephoned Ribbentrop that the visit was a big lemonade [farce].'"

12 January 1939, Vaughn Shoemaker, *Chicago Daily News* (United States)

The Old Lady's not in such good shape these days.

Japan, Germany, and Italy had all withdrawn from the League of Nations and Spain would do so later in the year. As a consequence, when in January China asked for sanctions against Japan, Foreign Secretary Lord Halifax declared that the absence of other countries from the League made the co-ordination of sanctions impossible. Halifax also found at the time that trying to end foreign intervention in Spain through the League had become futile.
The League had therefore become moribund in its attempts to deal with international issues.

17 January 1939, Cecil Orr, *Daily Record*

The Road to War   15

THE VICTORS!

With military help from Hitler and Mussolini, Barcelona was captured by the Nationalists on 26 January. Soon after, the rest of Catalonia fell with the Republican government fleeing for the French border. With their cause all but lost, the Republicans attempted to negotiate a peace, but Franco refused. On 28 March, 1939, the victorious Nationalists entered Madrid, and the bloody Spanish Civil War came to an end. Up to a million lives were lost in the conflict, the most devastating in Spanish history.

27 January 1939, Harold Hodges, *Western Mail*

Well, it looks like dirty weather, either way.

Whilst Hitler turned his attention to Poland demanding Danzig be incorporated into the German Reich as well as expecting the Polish state to also allow a rail easement across the Polish Corridor to East Prussia, Mussolini, meanwhile, demanded concessions from France with the Duce eyeing up the territorial acquisitions of Nice, Corsica, Tunisia, and Djibouti.

30 January 1939, Bob Rodger, *Daily Record*

GOEBBELS HAS A NIGHTMARE.

For years before 'The Great Dictator' was made, cartoonists had exploited the quite remarkable resemblance of Chaplin's moustache with Hitler's. Both men had been born four days apart. Chaplin had been planning a film on Hitler and from Nazi newsreels, he had carefully studied Hitler's mannerisms and the way he harangued large crowds. Chaplin also watched Leni Riefenstahl's propaganda documentary 'Triumph of the Will' (1935) several times to make sure that he knew Nazi rituals. His incredible talent for mimicry did the rest. Filming began in September 1939 and lasted more than a year. Chaplin released the movie in October 1940. Hitler supposedly demanded a copy and screened it in his private theatre twice.

12 February 1939, Thomas Challen 'Tac', *Sunday Pictorial*

IT GROWS WITH THE REICH!

On 15 March, Hitler ordered German troops to invade and occupy the Czech provinces of Bohemia and Moravia in the rump Czechoslovak state, which was in flagrant violation of the Munich Agreement. This convinced Britain and France that there were no limits to Hitler's territorial ambitions.

17 March 1939, Harold Hodges, *Western Mail*

THE DOUBLE CROSS!

Chamberlain, had been expecting Hitler to keep his word over Munich, and was 'shocked' beyond words by Hitler's cynical disregard of his commitments. On 17 March, Chamberlain gave a speech saying that he could not trust Hitler not to invade other countries.

19 March 1939, Thomas Challen 'Tac', *Sunday Pictorial*

Nazi Germany's occupation of the rest of Czechoslovakia was the first time the Third Reich had invaded territories which were not inhabited by a majority of Germans. According to *John Bull*: 'Hitler's banditry has changed the many voices in this country into one great voice crying "Halt!" Gone are the dissensions, the quarrels, the accusations. In the face of the threat, the nation is united behind its leaders. From now on, Britain knows better than to believe the dove-like cooings which come from Berlin in the intervals'

25 March 1939, Kimon Marengo 'Kem', *John Bull*

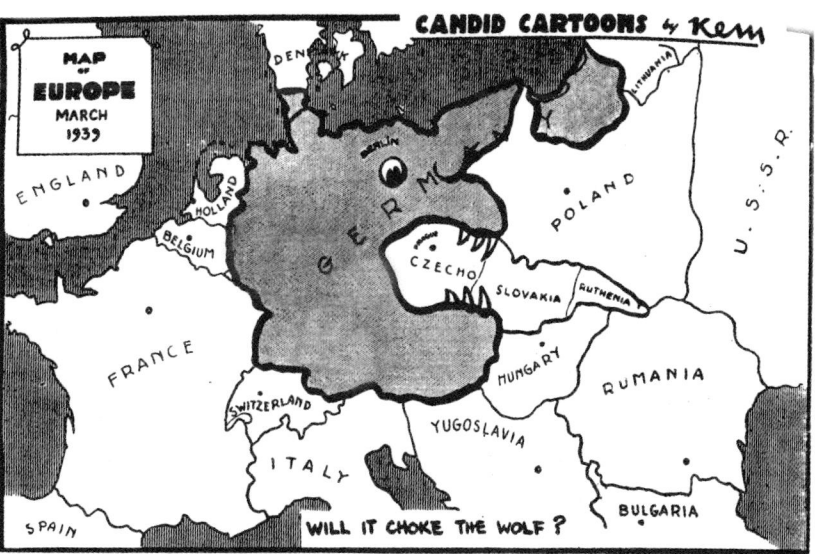

The Road to War

ACTIONS SPEAK LOUDER THAN WORDS!

After Hitler's annexation of Czechoslovakia, Britain and France now pledged support for Greece, Romania and Poland. The French also wanted a pact with the Soviet Union who demanded a guarantee of free passage across Poland in the event of war. Poland was vehemently against this believing the Soviets would not leave voluntarily. In any case it was clear that Stalin was put off such a pact after Munich from which he had been excluded. He was also concerned and disturbed by the Franco-British procrastinations.

1 April 1939, George Aria, *Sun* (Sydney, Australia)

THE GREAT DEPARTURE

Outraged public opinion in Britain over the German annexation of what remained of Czechoslovakia resulted in a new tough stance taken by Chamberlain in issuing a formal guarantee of Poland's borders on 31 March. The French Government then offered a similar guarantee. When Hitler heard about Chamberlain's support for Poland, he flew into a rage and shouted against the British: "I'll cook them a stew they'll choke on!"

4 April 1939, George Middleton, *Birmingham Gazette*

BACK TO THE JAWS OF THE JUNGLE

Prompted by Stalin's speech of 10 March, in which he said that the USSR stood 'for the support of nations which were the victims of aggression and were fighting for the independence of their country', the British government was encouraged 'to hope that the Soviets were prepared to co-operate in an effort to restrain further aggression in Europe. Stalin proposed an anti-Nazi alliance with Britain and France, and proposed moving a million Russian troops complete with supplies and weapons to the German border providing Polish objections be overcome to allow the Red Army crossing its territory.

11 April 1939, Harold Hodges, *Western Mail*

IMPERIAL CAESAR!

Having conquered Abyssinia, Mussolini invaded Albania on 7 April with a force of 100,000 men and 600 aircraft. The Albanian army that faced them had only 15,000 badly equipped troops. By the very first day of fighting, all ports were in Italian hands with King Zog being forced into exile in Greece. On 12 April, Albania surrendered to Italy and became part of the newly formed Italian Empire.

11 April 1939, George Whitelaw, *Daily Herald*

This was the last time Hitler would ever feature in a cartoon in any German published newspaper or magazine. Hitter had denounced the Treaty of Versailles as a form of enslavement of the German people. Up until the end of 1938, every move of Hitler's had been justified as helping to undo the injustice of the Treaty of Versailles. However, in March 1939 Hitler had gone beyond simply undoing the treaty and had begun to expand the German Reich.

16 April 1939, Oskar Garvens, *Kladderadatsch* **(Berlin, Germany)**

1919

Clemenceau: "I've waited 49 years for this day!"

1939

Adolf Hitler: "I've waited 20 years for this day!"

The Road to War

ANOTHER NEW DEAL

President Roosevelt addressed an appeal for peace to Hitler, sounding him out so as to learn his minimum terms for a pledge of lasting peace. He asked him if he was prepared to give an assurance that Germany would not attack or invade any other European nation. Hitler replied to 'Herr Roosevelt' stating that Germany only had peaceful intentions toward its neighbours and declared that he: "had not thought of proceeding in any way against Poland."

6 May 1939, Jim Russell, *Smith's Weekly*. (Sydney, Australia)

On 27 April, and in response to Hitler's continued belligerence, the British Government introduced conscription for all fit and able men aged 20 to 21 to undertake six months' military training. By the end of 1939 more than 1.5 million men had been conscripted to join the British armed forces.

6 May 1939, Kimon Marengo 'Kem', *John Bull*

IN THE BAG

Italy and Germany signed a military and political alliance known as the 'Pact of Steel'. It committed both countries to support the other if one of them became involved in a war. However, Ribbentrop only got Italian agreement after falsely assuring Mussolini that there would be no war for the next three years. Mussolini's son-in-law, Ciano, realised that the pact was potentially very damaging for Italy but Mussolini was more concerned with the prestige of allying with Europe's most potent power rather than the politics of it.

10 May 1939, George Whitelaw, *Daily Herald*

"OLD BILL" Sees the World

"Things look a bit better today, Maggie. They've had talks, leading to conversations, which have been followed by an understanding to have further talks."

After Hitler had signed a military pact with Italy and announced that he would no longer honour Germany's non-aggression pact with Poland, Britain promised to assist Poland if it was attacked. These events contributed to the buildup of tensions in Europe that would eventually lead to war in September.

17 May 1939, Bruce Bairnsfather, *The Bystander*

There's a long, sticky trail winding

"We know the difference between words and acts, but the difference must be noticed in England." – M. Molotov, Commissar for Foreign Affairs

Chamberlain realised that the guarantee given to Poland would be less effective without the Soviet Union's involvement. However, he was unenthusiastic about forming an alliance with them. He wrote to a friend: 'I must confess to the most profound distrust of Russia. I have no belief whatever in her ability to maintain an effective offensive, even if she wanted to. And I distrust her motives, which seem to me to have little connection with our ideas of liberty, and to be concerned only with getting everyone else by the ears.' Lord Halifax had been invited to Moscow for talks by the Russians but sent instead an underling, Sir William Strang, to carry out the talks with Molotov, the new Soviet Foreign Minister. The talks quickly stalled as a result of the British Government's continued distrust of the Soviet Union.

10 June 1939, George Aria, *Sun* (Sydney, Australia)

The Road to War

The Soviet cartoonist compares Chamberlain's hurry to come to an arrangement with Hitler at Munich in comparison with the way the British and French were dragging their feet over a possible defensive pact with the Russians. The Anglo-French plane reads: "For communications with Munich and Berlin". The 'car' driven by the British and French diplomats reads: "We are hurrying to talks in Moscow".

16 June 1939, Boris Efimov, *Izvestia* (Soviet Union)

In a speech to Parliament Chamberlain stated: "We have been reminded that Europe is not the only centre of disturbance in the world by recent events in the Far East. A local dispute between ourselves and the Japanese over the alleged complicity of certain Chinese in a murder has been followed by a blockade at the British concession in Tientsin, and by high-handed and intolerably insulting treatment of British subjects by Japanese soldiers." He warned the Japanese that he would: "not tolerate British nationals being subjected to such treatment as we have heard of in Tientsin, and no British Government could submit to dictation from another power as to its foreign policy."

28 June 1939, Don Angus, *Truth* (New Zealand)

"We must all consider July, August, and September as months in which tension in Europe will become most severe." – Mr. Winston Churchill.

Churchill published a collection of newspaper articles he had written about the threat posed by Hitler. Clement Attlee spoke for many when he said: "It must be a melancholy satisfaction to see how right you were." The public demand to bring back Churchill continued to grow. However, Chamberlain was still strongly opposed to him, believing that Churchill's inclusion in the Cabinet would frustrate his efforts to appease Hitler.

30 June 1939, Cecil Orr, *Daily Record*

MUSIC FOR DANZIG

Hitler saw the British guarantee to Poland as an attempt to encircle Germany and proclaimed, "I shall brew them a devil's drink". Apart from ordering a build-up of German troops on the Polish border, Hitler started making statements about increasing German intolerance for Polish "atrocities" to German citizens in Danzig.

2 July 1939, Thomas Challen 'Tac', *Sunday Pictorial*

WILL THE BLACK-OUT MAKE HIM STOP TO THINK?

The British Air Ministry had predicted that should war break out, Britain would be bombed at night by the German Luftwaffe. One of the very few precautions the country could take was the elimination of man-made light. In July, the British government distributed Public Information leaflets which set out the need for the general blackout. On 11 August, the first blackout was practised in London as the threat of war loomed. It was watched by massive crowds of spectators.

13 July 1939, Harry Thackray 'Thack', *Leeds Mercury*

STALIN: I wonder was Munich before I was born?

The Axis powers now vied with Britain and France to reach a strategic arrangement with the Soviet Union. However, because Chamberlain was lukewarm about any agreement with Stalin, British negotiators did not arrive in Moscow until 11 August. By that time, the Nazis had laid the groundwork for a Nazi-Soviet pact. Worse still, the Russians were insulted that Chamberlain sent second-rank military officers to Moscow. He also instructed his negotiators not to rush into anything at first, thus they moved at a snail's pace during the initial discussions, frustrating the Russians. All of these complications served to convince Stalin that Poland and its Western Allies were not serious about seeking a military alliance against Hitler.

15 July 1939, Alexander Saroukhan, *Akher Sa'a* **(Cairo, Egypt)**

"THERE'S A LULL IN EUROPE."

[In view of the international situation, the Labour Party is demanding that Parliament's summer holiday be shortened — and the Government is resisting this demand].

Despite the rising tensions in Europe, Chamberlain introduced a motion to adjourn the House of Commons for summer recess until 3 October. The motion passed and an attempted amendment by the Labour opposition to shorten the length of adjournment to 21 August was defeated.

28 July 1939, George Whitelaw, *Daily Herald*

An American view of Britain and France's failed attempts to appease Hitler.

28 August 1939, Jim Berryman, *Washington Evening Star* (United States)

AND FINALLY HEAVEN

On 22 August, Hitler gave a speech to his senior Wehrmacht Generals. In regards to world domination he said: "Poland will be depopulated and settled with Germans. My pact with the Poles was merely conceived of as a gaining of time. As for the rest, gentlemen, the fate of Russia will be exactly the same as I am now going through with in the case of Poland. After Stalin's death — he is a very sick man — we will break the Soviet Union. Then there will begin the dawn of the German rule of the earth."

29 August 1939, Will Mahony, *Daily News* (Australia)

HORRIBLE THOUGHT?

German Foreign Minister Joachim von Ribbentrop (bottom left) negotiated the Nazi-Soviet Pact with his Russian counterpart Vyacheslav Molotov. The pact was an agreement of convenience between two bitter ideologically opposed enemies. It permitted them to carve up Poland, while pledging not to attack each other for 10 years. Less than two years later, however, Hitler launched an invasion of the Soviet Union.

1 September 1939, W H Woodburn (Hengest), *Manchester Evening News*

NEVILLE'S KEYBOARD

Despite the inference here that he stood firm over Britain's guarantee to Poland, Chamberlain was still trying to negotiate with Hitler through the British Ambassador and an intermediary (Birger Dahlerus, a Swedish businessman, who was smuggled in and out of 10 Downing Street).

1 September 1939, George Middleton, *Birmingham Gazette*

This cartoon was left unpublished because by the time it was ready for publication, it had been superseded by events as German forces had already invaded Poland.

1 September 1939, (Unpublished) Will Mahony, *Daily News* **(Australia)**

ONWARD!

Despite a British and French ultimatum, Hitler refused to suspend his attack on Poland. Consequently, both Britain and France then declared war on Germany on 3 September. The Second World War had begun.

3 September 1939, Thomas Challen 'Tac', *Sunday Pictorial*

26   THE SECOND WORLD WAR IN CARTOONS

2
The Phoney War

"O.K., 'itler."

The cartoonist pays homage to Bruce Bairnsfather's grumbling walrus-moustached 'Old Bill' who, during the First World War had embodied the everyman British soldier. As the *Lethbridge Herald* commented in 1920: 'He is a type that took things as they found them, and made the best of them. It was the spirit of the 'Old Bills' that won the war.'

4 September 1939, Bob Rodger, *Daily Record*

ONE FOR ALL AND ALL FOR ONE

Britain called upon countries from across the British Empire for military assistance. Within days Australia, New Zealand, Canada, British India and South Africa had all declared war on Germany. Their contribution in terms of manpower and material would be critical to the Allied war-effort.

7 September 1939, Bill Falconer 'Con', *Daily Sketch*

The Gestapo has been given the task of picking up British propaganda leaflets, which all Germans are forbidden to read.

The first leaflets dropped over Germany by the RAF called upon the German people to overthrow Hitler. During September some 20 million propaganda leaflets were dropped. According to an overly-optimistic report in the *Scotsman*: 'Nothing has struck the popular imagination more than the dissemination of leaflets on German soil. The fact that British aeroplanes have made three flights for the purpose without meeting serious opposition suggests that the German defence is less vigilant than might have been expected. No doubt the most stringent measures are being taken to prevent the circulation of the leaflets, but the mere fact that their possession is forbidden will make them more treasured, and the assistance of underground organisations can be counted upon.'

11 September 1939, Bob Rodger, *Daily Record*

The spade will win this war.

In June 1939 the Women's Land Army had been officially formed, and by the outbreak of the war, roughly 17,000 volunteers had been registered and were ready to be sent out to work. However, the uptake of land girl labour by male farmers was initially slow due to pre-existing prejudices about women's capability to perform labour intensive farm work.

13 September 1939, Bill Falconer 'Con', *Daily Sketch*

AWAITING THE CATCH

CHAMBERLAIN: Take a fisherman's tip, John! Exercise patience!

The submarine war began almost immediately when a German submarine fired on the British passenger liner Athenia. The ship sank the next day, after most of its passengers had been rescued. One hundred and twelve people lost their lives, including 28 Americans. The U-boat had opened fire despite explicit orders not to fire on passenger ships. In the first four months of the war 221 ships were sunk.

15 September 1939, Harold Hodges, *Western Mail*

"One for me, one for you, one for me . . ."

The implication in this cartoon is that Britain and France would take the offensive against Germany. In reality, there was no major combat involving the Siegfried Line, except for a minor offensive by the French. Instead, both sides remained in a safe position behind their defences, during the so-called Phoney War.

17 September 1939, Percy Walmsley 'Lees', *Sunday Graphic*

Neighbours, eh?

Despite their valiant fight against the German Army, any chance of the Poles holding out were dashed on 17 September when Stalin instructed Soviet forces to invade the part of Poland granted him under the Molotov-Ribbentrop Pact.

18 September 1939, Bill Falconer 'Con', *Daily Sketch*

THE WEDDING MARCH.

According to the *Gloucestershire Echo*: 'Our preoccupation with the struggle against Germany should not blind us to the rapid advance of Russian influence among the Baltic States. Without a single word of protest from the Nazis, the Bolshevists are engaged in establishing themselves as the dominant Power in the only sea where the German Navy was until a couple of months ago supreme.'

25 September 1939, Percy Walmsley 'Lees', *Sunday Graphic*

TRY THE BACK POCKET, ADOLF!

Dr. Goebbels denies the statement by the American journalist, Mr. Knickerbocker, that he and other Nazi leaders have transferred fortunes abroad.

American journalist, Hubert R Knickerbocker claimed to have the evidence to show that Goebbels, Goering, Hess, Ribbentrop, Ley, and Himmler had invested fortunes abroad totalling 34 million dollars. The *Paris Soir* contained a long-signed article by Knickerbocker in which he had given details in support on his allegation.

27 September 1939, Harry Heap, *The Star* (Sheffield)

"LIVING SPACE"

In total, roughly 200,000 Poles died during the month of September. This was characterised by the indiscriminate and deliberate targeting of the civilian population by the Germans. According to Hannen Swaffer in *John Bull*:

"Heil, Hitler," Lord of Lies and King of Death,
"Heil, Hitler," bullying Nazis yell,
While martyred Poland draws a dying breath,
"Heil, Hitler," shout the fiends in Hell,
While mothers curse what was your mother's name,
And babes weep where their fathers fell,
You have but Anti-Christ to shame,
"Heil, Hitler," shout the fiends in Hell,
Hitler's inferno's realm is now your own,
Even the Devil yields to you his throne.

30 September 1939, Kimon Marengo 'Kem', *John Bull*

As Good As New

On 6 October, Hitler gave a speech in the Reichstag offering the olive branch of peace to France and Britain. He claimed that if the war should continue: "One day there will again be a frontier between Germany and France, but instead of flourishing towns there will be ruins and endless graveyards." This, he said, was his last offer, and as an alternative a war of annihilation would follow and Europe reduced to ruins. "The Poland of the Versailles Treaty will never rise again."

9 October 1939, Cecil Orr, *Daily Record*

ADOLF: "And to think I complained about being encircled!"

According to the *Gloucestershire Echo*: 'Ever since the non-aggression pact with Germany, Russia has steadily pursued a policy of unabashed self-interest. She has considerably narrowed the sphere of German influence, so that the encirclement which has been Hitler's nightmare for years has become a reality. Shut in on the east by Russia waiting and ready to exploit the confusions of Europe for her own ulterior ends, Germany now has to face the Allies in the West.'

16 October 1939, George Whitelaw, *Daily Herald*

THE REJECTED "OUTSTRETCHED HAND"

Chamberlain addressed the House of Commons on 12 October and declared Hitler's proposals to be vague and uncertain, and did not address the righting the wrongs done to Czechoslovakia and Poland. He said that no further reliance could be placed on Hitler's promises and that "acts — not words alone — must be forthcoming" if peace was to come. In turn, an official German statement on 13 October declared that Chamberlain, by rejecting Hitler's peace offer, had deliberately chosen war.

16 October 1939, Harry Thackray 'Thack', *Leeds Mercury*

IT IS complained that we have too many little Hitlers in this country.

During the early stages of the war a new term of abuse entered the English language. To call someone "a little Hitler" meant he was a menial functionary who employed what power he had in order to annoy and frustrate others for his own gratification.

18 October 1939, Cecil Orr, *Daily Record*

The Rainy Season

President Roosevelt sought American participation on the side of Britain and France. Isolationists fought his legislative proposals, beginning with repeal of the arms embargo and ending with the convoying of supplies to Britain. The America First Committee, however, so effectively mobilized anti-interventionist opinion as to make the president more cautious in his diplomacy.

20 October 1939, Harry Larimer, *News-Sentinel* (United States)

Swelling The "Nett" Total!

On Friday the 13 October, the RAF and the Royal Navy destroyed three U-boats, two in the North Sea and the other in the Atlantic. The Admiralty announced 'that Friday the 13th of October has proved an unlucky day for the U-boats.'

25 October 1939, Harry Heap, *The Star* (Sheffield)

Nasty Man!

According to the *Daily Herald*: 'Winston Churchill declared that Britain will fight until the baneful domination of "that evil man" has been ended. In a broadcast which was heard by millions of people around the world, he said: "Now we are at war, and we are going to make war and persevere in making war, until the other side have had enough of it. You may take it absolutely for certain that either all that Britain and France stand for in the modern world will go down, or that Hitler, the Nazi regime, and the recurring German or Prussian menace to Europe will be broken and destroyed."'

13 November 1939, Harry Heap, *The Star* (Sheffield)

Armistice Day

On the eve of the first Remembrance Day of the war, the *Daily Record* stated that: 'News late last night suggested that Herr Hitler has at last made his mind up as to his course of action — he has taken eight weeks over it — and that Holland is to be the victim.'

11 November 1939, Cecil Orr, *Daily Record*

THE FRIEND OF THE CHILDREN

On 18 November the Dutch liner, the Simon Bolivar, struck two German mines in the North Sea, and sank with the loss of over 120 lives, including women and children. A Czech woman passenger stated: "I shall never forget the sight of women, clutching their babies in their arms, being drowned before my eyes." The Admiralty said that this 'was a further example of the utter disregard of international law and the dictates of humanity shown by the German Government.'

21 November 1939, George Whitelaw, *Daily Herald*

EACH FOR ONE AND ONE FOR ALL — A special contingent of the Gestapo has been let loose on Poland.

According to the *Daily Mail*: 'The Death's Head battalion of the Nazi Black Guard (S.S.) has arrived at Cracow, ancient capital of Poland, to "Start its duties" states the German wireless. The Death's Head battalion is a special Gestapo unit generally used to suppress anti-Nazi activities or organize Jew-baiting. It also acts as Hitler's body-guard.'

22 November 1939, Bill Falconer 'Con', *Daily Sketch*

Never mind, Mein Fuehrer, if our battleships daren't go out, our mines CAN!

According to the *Edinburgh Evening News*: 'The Government appear to be in no doubt that the German mines which are causing such havoc are of the magnetic type. Sir John Simon, Chancellor of the Exchequer, described them as "this latest abomination of German savagery." He also spoke of magnetic mines being secretly deposited in the channels of the sea in order to blow up, without warning, neutral and British shipping alike and to destroy innocent lives — women, children and unarmed men — in breach of the rules of war, which Germany only two months ago had expressly promised to obey.'

26 November 1939, Percy Walmsley 'Lees', *Sunday Graphic*

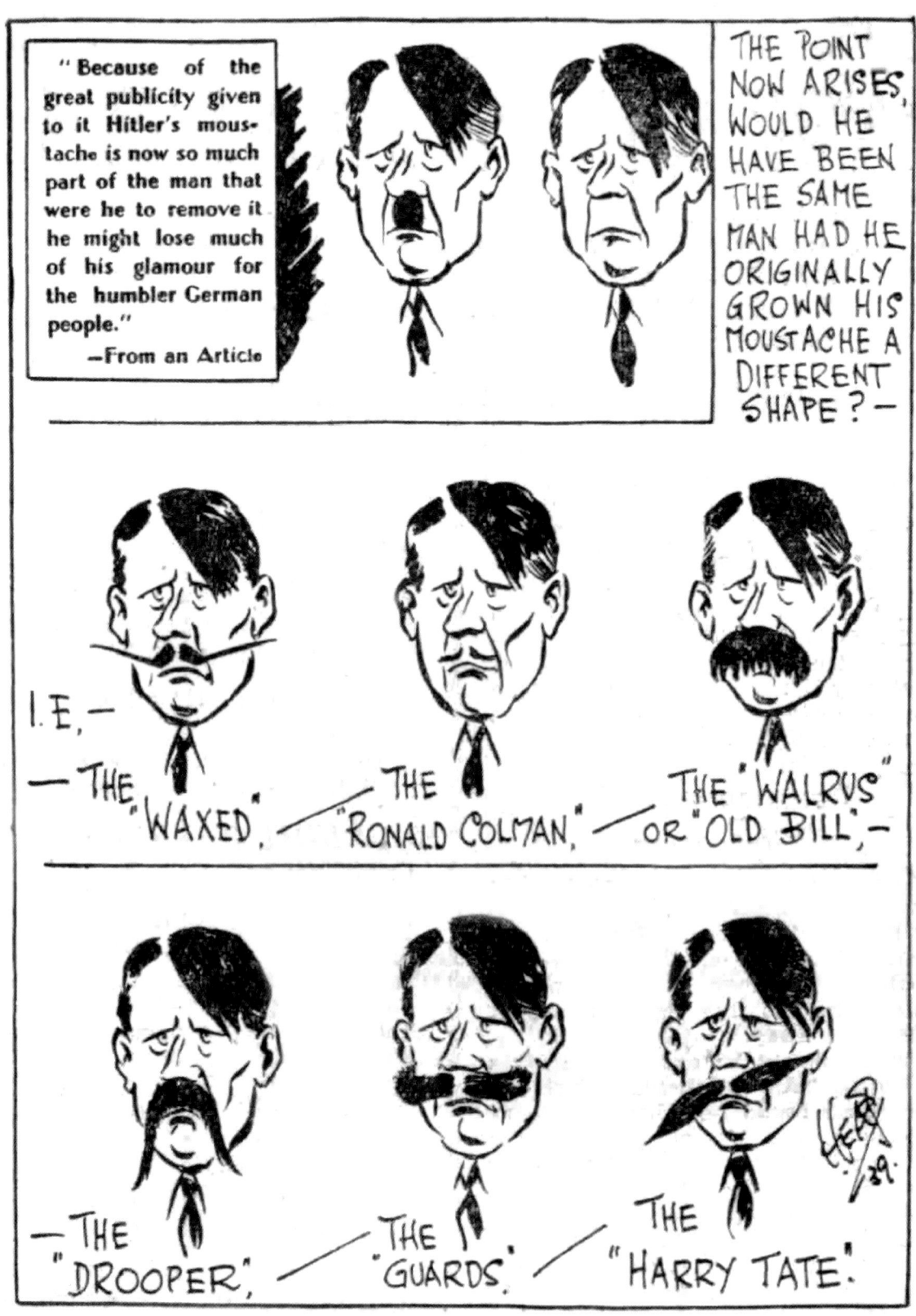

BEHIND THE MOUSTACHE

It has recently been revealed that Hitler's toothbrush moustache was as a result of a direct order, whilst in the trenches during the First World War, to trim down his full Bavarian moustache so that his gas mask would fit over his mouth properly. This order had been issued in response to British mustard gas attacks. Ronald Coleman was a Hollywood film star whilst Harry Tate was a comedian who wore a false moustache, which he used to express all kinds of emotion by twitching or moving it.

29 November 1939, Harry Heap, *The Star* (Sheffield)

Stalin and the Finnish President
Taking a Leaf Out of Hitler's Book

After Finland rejected an ultimatum to concede a considerable portion of its territory to the Soviet Union, Stalin's Red Army invaded the country with the intention of installing a puppet Communist Finnish government and eliminating a potentially hostile presence along his country's border.

30 November 1939, Bill Falconer 'Con', *Daily Sketch*

LITTLE SIR ECHO!

In a headline stating 'Stalin's ally is embarrassed' the *Manchester Evening News* reported: 'Neutral observers in Berlin report that official German circles are embarrassed in their attitude towards the Russo-Finnish conflict. This is revealed by the fact that their efforts are concentrated on the publication of excuses why Germany must remain aloof. It is recognised that the general public sympathises with the Finns and this also explains why news of the Soviet aggression was held back from them.'

3 December 1939, Percy Walmsley 'Lees', *Sunday Graphic*

TRYING TO GET BACK TO EARTH!

According to the *Nottingham Journal*: 'Herr Hitler is apparently trying to persuade Dr Schacht, Germany's financial wizard, to come back and straighten out the Reich's money troubles. From a neutral source the *Press Association* learns that Dr Funk and his experts have been working on a number of drastic schemes for financing the war, — but Hitler in hesitating to give them his approval; for Rudolf Hess has told him that the people must not be asked for any more big sacrifices just yet. In desperation the Fuhrer is, it is said, turning to the man who has saved Germany so many times before.'

14 December 1939, George Whitelaw, *Daily Herald*

The Phoney War

RATS TO THEIR HOLES

The Battle of the River Plate, the first naval battle of the Second World War, was fought on 13 December in the South Atlantic. The German heavy cruiser Admiral Graf Spee had been sinking merchant ships regularly, but was tracked down off the coasts of Argentina and Uruguay by three British cruisers. In battle the Graf Spee was hit more than fifty times and was forced to take refuge in Uruguayan waters. Churchill had said during the First World War that if the German fleet 'did not come out and fight they would be dug out like rats in a hole'.

16 December 1939, Stan Cross, *Smith's Weekly* (Australia)

Captain Langsdorf to Hitler: "Hadn't You Better Follow My Example?"

On 17 December, the battle-damaged Graf Spee limped out of the port of Montevideo into the estuary of the River Plate for what was expected to be a decisive clash with the Royal Navy. Captain Hans Langsdorff, believed he was facing impossible odds against a superior force and defied Hitler's order to fight to the last man by scuttling the Graf Spee. Three days later, Langsdorff committed suicide, shooting himself in the head in a Buenos Aires hotel room. At the time it was falsely reported that he had killed himself in protest against Hitler's order to scuttle the battleship.

21 December 1939, Bill Falconer 'Con', *Daily Sketch*

THE BELOVED FUEHRER IS ON HOLIDAY

Hitler left Berlin for his Christmas retreat in the Bavarian Alps near Berchtesgaden. A month earlier, he had narrowly survived an assassination attempt in a Munich beer hall when he had left the venue earlier than expected. According to the *Daily Herald*: 'That evil man Hitler is being hidden from those of his admirers who express themselves with bombs. His whereabouts are being kept secret. For instance, all the time he was at Munich, his personal flag was kept flying over the Chancellery in Berlin. Every German over 15 is being compelled to carry his identification card, as part of the "comb-out" following the Munich explosion.'

22 December 1939, Wyndham Robinson, *Star*

Hitler's "Sink-on-Sight" Navy

After the scuttling of the Graf Spee, German ships were ordered to scuttle themselves rather than be captured by British vessels. According to the *New York World Telegram*: 'There is a certain bravery about the person who has the courage to pull the trigger against his own temple, but there is deep cowardice in the policy of the overlord from afar for the order that causes the act. Scuttling is a reflection of the long-established fact of life, that the bully is yellow at heart, that the Germans have once more fallen under a bully leadership, that he is scuttling his way out when things turn against him and that the Langsdorffs, the Spees and the Columbuses are the price the nation pays for having a bully at the top.'

24 December 1939, Percy Walmsley 'Lees', *Sunday Graphic*

THE TWIST

After Britain and France had declared war on Germany, President Roosevelt invoked the provisions of the Neutrality Act. However, within weeks, he asked Congress to revise the legislation because it had indirectly aided the Germans. A 'cash-and-carry' provision in the Neutrality Act permitted the sale of arms to European warring parties as long as they paid for them in cash and took them away across the Atlantic in their own ships. Roosevelt believed the provision would aid France and Britain as they already controlled the seas.

28 December 1939, C. A. Munro,
***Civil and Military Gazette* (Lahore, India)**

KEPT WAITING

In a prophetic New Year message to the Nazi party Hitler said: "The German people did not want this fight. Up to the last minute I tried to offer England our friendship, and after Poland's elimination I was willing to make proposals that would have secured peace in Europe for a long time. They had prepared and were unwilling to cancel their plans for the destruction of Germany. These warmongers want war. They shall have it. May 1940 will bring the decision. Come what may it will be our victory."

4 January 1940, Clive Uptton, *Daily Sketch*

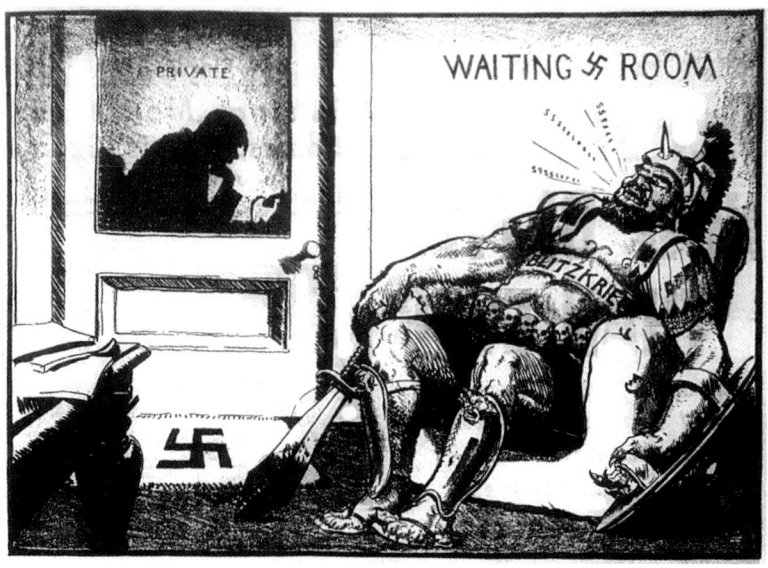

Prisoner of War.

(Newspapers mustn't talk about the weather)

With the headline 'Most popular topic barred', the *South London Observer* reported: 'The Censor will not allow any references to the weather because, he says, the Meteorological Department of the Air Ministry are certain that any statement of climatic conditions in these happy isles would be conveyed to the enemy. It is more than probable that the enemy gets reports from Britain about the weather as regularly as does our own Air Ministry. The science and art of intercommunication are vastly different from the days of the last war, and it is difficult to believe that there is any valid reason for depriving the British public of the satisfaction of knowing how bad or how good the weather is elsewhere in the country compared with that which they are enjoying. We may, however, still talk about it.'

5 January 1940, Cecil Orr, *Daily Record*

A WELL-EARNED REST!

Leslie Hore-Belisha, having been a successful Minister of Transport (he had reduced the number of road accidents by introducing Belisha beacons at pedestrian crossings) and an equally successful stint as Minister of War, (having improved conditions and pay for serving soldiers) was suddenly and mysteriously fired from his post. According to the *Daily News*: 'Leslie Hore-Belisha and Neville Chamberlain had taken elaborate pains not to explain why the one had been dismissed by the other from the War Ministry.'

7 January 1940, C. A. Munro, *Civil and Military Gazette* (Lahore, India)

SECOND THOUGHTS ARE BEST

German raiders attacking unarmed vessels off the British coast meant that the Government's scheme to evacuate children to safety in Canada, South Africa, Australia and New Zealand became ever more hazardous.

13 January 1940, Harold Hodges, *Western Mail*

'WE ARE SAILING AGAINST ENGLAND' — Nazi Hymn Of Hate . . .

According to the Minister for Economic Warfare, Ronald Cross, Britain had accomplished in four and a half months of economic warfare against Germany what took two years to accomplish in the First World War. According to Cross: "We are looking forward to the day when we shall have so throttled Germany's economic life that she can no longer sustain her war effort. We believe we shall greatly hasten the day of victory and so save the lives of men." His speech in the Commons was cheered by all members of the House.

19 January 1940, Clive Upton, *Daily Sketch*

The Phoney War 41

'INNOCENT' BYSTANDER

Heavily outnumbered Finnish forces put up a skilful and effective defence against the Russian military onslaught. Global opinion had by now rallied to their cause, especially amongst the western democracies. According to *The Times*, the Finns were seen as good democrats 'fighting with the heroic loyalty characteristic of a free people when its liberty is at stake.'

21 January 1940, Percy Walmsley 'Lees', *Sunday Graphic*

Sixty-five M.P.'s, it is announced, have joined the Army

According to the *Daily Record*: '65 M.P.'s were serving in the army apart from those holding honorary positions. Their names are given in a written answer yesterday. Ranks range from Second Lieutenants to Colonel.'

22 January 1940, Cecil Orr, *Daily Record*

The Bogey-Man

In a radio broadcast on 20 January, Churchill was scathing of the neutral nations, saying that they all hoped that the storm would pass "before their turn comes to be devoured. But I fear — I fear greatly — the storm will not pass. It will rage and it will roar, ever more loudly, ever more widely . . . What would happen if all these neutral nations . . . were with one spontaneous impulse to do their duty in accordance with the Covenant of the League, and were to stand together with the British and French Empires against aggression and wrong?"

24 January 1940, Cecil Orr, *Daily Record*

TIME MARCHES ON!

Most effective among the Nazis transmitting to Britain was William Joyce. This Irish-American fascist, known in Britain as Lord Haw-Haw, won a large audience during the 'phoney war' for broadcasting anti-British propaganda on behalf of Nazi Germany. His trademark call sign was delivered in his unmistakable accent: "Jairmany calling, Jairmany calling".

28 January 1940, Thomas Challen 'Tac', *Sunday Pictorial*

The Phoney War   43

THE BIGGER THEY ARE THE HARDER THEY FALL

Finnish ski troops used the rugged snow-covered landscape to conduct hit-and-run attacks on isolated Soviet units. Their guerilla tactics were aided by the freezing Finnish winter, which bogged the Soviets down and made their soldiers easy to spot against snowy terrain. One Finnish sniper, a farmer named Simo Häyhä, was eventually credited with over 500 kills.

30 January 1940, Clive Uptton, *Daily Sketch*

ON POINT DUTY

"The Germans grant our sailors the inestimable privilege of living dangerously" . . . neutral comment.

According to the *Berwick Advertiser* on 1 February: 'Within forty-eight hours of two vessels having been mined, another two neutral steamers had met their doom in the same area of the North Sea off the Northumberland coast.'

5 February 1940, Clive Uptton, *Daily Sketch*

President Roosevelt sent his closest foreign policy adviser, Sumner Welles, to assess the war situation in Europe in order to pursue and promote an American-brokered peace. Roosevelt wanted it made clear that he was prepared to act as a mediator to "reduce and reconcile" the conflict between Germany, Britain and France.

12 February 1940, Harold Hodges, *Western Mail*

KEEPING IT DARK — Probable effect of the Fougasse anti-gossip posters at the Ministry of Information.

According to the *Birmingham Mail*: 'The need for the campaign against careless talk which the Ministry of Information started today is obvious to anyone who travels much about the country. On provincial journeys a colleague has heard more details of shipping and troop movements than he has heard in Fleet Street. The existing posters seem to have made little impression, though the new Fougasse series must. Foreigners who saw them today thought them flippant, but they have the Bairnsfather touch which should make them popular everywhere, and that is what is needed.'

8 February 1940, George Middleton, *Birmingham Gazette*

"HUSH, HUSH" CAMPAIGN

Sir John Reith (centre), Minister of Information, with Sir Kenneth Lee (Director-General), and the artist Fougasse (right), inspecting anti-gossip campaign posters at the Ministry yesterday.

7 February 1940 *Birmingham Mail*

The Phoney War 45

The Russian attack against the strong Mannerheim Line continues with unabated fury.

According to the *Western Times*: 'During the last war we used to speak of the Russian steam roller. The crushing weight of that same steam roller is now crunching itself against the Mannerheim defences of Finland. Not since the famous battles of the Great War has the world seen such fierce and such desperate fighting. Anxious for the Soviet's prestige; anxious, too, lest he be drawn into deeper waters than he had bargained for, Stalin has ordered his Commander-in-Chief to press on regardless of sacrifices. That order is being obeyed at a terrible cost in men and material. But the Finns, with unrivalled heroism, are holding out and repulsing relentless attacks with amazing courage and skill.'

14 February 1940, Arthur Potts 'Spot', *Bristol Evening World*

NORWAY PROTESTS

The German tanker Altmark entered neutral Norwegian waters, carrying 299 British prisoners who had been picked up from ships sunk by the Graf Spee in the South Atlantic. HMS Cossack followed Altmark and on 16 February Churchill personally wrote the order to the Cossack's captain: 'You should board Altmark, liberate the prisoners and take possession of the ship.' In the ensuing fight, the Altmark ran aground and the British took control of the ship, releasing all prisoners and killing seven Germans. Norway's reaction to this breach of their neutrality can be summed up in the words with which the Norwegian Prime Minister greeted Britain's Minister in Oslo: "I have asked you to come to express the strong consternation and indignation that we feel at this gross violation of Norwegian territorial waters . . . we cannot doubt that the British Government will give full satisfaction at once."

19 February 1940, Harold Hodges, *Western Mail*

A million Poles may soon be toiling under the Nazi yoke in Germany. Goering has promised this number to farmers of the Reich to assist in the work of food production.

Nazi labour officials in Poland had stated that all Poles between the ages of 18 and 60 would be subject to compulsory public labour. By the end of February there were already nearly one million Polish forced labourers in Germany who were mostly employed in agriculture.

21 February 1940, Arthur Potts 'Spot', *Bristol Evening World*

Stalin: Well, I've got millions of 'em . . . (The Finns have wiped out 20,000 more Reds.)

During the war with Finland, Soviet troops, suffered huge casualties. One Finnish Soldier was purported to have said: "So many Russians — where will we bury them all?" As a consequence the eventual Soviet victory came at a great cost. Nikita Khrushchev later wrote: 'All of us sensed in our victory a defeat by the Finns.'

21 February 1940, Clive Uptton, *Daily Sketch*

STREET NOISES AT SILVERTOWN

Two anti-war candidates, a Communist and a Fascist, opposed one another and the Labour candidate in the Silvertown (West Ham) by-election. They were Thomas Moran, a senior member of the British Union of Fascists and Harry Pollitt, General Secretary of the Communist Party of Great Britain. Moran's campaign, which was almost exclusively anti-Semitic, secured only 151 votes compared to 966 for Harry Pollitt. The Labour candidate won with 14,343 votes.

22 February 1940, Wyndham Robinson, *Star*

In a radio broadcast Hitler defined German war aims: "We have our own spheres, Central Europe was built by us, not by the British. In this territory we will live, and not allow our life to be endangered. We will not tolerate any combination against us. We demand the return of the Colonies stolen from us a by capitalistic plutocrats."

26 February 1940, William Furnival, *Lancashire Evening Post*

THE ALLIES — AS HERR HITLER SEES US

According to the Nazi Party organ, *Voelkischer Beobachter*: 'The Jews will now be busier than ever pulling strings behind the scenes.' It then went on to publish a long list of British Cabinet Ministers, MPs and others, who, it said, 'are or have Jewish connections, by marriage or otherwise.' It concluded by stating: 'As Cabinet and Parliamentary posts are occupied by Jews and Jewish comrades, the Jews exert influence throughout England.'

27 February 1940, C. A. Munro, *Civil and Military Gazette* (Lahore, India)

"AND WHAT, SIR, ARE YOUR INTENTIONS?"

President Roosevelt's peace envoy, Sumner Welles, arrived in Berlin for discussions with Hitler, who insisted that the Allied war aim was 'annihilation', that of Germany 'peace'. He lectured Welles on all he had done to maintain peace with England and France. According to the *Press Association*: 'Germany is exploiting the visit of Mr Sumner Welles to Europe to launch a "peace offensive" . . . Hitler, it is stated, will say that he is ready for peace, but M. Daladier and Mr Chamberlain will declare that they do not want peace. It will then be clear, according to the radio statements, who will bear the responsibility for the continuation of the war.'

1 March 1940, Bill Crawford, *Newark News* **(United States)**

"WON'T YOU SIT DOWN?"

It is reported that Hitler will not discuss any peace terms which include the surrender of any of his "acquisitions."

5 March 1940, George Whitelaw, *Daily Herald*

NOW ISN'T THAT NICE TO KNOW!

From the start of the Russo-Finnish War, Britain and France had supplied the Finns with weapons and war materials. Both British and French governments also started to consider sending an expeditionary force to fight the Soviets. Such a move would have meant being at war with both the Soviet Union and Germany. Fortunately, the signing of the Finno-Soviet Peace treaty ended any Allied plans for intervention on Finland's behalf.

5 March 1940, C. A. Munro, *Civil and Military Gazette* **(Lahore, India)**

THE 'HAPPY' ENDING

By March, the Soviet forces had regrouped, strengthened, and broken through the Finnish defences, forcing them to agree to an unfavourable peace treaty. In the end, the Soviet Union lost about a hundred times more soldiers than Finland, although the latter lost almost a tenth of its territory to the former.

17 March 1940, Percy Walmsley 'Lees', *Sunday Graphic*

The Phoney War

According to the *Manchester Evening News*: 'Old iron will buy a Goering autograph in Germany now. A 12-day campaign to collect old metal for Hitler's birthday on 20 April begins today with the opening of 350 centres in Berlin and thousands throughout the Reich to receive contributions from dutiful citizens. In return for their old metal, contributors will receive a certificate bearing pictures of guns and Field-Marshal Goering's signature. The campaign is aimed entirely at the collection of copper, brass, bronze, tin, lead, nickel, and German silver. Newspapers ask the public to search their homes, offices, and factories for ashtrays, pots, pans, cups, plates, railings, gates, statues, coats of arms, and wall decorations and to hand them over to the authorities.'

27 March 1940, Wyndham Robinson, *Star*

"WELLE, SUMNER, WELLE ?"

According to the *Daily Mirror*: 'Mr. Sumner Welles arrived in Washington on his return from his European tour, and conferred with President Roosevelt. Friends who travelled with Mr. Welles said that they believed that he had found the possibilities of peace hopeless.' Roosevelt then made a statement stating that there was 'scant immediate prospect of a stable peace'.

28 March 1940, W. H. Woodburn 'Hengest', *Manchester Evening News*

CLOSING IN ON HIM

In a radio broadcast, Churchill called for the war to be intensified by tightening the blockade on Germany. He called for the adoption of exceptionally strong measures against the neutrals, so as to force them to give up supplying the Germans with goods that she required to continue the war.

2 April 1940, Harold Hodges, *Western Mail*

"Sorry, gu'vnor, but your hat keeps getting in the way of our stones." (Neutral trade with Germany is causing the Premier some concern.)

Chamberlain also announced that the Allies intended to intensify the blockade to the utmost, and that various neutrals with which the Allies had concluded agreements with must guarantee to limit their future trade with Germany. Churchill meanwhile accused neutral country's supplying Germany with raw materials of prolonging the war: "The fact that many of the smaller States of Europ are terrorised by Nazi violence and brutality into supplying Germany with the materials of modern war, may condemn the whole world to a prolonged ordeal, with grievous consequences in many lands."

4 April 1940, Arthur Potts 'Spot', *Bristol Evening World*

In a confident speech to the Conservative and Unionist Associations, Neville Chamberlain showed contempt for the Nazis and declared that Hitler had "missed the bus" and after seven months of war he felt "ten times as confident of victory" than he had done at the start. He went on to say: "I do not believe in its whole history the nation has ever been so completely united upon the broad aims of our policy, and upon our determination to carry on this fight until we have achieved our purpose."

5 April 1940, Wyndham Robinson, *Star*

The Phoney War 51

FILLING THE GAPS (Vigorous measures to tighten the blockade have been put into action by Mr. Chamberlain and the French Premier, Mr. Reynaud.)

8 April 1940, Clive Uptton, *Daily Sketch*

HAUNTED!

Mr. Churchill's appointment as chief of the Navy, Army and Air Committee has aroused fresh fury in Germany.

On 3 April, Chamberlain carried out a reshuffle of his war ministry. Churchill was made chairman of the Military Co-ordination Committee, which consisted of two other ministers and three chiefs of staff who would make strategic proposals to the War Cabinet. The public reacted enthusiastically to the move, including in America where *Associated Press* special correspondent DeWitt Mackenzie said that the appointment represented 'one of the most constructive moves towards victory which have been made for the Allied cause'.

8 April 1940, Stuart Peterson Sydney, *Sun* (Australia)

TIGHTENING THE GRIP

With the headline 'The Iron Blockade' the *Berks and Oxon Advertiser* reported that: 'In 1938 Germany imported 22 million tons of iron ore. Of this total, ten million came from countries from which the war immediately shut her off and ten million from Norway and Sweden. Of this remaining ten million tons, less than 5,000 came through Baltic ports, the remainder through Narvik. By his invasion of Norway, Hitler has enabled the British Navy to prevent a single ton from reaching Germany through Narvik.'

9 April 1940, George Middleton, *Birmingham Gazette*

HERE THEY COME — I HOPE!

On 9 April, German warships entered major Norwegian ports, from Narvik to Oslo and were able to slip through the mines Britain had laid around Norwegian ports because local garrisons were ordered to allow the Germans to land unopposed. The order had come from a Norwegian commander loyal to Norway's pro-fascist former foreign minister Vidkun Quisling.

10 April 1940, C. A. Munro, *Civil and Military Gazette* **(Lahore, India)**

Under the code name 'Operation Weserübung', Nazi Germany attacked Denmark and Norway. Denmark surrendered within hours and was occupied. The country was a useful base of operations for the fight against Norway. German planes dropped leaflets over Copenhagen calling for Danes to accept the German occupation peacefully, falsely claiming that Germany had occupied Denmark in order to protect it against an invasion by Great Britain and France.

14 April 1940, Bill Baker 'Pix', *Sunday Pictorial*

AS SHAKESPEARE SAID: "Something is rotten in the state of Denmark." Hamlet, Act I., Scene IV

Norway had successfully remained neutral throughout the First World War and now had hoped to remain neutral during the Second. However, Germany's unprovoked invasion of Norway changed all that. Poorly armed, the Norwegians resisted for two months but were forced to surrender on 9 June 1940.

14 April 1940, Stuart Peterson Sydney, *Sun* **(Australia)**

The Phoney War   53

By invading neutral Denmark, Germany was in direct violation of a German-Danish treaty of non-aggression which had been signed the previous year. The decision to occupy Denmark was taken to make it easier to invade the strategically more important Norway.

14 April 1940, Clive Uptton, *Daily Sketch*

THE SWEDE'S PREDICAMENT

After the occupation of Norway and Denmark, Germany pressurised Sweden into remaining neutral. Hitler feared that Sweden's entry into the war would jeopardise the delivery of iron ore and that if Russia attacked Sweden, it would be difficult for the Swedes to refuse Allied offers to intervene in Scandinavia. The Germans warned the Swedish government that they would take swift action if Allied troops entered the country. Greta Garbo was a Swedish American actress who was one of the most glamorous and popular movie stars of the inter-war period. The most famous quip attributed to Greta Garbo is the short and sardonic: "I want to be alone."

19 April 1940, Harold Hodges, *Western Mail*

THE ROMAN CANDLE

It was reported in the American press that Hitler, on the advice of General von Keitel, was encouraging Mussolini to actively throw in his forces with Germany in the soon to be expected offensive against the Allies. To induce Italy into the war, Germany was to offer Mussolini immediate support in Italy's Mediterranean claims and in her demand from Turkey that Italian ships should be given right of way through the Dardanelles.

5 May 1940, Bill Baker 'Pix', *Sunday Pictorial*

54   THE SECOND WORLD WAR IN CARTOONS

"NEITHER WAY."

According to the *Daily Worker*: 'As the facts about the terrible Norway affair are revealed day by day the anger of the people increases. Now they know the grim truth. But what conclusion is to be drawn from all this? A change of Government? Yes, without hesitation. Get rid of the Chamberlains, Churchills and Hoares who plunged us into this terrible war and whose policy threatens us with further disaster. But who is to replace them? A Government of Attlee, Lloyd George and Sinclair? Would these war advocates be any better than those they replace? The lesson of Norway is not the need for a "stronger" Government which will carry on the war with greater intensity, but a Government that will put an end to the war and bring peace to the peoples. The people are anxious and fearful. They are looking for a way out before the slaughter extends throughout Europe. At this moment of crisis a real Labour Opposition could bring the Government tumbling down and send a peace call which would echo through all of the warring countries. But these leaders do exactly the opposite. They come to the rescue of the warmongers, they use all of their power and influence to drive the workers to the slaughter.'

7 May 1940, Jimmy Friell 'Gabriel', *Daily Worker*

MORE POWER TO HIS ELBOW!

According to the *Daily Mirror*: 'Mr Chamberlain has decided to answer the critics of his handling of the Norway campaign by giving more power to Winston Churchill. In future, Mr Churchill will be the Minister in command of all naval, military and air operations. It was announced, weeks ago that Mr Churchill would take over the chairmanship of the Cabinet's defence committee, but, in fact, he has never had complete control of the Service departments. Many MP's have urged that Churchill's powers should be extended, and Mr Chamberlain's announcement today will stifle much criticism and prolong the life of the Government.'

9 May 1940, George Middleton, *Birmingham Gazette*

BUT SOME THINK IT ISNT GOOD ENOUGH

Chamberlain failed to justify the Government's handling of the Norwegian campaign, with his arguments being frequently met with jeers in the Commons. David Lloyd George called for his resignation stating that he had appealed "for sacrifice" and declared, "that the Prime Minister should give an example of sacrifice, because I tell him that there is nothing which would contribute more to victory in this war than that he should sacrifice the seals of office." When he stood to speak, Leo Amery evoked Cromwell's words by saying: "You have sat for too long for any good you have been doing. Depart, I say, and let us have done with you. In the name of God, go!" Harold Macmillan said that Amery's speech 'effectively destroyed the Chamberlain government'.

9 May 1940, S J Ray, *Kansas City Star* (United States)

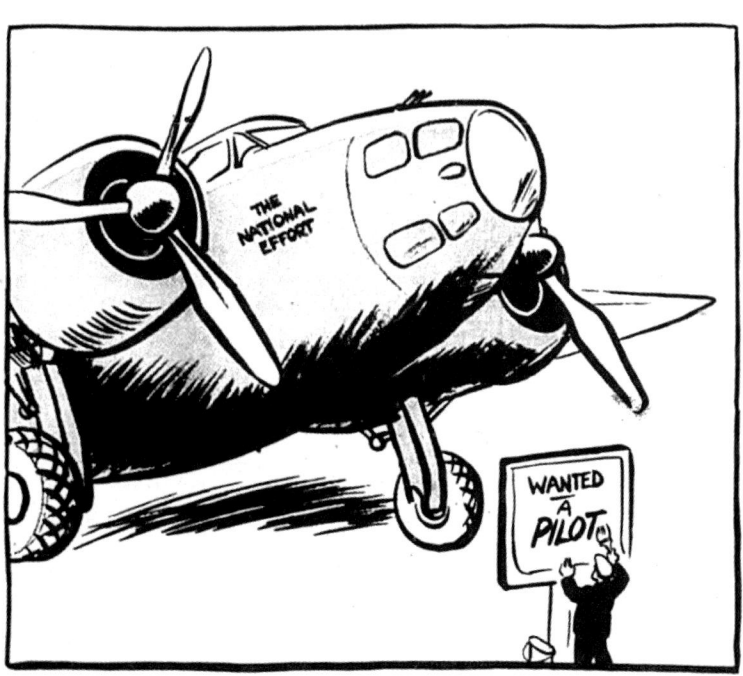

Having been humiliated over Norway, Chamberlain attempted to form a coalition government with the Labour and Liberal opposition. The leader of the Labour Party, Clement Attlee, confirmed that the party would be willing to join the Government, but not under Chamberlain. On 10 May, Chamberlain went to Buckingham Palace to offer his resignation to the King and advised him to send for Churchill, who then agreed to form a new government of national unity.

10 May 1940, Wyndham Robinson, *Star*

3
Britain's Finest Hour

[He's Broken Out Again!]

When the Germans invaded France, they avoided altogether the well defended and fortified Maginot Line by initially attacking through Belgium and the Netherlands.

10 May 1940, William Furnival, *Lancashire Evening Post*

BLITZKRIEG

Using the 'Blitzkrieg' techniques of fast-moving armoured formations supported by ground-attack aircraft, mobile artillery and mechanised infantry, German forces quickly overcame the Dutch and Belgian armies.

11 May 1940, George Finey, *Daily Telegraph* **(Sydney, Australia)**

DEAD WEIGHT

The new Premier is likely to go ahead with the war with ruthless enthusiasm.

Churchill appeared before the House of Commons and stated: "If you ask what is our policy, it is to wage war by sea, land and air with all our might . . . I have nothing to offer but blood, toil, tears and sweat." His words established a new more aggressive approach towards fighting the war.

11 May 1940, Arthur Potts 'Spot', *Bristol Evening World*

THE MASK DROPPED

With the headline 'Mask Dropped', the *Evening Dispatch* reported: "'The Fuhrer has decided to protect the neutrality of Belgium and Holland against the Franco-British aggressors," declared Ribbentrop, the German Foreign Minister, in his statement to German and foreign Press. "Great Britain and France have dropped the mask" he continued. "After the failure of Norway, the alarm was given in the Mediterranean. This was intended to veil the true aim — an attack on the Ruhr district of Germany via Belgium and Holland. This attack was secretly prepared a long time ago with the knowledge of Holland and Belgium. The news received during the last few days of invitations by the Belgian and Dutch Governments to British troops to land at Dutch and Belgian ports speak a clear language.'"

13 May 1940, Harold Hodges, *Western Mail*

The Beast Is Loose

See Uptton cartoon on page 52.

14 May 1940, Clive Uptton, *Daily Sketch*

"GO ON BOYS — THEY'VE GOT ME"

Having heavily bombed Rotterdam, the Germans threatened to bomb other large Dutch cities if Dutch forces refused to surrender. On 14 May the Dutch did so to prevent other cities from being destroyed.

15 May, 1940, W. H. Woodburn 'Hengest' *Manchester Evening News*

"The whole place afire and — me with this thing on my hands!"

Roosevelt was predisposed to help Britain but with the Presidential elections set for November, he did not want to risk alienating either Congress or the electors. America at the time was overwhelmingly isolationist. Polls still showed that 80% of Americans were against joining the war in Europe. To have openly supported Britain was deemed at the time to be electoral suicide.

16 May 1940, Arthur Potts 'Spot', *Bristol Evening World*

'Value of Slaves' The Germans are advancing even over their own dead and wounded. News item

According to the *Daily Sketch* War Correspondent Aubrey Hammond: 'The enemy hordes have been pressing on with such disregard of life that it is as though they were driven forward under some hypnotic influence. No masterly strategy has brought about the German successes. It Is simply a battering ram attack launched with at least half of Germany's offensive strength.'

22 May 1940, Clive Uptton, *Daily Sketch*

The Emergency Powers (Defence) Act, originally passed by Parliament at the start of the war, was extended on 22 May. The Act made 'provision for requiring persons to place themselves, their services and their property at the disposal of His Majesty . . . or for maintaining supplies or services essential to the life of the community'. As Churchill told President Roosevelt: "Democracy has to prove that it can provide a granite foundation for war against tyranny."

24 May 1940, Wyndham Robinson, *Star*

'Not So Fast — YOU!'

Lieutenant General Alan Brooke set up a defensive perimeter around Dunkirk, in order to allow the rest of the British Expeditionary Force to fall back towards the beaches, so as to be evacuated by the Royal Navy back to Britain.

26 May 1940, Percy Walmsley 'Lees', *Sunday Graphic*

CARRYING ON

According to the *Yorkshire Post*: 'The communique issued this morning read: The military situation has become graver as a result of the capitulation of the King of the Belgians, whose army was engaged at the side of the French and British. Although King Leopold's action opened the road to Dunkirk to the Germans the Allied Command has never lost its coolness for a moment. The watchword immediately went out " The British and French go on fighting."'

29 May 1940, Talbot Ellison, *Birmingham Mail*

Britain's Finest Hour

WINNING THEIR IRON CROSS

In order to disrupt Allied communications, the Luftwaffe deliberately bombed small towns and villages behind Allied lines, chasing the civilian population on to the roads and thus clogging them up. The Luftwaffe would then create further havoc and damage, machine-gunning the struggling refugees from the air. An American ambulance driver witnessed such scenes: "I saw German bombers open the full blast of their machine-guns on women, children and old men struggling along the roads loaded with whatever they could carry and intent only on escaping the danger."

1 June 1940, Harold Hodges, *Western Mail*

LEOPOLD LOOKS ON

The world is full of a number of things, I'm sure we should all be as happy as kings. — Robert Louis Stevenson

King Leopold III of Belgium's unconditional surrender left the British with no choice other than to evacuate its forces from the continent of Europe.

2 June 1940, Carl Giles, *Reynolds News*

62 THE SECOND WORLD WAR IN CARTOONS

"We'll be back, Adolf"

Operation Dynamo, the successful evacuation of British and French troops from the beaches of Dunkirk took place between 27 May and 4 June. A total of 338 226 troops were successfully evacuated back to Britain.

2 June 1940, Percy Walmsley 'Lees', *Sunday Graphic*

"FOILED AGAIN"

"We shall meet the Germans again, and next time victory will be with us." — Lord Gort,

Lord Gort had been Commander-in-Chief of the British Expeditionary Force and had withdrawn British forces towards the coast on 25 May, disregarding orders to join French forces in a counter attack. This decision made the subsequent evacuation of British and French troops from Dunkirk possible. In the circumstances, the wisdom of ordering a retreat is not widely held in doubt: the BEF would otherwise have been annihilated.

3 June 1940, Talbot Ellison, *Birmingham Mail*

According to *John Bull*: 'Britain is strong. Britain is ready. The whole of the nation has been mobilised. Every man and woman is now a soldier. And all of us are in the front line. Hitler is determined to strike at these shores. His defeat does not rest alone on the men fighting grimly for us in Flanders, on the youngsters of the R.A.F. who have saved the Allied armies from disaster, on the Navy that is our greatest protection against invasion. It rests also on the people in the factories and offices, on the land and at home.'

8 June 1940, Kimon Evan Marengo 'Kem', *Daily Herald*

"If new enemies oppose us we may be sure that old and new friends will arise to help us." — Mackenzie King

According to a *New York Times* dispatch from Rome a 'straight warning' regarding the consequences of Italian intervention in the war had been given to Mussolini by President Roosevelt.

The dispatch stated: 'According to all accounts President Roosevelt has told Signor Mussolini that if he intervened it would precipitate a series of interventions, including that of the United States.

Some, however, believe it is not a question of hesitation, but that Italy is refraining from action at the insistence of Hitler, who may be anxious that the war should not at present be extended to the Mediterranean.'

10 June 1940, Clive Uptton, *Daily Sketch*

The Man Who Would Play With Fire

On 10 June, with the French in full retreat and the British evacuating its forces from Dunkirk, Mussolini declared war on France and Britain, though he had not consulted his own government or the advisory Grand Council of Fascism. The following day, he sent the Italian Royal Air Force to attack French bases in Tunisia, North Africa, and on the French Mediterranean island of Corsica, as well as British installations on the strategically located fortress island of Malta.

12 June 1940, Arthur Potts 'Spot', *Bristol Evening World*

WE STAND ALONE

With the heading 'Men who guard Britain' the *North Eastern Gazette* reported: 'Nearly three million men, forming what might be called an international army, are resting on their haversacks in Great Britain, prepared to stem and stop the avalanche of Nazism making its final plunge. In this glorious stand, which Britain has decided to make alone if necessary, there has flocked to her aid nationals from those countries which have fallen beneath the heel of Germany. These foreigners, who have rallied around the standard of liberty, are all trained soldiers and men who have had practical fighting experience.'

19 June 1940, Arthur Potts 'Spot', *Bristol Evening World*

History Repeats

On 22 June, the French officially surrendered to the Germans. The armistice agreement was signed in the same railway carriage in which the Germans had been forced to sign the surrender at the end of the First World War. Meanwhile, the British fought on alone, with Churchill proclaiming that it would be Britain's 'finest hour'.

23 June 1940, Fred O. Seibel, *Richmond Times-Dispatch* **(Virginia, United States)**

Britain's Finest Hour

The True Spirit of Gaul

On 18 June, General Charles de Gaulle made a broadcast to German occupied France, rallying the French Resistance to "fight on to uphold the honour of France." With Petain's government having signed an armistice with Germany, de Gaulle refused to accept that the fight for his country was over; "Quoi qu'il arrive, la flamme de la résistance française ne doit pas s'éteindre et ne s'éteindra pas". De Gaulle was recognised by Churchill as "the leader of all Free Frenchmen, wherever they may be."

24 June 1940, W. H. Woodburn 'Hengest', *Manchester Evening News*

THE PUPPET

Churchill made it clear that the Petain Government would be regarded as having delivered itself over to the enemy. Vichy France was established after the armistice, and took its name from the government's administrative centre in Vichy. While officially neutral in the war, Vichy actively collaborated with Hitler and the Nazis, including, to some degree, with their racial policies.

26 June 1940, Talbot Ellison, *Birmingham Mail*

According to the *Daily Record*: 'It is expected that the Italian peace terms to France will bear a superficial appearance of moderation. This is under Hitler's pressure and a repetition of the old Nazi trick, used in the case of Czechoslovakia, of reassuring the victim while there is still any possibility of his resisting.'

26 June 1940, Cecil Orr, *Daily Record*

The Flag Still Flies

According to the *Daily Record*, de Valera stated: 'that the country was in danger of invasion. The geographical position of Ireland made it a tempting place for any belligerent. The war had taken a very quick turn recently and instead of removing the danger had only brought it nearer and made it more threatening. But if they had time to organise, he had no doubt that they could render an attempted Invasion very unattractive.'

28 June 1940, Cecil Orr, *Daily Record*

THE SPIRIT OF BRITAIN

According to *John Bull*: 'Now that France Is conquered, Great Britain, with the Empire, has to face the might of Germany alone. She can do it, but for the next three months we shall need our utmost fortitude. Hitler is staking everything upon victory before the winter. We are staking not only our lives and our freedom, but the fate of civilisation, upon holding fast until the darkening days begin to lighten our tremendous task. The testing time is now. With each week of dauntless resistance our strength will grow and his decline. And so each to his post of duty!

29 June 1940, Kimon Evan Marengo 'Kem', *John Bull*

Friendly Relations

Having already partitioned the eastern part of Poland, Stalin had by July also swallowed up the Baltic States of Latvia, Lithuania and Estonia, Finland and parts of Romania which all now came into the Soviet sphere of influence. Hitler, along with Mussolini, basically controlled the rest of Europe. A number of observers, correctly as it turned out, believed that the competing Fascist and Communist states would eventually turn on each other.

1 July 1940, Cecil Orr, *Daily Record*

THE LOOTER

According to the *Manchester Evening News*: 'The vultures are already beginning to descend upon what they believe to be the carcases of the French and British Empires. The first in this ignoble and premature game of grab is Japan, who speaks to France and to Britain with a new voice since the German success in the Battle of France . . . It is plain that if the European War seems likely to weaken British strength in the East Japan will not hesitate to attack British and French possessions there by force of arms.'

3 July 1940, W. H. Woodburn 'Hengest', *Manchester Evening News*

Britain's Finest Hour

Tragic Victory

As part of the Armistice, France had agreed to transfer its warships to German control. Part of that fleet was at the naval base at Mers El Kébir, near Oran, on the coast of French Algeria. On 3 July, in one of the hardest decisions Churchill had to make during the war, British warships opened fire on the French fleet. More than 1,250 French sailors were killed and most of the ships disabled. Seven months later Harry Hopkins told a member of Churchill's Private Office that it was Britain's action at Oran that convinced Roosevelt that Britain would continue to fight.

7 July 1940, Fred O. Seibel, *Richmond Times-Dispatch* (Virginia, United States)

According to the *Manchester Evening News*: 'Steps are about to be taken, writes our London correspondent, for recruiting all available British man-power for the supreme task of national defence. Mr. Ernest Bevin has wide compulsory powers he has not yet fully exercised. Mr. Bevin, however, dislikes the word "compulsion." He has found that "co-operation" yields bigger dividends, but the fact remains that there are gaps which must be filled by the civilian defender. A.R.P. has to be brought to the peak of efficiency and this cannot be achieved while there is a shortage of man-power. Sir John Anderson admits that the voluntary spirit has enabled most local authorities to put up a splendid show in civil defence, but in some places there is still need for further recruits.'

10 July 1940, Cecil Orr, *Daily Record*

A million men of the L.D.V. are watching and waiting for Hitler's threatened attack on this country.

In May, the British government, fearing a German invasion, had made an urgent appeal on the radio for volunteers to join a part-time defence force called the Local Defence Volunteers. The appeal was aimed at men who were ineligible or unfit to serve in the military. The LDV was soon given the more inspiring name of 'Home Guard' but had been launched without funding. This meant that for a while, the men found themselves without adequate uniforms or equipment. However, by the end of 1940, the Home Guard had developed into a well-trained and efficient force of 1.7 million men.

10 July 1940, Arthur Potts 'Spot', *Bristol Evening World*

Another Tight Little Isle

Four years after abdicating, the Duke of Windsor was sent to the Bahamas to take up Governorship of the island. Sourly referring to the Bahamas as "a third-rate colony", the Duke reluctantly accepted the appointment. The real reason behind his and his wife's exile was to keep their brazen Nazi sympathies quiet and stop them communicating with the enemy. Politically naive, the Duke had been routinely courted by Nazi agents, some of whom suggested he would be re-installed as a puppet king if the Germans conquered Britain, and he was also given to making defeatist statements.

11 July 1940, Fred O. Seibel, *Richmond Times-Dispatch* **(Virginia, United States)**

Britain's Finest Hour 71

POTZKRIEG

The Minister for Aircraft Production, Lord Beaverbrook, issued a manifesto through the newspapers "We will turn your pots and pans into Spitfires and Hurricanes, Blenheims and Wellingtons". Housewives were encouraged to hand over all their aluminium utensils for use in the manufacture of aircraft. Mountains of pots and pans and bathroom fittings were handed over for recycling. Ironically, most of this aluminium was never used.

12 July 1940, Cecil Orr, *Daily Record*

MR. CHURCHILL'S BILLPOSTER

On 14 July, Winston Churchill gave a radio address declaring that Britain would fight on alone, saying that "be the ordeal sharp or long, or both, we shall seek no terms, we shall tolerate no parley; we may show mercy — we shall ask for none."

16 July 1940, George Middleton, *Birmingham Gazette*

THE LITTLE CAESAR

According to the *Western Mail*: 'It was disclosed in an Admiralty communiqué last night that the Italian force which ran away when British warships were sighted in the Mediterranean last week included two battleships, many cruisers, and approximately 25 destroyers. Having chased them until it was within sight of land the British Fleet waited until evening in the hope that the Italians would come out and fight. But except for sending out waves of bombers the Italians made no attempt to test their strength in a naval battle.'

16 July 1940, Harold Hodges, *Western Mail*

"DO YOU THINK HE WILL FIGHT?"

20 July 1940, Kimon Evan Marengo (Kem), *Daily Herald*

I APPEAL ONCE MORE TO ENGLAND

According to the *Yorkshire Post*: 'Hitler addressing the Reichstag in Berlin last night, said: "I wish to appeal once more for the last time to commonsense. I speak as a victor proposing a reasonable peace — not as a victor demanding the capitulation of the vanquished. There are no grounds for the prolongation of the war," he said. Hitler left his listeners in no doubt that any peace would be on German terms.'

22 July 1940, Will Mahony, *Sydney Daily News* (Australia)

THAT'S THE WAY THE MONEY GOES!

According to the *Western Mail*: 'R.A.F. bombers dealt more severe blows at the German Air Force, says an Air Ministry statement. The chosen targets were the factories which build aircraft, the oil refineries which supply them with fuel, and the aerodromes from which they take off to raid Britain's towns and shipping. At Paderborn (east of the Ruhr) bombs were dropped on stores and assembly sheds, while the nearby landing ground was pocked with craters. At Diepholz, north-east of Osnabruck, more sheds and equipment dumps were set on fire. At Ghent a factory was smashed. At Bremen. Monheim, Hamburg, Gelsenkirchen, and Ghent oil tanks were hit and large fires started as the fuel spread over the yards. Pilots reported terrific explosions as one oil tank after another burst, and great beacons of flame lit up the countryside.'

24 July 1940, Clive Uptton, *Daily Sketch*

The progress of Lord Beaverbrook's drive for air supremacy is causing grave misgivings in Germany

In the four months before he took over, Britain had built just 638 fighters. He tripled fighter production in the following four months. Beaverbrook's output became 2.5 times greater than that of the Third Reich's. Beaverbrook set production quotas 15% higher than British plane makers had originally done and inspired people with what seemed to be unrealistic targets. The war of attrition took its toll from July to the end of the battle in early October. German fighter strength fell from 725 to 275. With production outpacing losses, RAF fighter planes rose from 644 to 732.

25 July 1940, Arthur Potts 'Spot', *Bristol Evening World*

SWAT THOSE WASPS! — The Japanese nuisance is becoming more acute

According to the *Bristol Evening World*: 'Japan today proclaimed their new policy. It visualises the establishment of "a great East Asiatic sphere of common prosperity" including the South Sea region, French Indo-China, and the Netherlands East Indies, with Japan, Manchukuo, and China as the mainstay. In the words of the Japanese Foreign Minister, Mr. Matsuoka, a diplomatic offensive would be launched by giving up for good the "pat on the back for everybody" policy. "Japan." he said, "would never endeavour to shake hands with those foreign countries which refuse cooperation with her."'

1 August 1940, Arthur Potts 'Spot', *Bristol Evening World*

"YEAH, THAT SURE IS MY LEG"

In reaction to the advance of the Japanese Army into Southern Indochina the United States government announced a ban on oil exports to Japan. Following this, a perception grew within the Japanese Army that their country was in danger of running out of resources. According to the *Scotsman*: 'Japan made representations to the United States against the imposition of the embargo on the export of aviation petrol to places outside the Western Hemisphere.'

2 August 1940, W. H. Woodburn 'Hengest',
Manchester Evening News

'Grr-r-r-r!'

With the threat of imminent Nazi invasion hanging over the country, the Minister of Information, Alfred Duff Cooper, thought it important for the government to know the state of public morale. He organised what was called a 'Social Survey' to find out. As his volunteer spies fanned out across the country to question people in food queues and at bus stops, the press gave them a nickname that quickly caught on: 'Cooper's snoopers'. Such prying into people's private opinions was widely deemed offensive, authoritarian, distinctly un-British and compared to the Gestapo. Duff Cooper was soon replaced as Minister for Information and the scheme abandoned.

2 August 1940, Clive Uptton, *Daily Sketch*

NO RELAXATION!

"Our sense of growing strength and preparedness must not lead to slightest relaxation of vigilance or moral alertness." — Premier's message to nation.

Churchill issued a statement warning the country that the possibility of German invasion "has by no means passed away. The fact that the Germans are now putting about rumours that they do not intend an invasion should be regarded with a double dose of the suspicion which attaches to all their utterances."

5 August 1940, Harold Hodges, *Western Mail*

THE BEATER WHO DIDN'T PUT HIS BIRDS UP

Adolf Hitler called for preparations to be made for the invasion of Britain. He demanded that "the British Air Force must be eliminated to such an extent that it will be incapable of putting up any sustained opposition to the invading troops." The Luftwaffe planned to destroy the aircraft of Fighter Command, either on the ground or in the air. Consequently, airfields and radar stations became the focus of German bombing.

6 August 1940, George Middleton, *Birmingham Gazette*

"FEEDING THE BRUTE."

According to the *Western Mail*: 'Relief food reaching Nazi conquered countries from the United States this winter may be limited largely to supplies for children in areas not occupied by German troops. It was stated that the British authorities appeared to be sympathetic to informal proposals from the American Red Cross that the food for children in unoccupied France be permitted to pass through the blockade. President Roosevelt has established machinery to administer a $60 million fund appropriated by Congress for war relief, and the American Red Cross has advised the Franco-German armistice commission of the manner in which the relief organisation operates. Nothing has been heard from the commission, it is reliably stated and the Red Cross will not make formal proposals to Britain for passage through the blockade until it learns what latitude may be expected during negotiations now in progress.

8 August 1940, Harold Hodges, *Western Mail*

Egypt is well prepared to resist any Italian assault from Libya

According to the *North Eastern Gazette*: 'Mussolini has launched his great attack in Africa. Already he has one army advancing into British Somaliland from Abyssinia. His large forces in Libya are expected to strike at Egypt and the Sudan at any moment. The Duce is faithfully imitating the tactics which Hitler's troops have employed in Europe. Heavy air attacks on our forces and fortified positions have preceded advances by motorised units, backed by considerable numbers of native infantry.'

10 August 1940, Arthur Potts 'Spot', *Bristol Evening World*

' — in a badly damaged condition, and probably beyond repair.'

On 13 August, Hitler unleashed the Luftwaffe's main offensive against air bases, aircraft factories and against radar stations in south-eastern England. To defend the country the British arranged more than 600 frontline fighters. Thanks to their superior equipment the British actually had the advantage against the German bombers that were mostly lightly armed, twin-engine planes. These aircraft in daylight were very vulnerable and so by the end of August, the Luftwaffe had lost more than 600 aircraft. By mid-September, British fighters were shooting down German bombers faster than German industry could produce them.

13 August 1940, Cecil Orr, *Daily Record*

THERE'S ONLY ONE TOPIC

On the day this cartoon was published, in the biggest air engagement of the Battle of Britain up to this point, the Luftwaffe attempted to overwhelm the RAF with a series of major air attacks. The Germans lost 76 aircraft to the British 34, and to the Germans the day became known as Black Thursday. On the 21 August, Churchill stated in the Commons that: "Never in the field of human conflict was so much owed by so many to so few. All hearts go out to the fighter pilots, whose brilliant actions we see with our own eyes day after day."

15 August 1940, George Whitelaw, *Daily Herald*

THE MAN WHO TAKES THE "F" OUT OF FLYING

With the headline 'The R.A.F. and Dr. Goebbels' the *Evening Telegraph* stated: 'One of Germany's leaders is apparently unperturbed by his country's air losses. This is Dr. Goebbels, the Propaganda Minister, who has a simple formula by which defeats may be turned into victories; humiliation to glory. The falsity of Dr. Goebbels's claims is manifest to all who claims have eyes to see. Remember that he has already, on paper or over the wireless, more than once sunk the British Fleet.

Now he is just as speedily shooting the R.A.F. out of the skies. Yet our Navy is still blockading Europe, and our airmen are still able effectively to defend our shores and to hit back, hard, in Germany itself.'

20 August 1940, George Whitelaw, *Daily Herald*

"AND THEN THERE WAS ONE"

On 20 August, an assassin called Ramon Mercader, acting on Stalin's orders, stabbed Trotsky with an ice pick, who died of his injuries the following day. With his nemesis murdered, Stalin could feel a deep satisfaction. The individual, who, more than any other, symbolised opposition to Stalinism, had been eliminated. Stalin was now the only survivor of Lenin's first politburo having had all the other members eliminated.

22 August 1940, W. H. Woodburn 'Hengest', *Manchester Evening News*

78   THE SECOND WORLD WAR IN CARTOONS

Thespian Tribulations

With Hitler considering postponing the invasion of Britain (he had claimed he would be in London by 15 August), Mussolini looked into the possibilities of invading Greece via newly conquered Albania.

24 August 1940, Cecil Orr, *Daily Record*

"PUSSOLINI"

According to the *Dundee Courier*: 'The very explicit report that the Italians had presented an ultimatum to Greece demanding her renunciation within 24 hours of the British guarantee of help is denied in Rome, and we should say was nothing more than a speculation put in the form of a statement of fact. The manner of the Dictators when they do present an ultimatum is to act before its delivery, and if Mussolini had presented one to Greece his armies would now be over the Albanian frontier and his fleet would be bombarding Corfu.

25 August 1940, Stuart Peterson, *Sydney Sun* (Australia)

"Look here, Goebbels — are you telling us the truth?"

With the headline 'Goebbels says "we're breaking the R.A.F"', the *Birmingham Gazette* reported: 'The German official news agency claims that 71 British planes were shot down today with 40 brought down round Portsmouth alone. According to well-informed sources the present raids on Britain are "only just the beginning." The agency declared that today, in contrast to yesterday's fighting, British planes were unable to maintain an unbroken fighter barrage in the air along the south coast, and adds: "This shows the first signs that their resistance is broken. The English fighters fled when the German escorting fighters appeared."'

26 August 1940, Arthur Potts 'Spot', *Bristol Evening World*

THE CHAIN OF FRIENDSHIP

On 3 September, President Roosevelt announced that he was sending 50 obsolete destroyers to Britain in exchange for 99-year leases on seven British bases in the western hemisphere (Newfoundland, Bermuda, several Caribbean islands and British Guiana). Churchill had originally asked for the warships in order to replenish British losses during the Norwegian campaign.

5 September 1940, George Butterworth, *Daily Dispatch*

Austrian Paperhanger Again

Following Britain's rejection of his final offer of a negotiated peace settlement, Hitler had ordered an immediate invasion of Britain to prevent the British army recovering from its defeat in France. The Luftwaffe's failure to achieve air supremacy in the Battle of Britain forced Hitler to postpone Operation Sealion indefinitely. The operation was never formally cancelled.

8 September 1940, Stuart Peterson, *Sydney Sun* **(Australia)**

Salute!

The Luftwaffe had originally concentrated its airpower against the RAF. The Germans were on the cusp of overwhelming the RAF when the accidental bombing of London occurred. Churchill interpreted this as a deliberate strike against defenceless civilians and, ordered the bombing of Berlin. Enraged, Hitler ordered the Luftwaffe to switch from their successful attacks against airfields and conduct a 'Blitz' bombing of London. While 'the Blitz' resulted in vast destruction, from a military perspective, the purely revenge attacks relieved the pressure on the RAF and allowed it to recover.

11 September 1940, Cecil Orr, *Daily Record*

The R.A.F. are steadily "extracting" Goering's airplanes.

With the headline 'Goering's Legions Begin to Face Defeat' the *Yorkshire Post* stated: 'The German air campaign against Britain completes three months this weekend, having been started in a mild form when the Nazi land forces ceased operating. The preliminary weeks were exploratory and gradually led up to the Blitzkrieg and, all told, the period cost the Germans two thousand planes and five thousand airmen. Experienced airmen are of the opinion that the Luftwaffe is facing defeat in the first great air operations the world has known, and if in 20 days from now Goering's legions score no advantage, a mortal blow will have been struck at German power and prestige.

13 September 1940, William Furnival, *Lancashire Evening Post*

Like Falling Leaves in Autumn

On 15 September, the Luftwaffe launched two huge bombing raids on London. as it was the day when RAF Fighter Command claimed what proved to be a decisive victory over the German Luftwaffe. It was claimed in the press that 'at least 175 German planes were shot down during mass attacks on Britain, 171 by R.A.F. fighters and four by anti-aircraft guns. Thirty of our fighters were lost, but ten of the pilots are safe.' In fact, Fighter Command shot down 56 German aircraft.

17 September 1940, Fred O. Seibel, *Richmond Times-Dispatch* **(Virginia, United States)**

Britain's Finest Hour 81

'NEIGHBOURS' It merely serves to unite the people. — U.S. comment

On 13 September, a single German raider dropped five bombs on Buckingham Palace, two of which exploded in the inner quadrangle, while King George VI and Queen Elizabeth were in residence.

A third bomb hit the Royal Chapel in the South Wing and a fourth was dropped on the forecourt, while the last fell near the Queen Victoria Memorial. The palace was left with significant damage with many of the windows completely shattered. After surviving the attack, the Queen Mother later said in a statement: "I am glad we have been bombed. It makes me feel I can look the East End in the face."

18 September 1940, Clive Uptton, *Daily Sketch*

" Will you come into our parlour?" said the spiders to the fly

According to the *Daily Record*: 'Hitler and Mussolini are working like beavers to make General Franco enter the war on their side. They menace him with dire consequences if Spain persists in her neutral attitude. Germans and Italians assure Franco that the time has arrived for sharing out the great French possessions in Africa. Spain claims the Oran province of Algeria, and a large slice of Morocco. Hitler has let Franco know that the Spanish claim can be satisfied only if Spain enters the war immediately.'

23 September 1940, Cecil Orr, *Daily Record*

Wind, weather and the R.A.F. seem to have induced Hitler to look towards the East.

With the headline 'Hitler And The East', the Foreign Editor of the *Daily Mail* stated: 'that the invasion of Britain was no longer the first item on Hitler's agenda. For the time being he has rolled up the map of Western Europe and is concentrating on a winter campaign in the Mediterranean in general and in the Eastern Mediterranean in particular. For one thing, the gales have scattered his armada, but the most important contribution to this decision is the fact that the R.A.F. have smashed his invasion ports and generally created havoc among his stores and the personnel attending them. Thus, the wisdom of our policy in refusing to see red because of the attacks on London and large provincial centres, and repay bomb for bomb, has been fully justified.'

23 September 1940, Arthur Potts 'Spot', *Bristol Evening World*

SUFFER LITTLE CHILDREN

The City of Benares known as the 'Children's Ship', was carrying evacuee children fleeing Britain for Canada when on 17 September it was torpedoed in mid-Atlantic by a U-boat. The ship sank in the early hours of 18 September, 600 miles off Ireland after its Royal Naval escort had deployed elsewhere. 87 children and 175 adults were lost and the sinking of the ship put an end to the short-lived policy of overseas evacuation.

24 September 1940, Will Mahony, *Sydney Daily News* **(Australia)**

DE GAULLE'S TASK

De Gaulle believed that he could persuade the French forces in Dakar, which were under Vichy French control, to join the Allied cause. Much would be gained by this. Another Vichy French colony changing sides would have great political impact. Also, the gold reserves of the Banque de France and the Polish government in exile were stored in Dakar; and the port of Dakar was far superior as a naval base to Freetown, Sierra Leone, which was the only Allied port in the area.

25 September 1940, Harold Hodges, *Western Mail*

"THANKS! AND NOW BACK IN THE BOTTLE"

The Battle of Dakar did not go as expected for de Gaulle and the Allies as Vichy forces refused to change sides. With the headline 'The Rebuff At Dakar', the *Belfast Telegraph* reported: 'The "hidden hand" working in support of the Vichy Government and in opposition to the "Free France" movement led by General de Gaulle has, for the time being at least, obtained a success at Dakar, and that important port, with the region adjoining it, must be considered as under pro-German control to a greater or less extent.

30 September 1940, George Butterworth, *Daily Dispatch*

A MACKEREL TO CATCH A SPRAT

Hitler encouraged Franco to enter the war on the Axis side. Gibraltar was offered as an incentive and would be taken by special Wehrmacht units and turned over to Spain. However, Franco refused the offer and emphasised Spain's need for large-scale military and economic assistance.

1 October 1940, George Middleton, *Birmingham Gazette*

Painful Perseverance

With the headline 'Blitzkrieg Failure' the *Belfast Telegraph* reported: 'It is two months since the German Air Force's Blitzkrieg was launched against Britain. Its objectives were the overthrow of Fighter Command and the destruction of the aerodromes on which it was based. Yet at the end of two months Germany's losses in the Battle of Britain are over 2,250 machines and approximately 5,500 airmen against 650 British machines and just over 300 pilots. Meanwhile the Bomber Command of the Royal Air Force has strengthened and lengthened its arm weekly, striking powerful blows at a wide variety of targets.'

2 October 1940, Cecil Orr, *Daily Record*

Air raids on Berlin continue to embarrass the Führer!

In retaliation for bombing London, a huge raid on Berlin was carried out by Bomber Command on 23-24 September. Berliners were horrified having believed Nazi official propaganda, that an air attack on Berlin was impossible. Goring had even said that if a single enemy bomber reached the German capital, then his name was not Goring it was "Meyer" (like the English saying "then I'm a Dutchman"). Hitler was furious and saw the attacks as a personal insult.

3 October 1940, Arthur Potts 'Spot', *Bristol Evening World*

War — The Destroyer

The Berlin correspondent of the *Aftonbladet* declared that they take the British attacks on Berlin and other places as a distinct sign that the British desire to continue the violent air warfare which has developed during recent days over the British Isles. 'Churchill will not respond to reason,' they say, 'therefore we are obliged to continue the reprisal attacks.'

11 October 1940, Fred O. Seibel, *Richmond Times-Dispatch* **(Virginia, United States)**

Britain's Finest Hour 85

According to the *Belfast Telegraph*: 'While the dangers of wishful thinking should be avoided, it seems likely that the results of the last two months' air fighting have had some effect on the Luftwaffe's morale. For the first time this creation of Goering, built up quickly, has discovered that numbers will not suffice against opponents who are fundamentally better trained and who are also better equipped. Britain's air strength has been carefully sustained and developed on a foundation of sound technical training.'

12 October 1940, Kimon Evan Marengo (Kem), *Daily Herald*

CARRIED UNANIMOUSLY

With the headline 'Balkan Defence Pack Rumoured' the *Newcastle Evening Chronicle* stated that: 'Reports reaching diplomatic circles in Bucharest today, suggest that a three-Power bloc between Jugoslavia, Greece and Turkey may be formed to resist a German or a German-Italian thrust towards Greece or Turkey.'

16 October 1940, Will Mahony, *Sydney Daily News* (Australia)

"Owner having no further use for same."

According to the *Dundee Courier*: 'The Burma Road closed three months ago in a vain effort to appease the Japanese war lords, is reopened today, and the date is marked in red in the Chinese calendar. They have assembled hundreds of lorries, properly camouflaged, at and near the point where the Burmese and Chinese sections of the road meet, and they have their well-thought-out plans for defeating the expected operations of the Japanese bombers from Indo-China. In this the good wishes of all the world, except Germany and Italy, are with them.'

18 October 1940, George Whitelaw, *Daily Herald*

"MICE, I SUPPOSE"

According to the *Daily Mirror*: 'R.A.F. raids on Berlin have produced a wisecrack. Instead of saying good night, Berliners now say "splitterfreie nacht" (splinterless). They are astonished that the R.A.F. raiders have been able to approach Berlin always from the same directions, despite Goering's boast. There is now considerable respect in Berlin for the R.A.F., he adds. Goering has revised his previous instructions to the public. They must now take shelter as soon as the alarm sounds instead of waiting for the drone of motors and the sound of anti-aircraft fire.'

19 October 1940, Geoffrey Evans, *Western Mail*

The Lion Grows Belligerent

Britain now stood as the last bastion of resistance against Nazi Germany. The *New York Herald-Tribune* stated: 'The old iron determination was there, underlying the whole, flashing through, in those carefully wrought phrases of which Mr. Churchill is the master. The note of confidence was stronger, and the tension less than in his earlier calls to arms. Many there must be in Europe who, doomed by the brute strength of a triumphant army to suffer silently, will take renewed courage from the British leader's touching close. His general confidence brought renewed relief to people who wonder, in spite of the courage being shown by the, British people, how long they can stand the German air raids. Churchill's insistence that Britain "will stick it out" was welcomed everywhere.'

24 October 1940, Cecil Orr, *Daily Record*

"There is every reason to believe that the Nazis are about to embark on a new and greater scheme than ever before for the falsification of news."

According to *Reuters*: 'Nazi officials apparently no longer hold out any prospect of a quick victory over Britain, for Goebbels said in a speech in Danzig that Germans knew Britain's downfall "must come some-day." "London is trembling under the hammer blows of the German air attack," he said.'

26 October 1940, Cecil Orr, *Daily Record*

THE ROAD TO NOWHERE

"I enter to-day the path of collaboration with Germany." — Pétain.

A week after meeting Hitler, Pétain made collaboration Vichy state policy, declaring on French radio: "I enter today on the path of collaboration", and inviting his countrymen to join him on the journey. He believed that improving relations with Germany was the only viable option for France.

1 November 1940, George Middleton, *Birmingham Gazette*

On 28 October, Mussolini, whose army already occupied Albania, invaded Greece in what proved to be a disastrous military campaign for the Duce's forces. Mussolini, fed up with playing second fiddle to Hitler according to the American press, surprised everyone with this move against Greece. Hitler denounced the move as a major strategic blunder. After just one week, the Greeks succeeded in pushing the Italian invaders back into Albania where they spent the next three months fighting for its life in a defensive battle.

3 November 1940, Percy Walmsley 'Lees', *Sunday Graphic*

Now's the time to catch him bending

According to the *Western Mail*: '"Hit Italy and hit her hard" seems to have become the nation's slogan, and it was good news that the R.A.F. had bombed Naples, the most distant objective in enemy territory it has yet attacked. Equally satisfactory is it to hear of British bombs falling on Italian-occupied Albania, including several Albanian ports. These exploits have done a great deal to hearten the Greeks, to whose unity and determination all the messages of correspondents on the spot give unstinted testimony.'

4 November 1940, Cecil Orr, *Daily Record*

SAM MAKES. DOUBLY SURE!

This cartoon appeared on the day of the 1940 American Presidential Election. Both President Roosevelt and his Republic opponent Wendell Willkie favoured a vigorous defence programme and all possible aid to Britain "short of war." Roosevelt would win a historic third term with 449 electoral votes compared to Willkie's 82.

5 November 1940, Harold Hodges, *Western Mail*

Eire Prime Minister, Éamon de Valera, followed a policy of strict neutrality for Ireland and refused to let British forces use Irish naval bases, despite German air raids on the city of Dublin. On 7 November he asserted that Ireland would resist by force any attempt to occupy the ports or to impair Ireland's sovereignty by any of the belligerents: "That is the determination of the government and of the people. Under no circumstances will this policy be departed from."

8 November 1940, Wyndham Robinson, *Star*

Britain's Finest Hour

1918-1940 : And the Old Spirit Still Lives.

According to the *Evening News*: 'What would the heroes who passed on in the Great War say to us if they were with us today? The confident reply surely is, "Keep the flag flying!" The roll of honour in 1914-18 was long and glorious, and here we are again today, and have been for many months, acknowledging the dauntless brave on sea, on land, and in the air. The standard of bravery in this war reaches to the heavens, but who showed the way? Truly, the men of 1914-18. Our men in 1914-18 never let us down. Nor will the men of today, many of whom served in the Great War, lack in shining courage.'

11 November 1940, Cecil Orr, *Daily Record*

MUSSO FEELS THE HEAT

According to the *Daily Record*: 'The surprising failure of the Italian campaign against the Greeks has improved our situation in the Eastern Mediterranean beyond all probable expectation. After this, Mussolini will know beyond doubt the trouble that awaits him in ferrying supplies and reinforcements from Italy across the Adriatic to his troops in Greece and Africa. Not even the Greek Islands a prize strategically well worth his attack on Greece, have fallen into his hands. On the contrary we have now been able to occupy them without breaking any laws of neutrality.'

12 November 1940, Harold Hodges, *Western Mail*

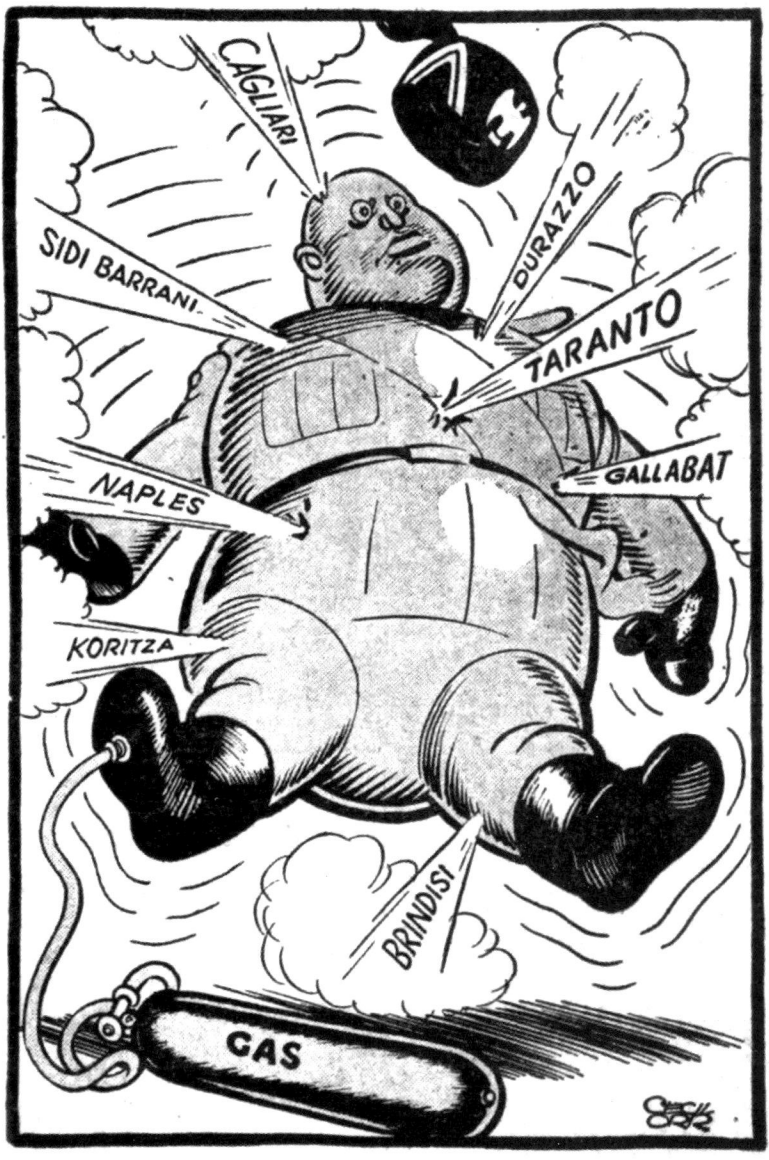

Exit the Bogy Man.

On the nights of 11 and 12 November, British torpedo bombers from HMS Illustrious decimated the Italian Navy at Taranto Bay. In an article entitled 'Blows for Italy', the *Advertiser* reported: 'Since the sinking of the Graf Spee the people of the British Empire have had no more heartening news than that announced by the Prime Minister of the crippling of the Italian fleet by the British Fleet Air Arm. Japanese planning staff studied the Taranto attack intensively when planning their successful attack on US naval forces at Pearl Harbor in 1941.

15 November 1940, Cecil Orr, *Daily Record*

SEND HIM TO COVENTRY

On 14 November the Luftwaffe launched its most devastating bombing raid of the war so far. Almost 500 German bombers attacked the manufacturing city of Coventry. According to the *Daily Herald*: 'The bombing of Coventry was as foul a deed as even Hitler has ever ordained. Clearly his airmen were instructed: "Don't worry If you cannot reach your industrial targets. Bomb and burn the city. Never mind if you fail to hit factories. Hit houses. Have no scruples about military objectives. Kill men, kill women, kill children. Destroy! Destroy! Destroy! Heil Hiller! Hell bloodshed! Heil pain!"

17 November 1940, Sidney Moon, *Sunday Dispatch*

Britain's Finest Hour

GREAT CITIZENS

Being a tribute to the city's auxiliary services!

On 24 November, 148 German bombers attacked Bristol. Coventry had suffered a devastating air raid 10 days earlier, but that night the Luftwaffe wreaked havoc on another historic city. More than 200 people died, 187 were seriously injured and 1,400 were made homeless. The German plan was to destroy the port and Bristol Aeroplane Company, but it was the city's mediaeval centre which bore the brunt of the bombs. The port was an important Luftwaffe target as a distribution centre for essential supplies and shipyards where warships were made and repaired. The Edward Colston statue was then seen as a symbol of both pride and defiance.

27 November 1940, Arthur Potts 'Spot', *Bristol Evening World*

The Mirror of Truth

According to the *Daily Record*: 'The Greek advance into Albania shows no signs of slackening. Pushing forward on all fronts the Greeks have now reached a point seven miles from Tepelini, which is only 30 miles from the key port of Valona. The capture of Tepelini would give the Greeks command of practically the whole of Southern Albania. Mussolini who is now being forced to admit Italian reverses, may make an inspection tour of the Albanian front within the next few days, according to reports in Rome.'

11 December 1940, Cecil Orr, *Daily Record*

The Soviet cartoonist mischievously highlights Britain's precarious financial position as by December, British bankruptcy was imminent. On 8 December, Churchill wrote a letter to this effect to Roosevelt. In it he stated: 'The more rapid and abundant the flow of munitions and ships which you are able to send us, the sooner will our dollar credits be exhausted. They are already, as you know, very heavily drawn upon by the payments we have made to date. Indeed, as you know the orders already placed or under negotiation . . . many times exceed the total exchange resources remaining at the disposal of Great Britain. The moment approaches when we shall no longer be able to pay cash for shipping and other supplies.'

18 December 1940, Boris Efimov, *Izvestia* **(Soviet Union)**

"OUR MAIN ARMY IS INTACT." — Rome Radio.

According to the *Derby Evening Telegraph*: 'In a brilliant action against Bardia, Australian troops have captured a quarter of the beleaguered Italian garrison, which was estimated at 20,000 men. A special communique from G.H.Q. in Cairo states: "Operations developing successfully. So far 5,000 prisoners have been captured."'

8 January 1941, George Whitelaw, *Daily Herald*

Britain's Finest Hour 93

The Talking Dummy

According to the *Daily Mirror*: 'The New Year will bring decisive events in the war against Hitler and his puppet Mussolini. Official spokesmen yesterday were confident in their predictions of R.A.F. expansion to a smashing force never yet seen, of a Victory Army finally equipped for action anywhere.'

9 January 1941, Cecil Orr, *Daily Record*

HOT EIRE

It was reported that nine Eire ships flying the Eire flag had been sunk off the coast of Ireland. Taoiseach Éamon de Valera told the Dáil that the loss of life and the sinkings had "occasioned feelings of deep resentment here" and that he had protested to the German government and lodged a claim for compensation, and "reserved all rights to which we are entitled by International Law." Rumours abounded that this was intended to intimidate the Irish into remaining neutral in spite of Anglo-American pressure for the use of Irish bases to help to protect convoys.

14 January 1941, George Whitelaw, *Daily Herald*

"REMEMBER ME?'

(Haile Selassie is raising the standard of revolt against Italian rule in Abyssinia.)

Haile Selassie returned from exile by crossing the border from Sudan into Ethiopia. The standard of the Lion of Judah was raised again. Two days later, he and a force of Ethiopian patriots joined British and African forces, which were already in Ethiopia. On 5 May 1941, Haile Selassie would enter Addis Ababa and personally address the Ethiopian people, exactly five years after the Italians had entered Addis Ababa:

15 January 1941, George Whitelaw, *Daily Herald*

VOICE FROM THE MINARET

Within two days of this cartoon being published, Tobruk was captured by Allied troops, during Operation Compass, an offensive against the Italian forces in Egypt and Cyrenaica. About 25,000 Italian personnel surrendered there, though the base itself was well-stocked with supplies. On 3 January, the British began their attack. After only three days, the Italians surrendered; Tobruk followed on January 24. All in all, another 75,000 Italians had surrendered.

19 January 1941, Percy Walmsley 'Lees', *Sunday Graphic*

At the Water's Edge

In order to bring Anthony Eden back as Foreign Secretary, Churchill persuaded Lord Halifax to take up the ambassadorship to Washington. President Roosevelt underlined the importance of his arrival by waiving diplomatic precedent and sailing out on his yacht, Potomac, to personally greet the Ambassador. He proceeded to entertain Halifax and his wife, Dorothy, to tea on board.

26 January 1941, Fred O. Seibel, *Richmond Times-Dispatch* (Virginia, United States)

Britain's Finest Hour

THE GIRLS THEY LEAVE BEHIND 'EM

From 1941, it became compulsory for women aged between 18 and 60 to register for war work. They fulfilled roles such as mechanics, engineers, munitions workers, air raid wardens, bus and fire engine drivers. By 1943, almost 90 per cent of single women and 80 per cent of married women were working in factories, on the land or in the armed forces.

31 January 1941, Clive Uptton, *Daily Sketch*

Exile's Dream of Home

According to the *Newcastle Journal*: 'British United Press war correspondent at Derna states that British guns are lumbering past Derna as General Wavell's victorious army continues to move Westward. The Imperial forces rejoiced at the sight of Derna with its splashes of green foliage in the surrounding countryside and the groups of palm trees affording restful shade. The trees there were the first they had seen for weeks but the advance relentlessly continues.' Before the war, the stereotypical view of Italians was as ice-cream salesmen.

3 February 1941, Cecil Orr, *Daily Record*

The Lease-and-Lend Bill is being hurried through the U.S. legislature despite Hitlers U-boat threat.

According to the *Gloucester Citizen*: 'Generally phlegmatic reception is accorded here to Hitler's speech in the Munich Beer Cellar. Attention centres in the threat of intensified submarine warfare which the "*New York Times*" and the "*New York Herald Tribune*" both interpret as a challenge to the capacity of the United States to deliver war material overseas.'

4 February 1941, Arthur Potts 'Spot', *Bristol Evening World*

Petain offered Laval a cabinet seat in the Vichy government, but the offer was refused because the latter did not want to accept a secondary position in the government. According to the *Daily Herald*: 'Laval, as Premier by the grace of Hitler, would direct France's foreign policy, anyway — in the interest of Germany. As Minister of the Interior be would have all police powers for dealing with his enemies in the Fascist way. True to Nazi form, Laval has apparently demanded more, he wanted to become Premier, Foreign Minister and Minister of the Interior as well.'

10 February 1941, William Furnival, *Lancashire Evening Post*

Britain's Finest Hour 97

According to the *Daily Herald*: 'Italians in Libya and East Africa are retreating faster than ever — with our troops hot in pursuit. At the moment, especially in Libya, the chase covers thirty miles a day — "a marked speeding up in the tempo of our advances" as a military spokesman in Cairo described it. Graziani's army is in full flight towards Benghazi leaving the roads littered with war materials and vehicles. Of Graziani, the Italian Commander-in-Chief, no news has so far been received. By another masterstroke of strategy, General Wavell has driven him once more to seek safety in flight.'

11 February 1941, Cecil Orr, *Daily Record*

Master Strategist Seeks Inspiration

Churchill in a speech on the next phase of the war, turned to the subject of Hitler's next move:

"What has that wicked man, whose crime-stained regime and system are at bay and in the toils — what has he been preparing during these winter months. What new devilry is he planning? What new small country will be overrun? What fresh form of assault will he make on our island home that stands between him and the domination of the world? We may be sure that the war is soon going to enter upon a phase of greater violence."

18 February 1941, Cecil Orr, *Daily Record*

The Australians have arrived at Singapore to keep the Axis steady in the East.

According to the *Daily Mirror*: 'An Australian Imperial Force, many thousands strong, reached Singapore yesterday bringing to the Empire's Pacific defences the largest and most powerful reinforcement of men and guns that has ever arrived under a single convoy. A few hours after disembarking from the great liners which transported them under an Australian and British naval escort, the Australians entrained for prepared defence stations on the Malayan peninsula.'

20 February 1941, Arthur Potts 'Spot',
Bristol Evening World

HON. CONVERSATION

"Hon. Friend will accept my humble assurance that I did not knock upon door. Yes please?"
"Will Hon. Friend perceive that there is no Hon. door?"

According to the *Daily Mirror*: 'Mr. Churchill has told Japan there can be no question of compromise or parley in the cause for which were fighting: "It is a cause in no way concerned with territory, trade or material gains," he said "It affects the whole future of humanity." That snub of Japan's offer of "mediation" was revealed in Parliament yesterday by the Foreign Under Secretary.

27 February 1941, George Middleton,
Birmingham Gazette

Leaving no stone unturned

With the headline '7 British Columns Are Carving Up Italian East Africa' the *Manchester Evening News* reported that: 'With only a fraction of the 500,000 men Mussolini used to conquer Abyssinia, seven advances by British columns are routing the Italians on all fronts and threatening to strip the Duce of his East-African Empire. In the six weeks of their offensive the attackers have made important inroads into Italy's East African forces. Considerable casualties have been inflicted, at least 15,000 prisoners taken, and much material secured.'

3 March 1941, Cecil Orr, *Daily Record*

NO CAUSE FOR ALARM

With the headline 'Attack On Greece In 48 Hours' the *Northern Whig* reported that: 'as the threat to Greece and Turkey increases, Sofia reports that Britain is sending all the equipment she could spare to Turkey, the one power able to harass any German march into Greece. Neutral military observers in Sofia expressed the view that German troops massed on the Bulgarian frontiers with Greece and Turkey may attack Eastern Macedonia and Thrace within 48 hours.' Stalin would soon ignore information from various sources on Hitler's intention to invade the Soviet Union.

9 March 1941, Percy Walmsley 'Lees', *Sunday Graphic*

THE NEW "OLD BILL."

With Britain no longer able to pay cash for war materials and food, as required by United States law, President Roosevelt introduced a 'Lend-Lease' Bill into the American Congress in January. Though bitterly contested by isolationists, the bill became law on 11 March. The Act allowed the United States to lend or lease war supplies to any nation deemed "vital to the defence of the United States".

10 March 1941, George Butterworth, *Daily Dispatch*

100   THE SECOND WORLD WAR IN CARTOONS

HOLDING THE WHEEL

According to the *Belfast Telegraph* the Nazis had put their hopes in Admiral Darlan to act as an instrument for carrying out their demands. He had 'been vested practically full power to control the French Government, subject only to Marshal Petain's veto. Marshal Petain could be forced to resign his position as head of the French Administration. What the Nazis want, of course, is the French Fleet and use of its bases on either side of the Mediterranean, in the hope of making the British position there one of much difficulty.'

12 March 1941, George Middleton, *Birmingham Gazette*

R.A.F. night fighters are taking an increasing toll on Goering's Luftwaffe.

Initially, RAF Fighter Command found it almost impossible to target German night bombers, who operated with virtual immunity from being shot down. With the advent of new radar equipment, R.A.F ground control operators could now view a radar map of incoming German night bombers, and guide night-fighters towards them. In March, 22 German bombers were shot down. The following month, the figure was 48 and in May almost 100 enemy aircraft were destroyed by RAF night-fighters. German night raids then tailed off as Luftwaffe bomber units were deployed elsewhere.

15 March 1941, Arthur Potts 'Spot', *Bristol Evening World*

BOGEY — BOGEY!

According to the *Portsmouth Evening News*: 'Winston Churchill and the indomitable courage of the British people were described as Britain's secret weapons by Sir Douglas Hacking, Chairman of the Conservative Party at the opening of War Weapons Week in Dorking: "When Hitler started out to subdue the world to his rule, we had two secret weapons that he never dreamed of. The first is the indomitable courage of the people of Britain and the Empire — a bulldog people who once they got their teeth in would never let go. Our second secret weapon is Winston Churchill. In this our greatest hour, we are fortunate indeed to be fighting under the incomparable leadership of a very great leader. Today he is not only the embodiment of the spirit of Britain, he is our bulldog leader, whom Britons, nay, the whole world of free men, place their implicit trust."'

17 March 1941, W. H. Woodburn 'Hengest', *Manchester Evening News*

SECOND THOUGHTS

Hitler having proved unable to persuade Yugoslav Prime Minister Dragisa Cvetkovic to formally join the Axis, gave Yugoslavia an ultimatum to join within five days or face invasion. With an anti-German uprising in Yugoslavia, Hitler maintained that the country must now be regarded as an enemy and be destroyed as quickly as possible.

18 March 1941, Wyndham Robinson, *Star*

"NOW, WHAT ABOUT A FEW MORE CHURCHES, HERMY?"

According to the *Daily Herald*: 'A doctor stood amid ruins of a London hospital at which he is senior medical officer. "It might have been worse," he said. It was one of five hit in Wednesday night's Blitz. While more than 100 patients were trying to sleep in this hospital two high explosive bombs dropped on it. Floors crashed on top of five nurses, burying them in debris. Other nurses ran to the rescue and dug them out with their bare hands. While guns roared, incendiaries blazed. and bombs crumped all round them the rescued nurses, their rescuers and the doctors got all the patients out of their beds on to stretchers and into ambulances.'

21 March 1941, George Whitelaw, *Daily Herald*

Tell me laddie, who is this fellow Hitler?

According to the *Sunderland Echo*: 'Mussolini's East African Empire, founded upon aggression, fostered by Fascism and fortified by the "lath-and-plaster" bulwarks of propaganda, crumbled to dust under the force of hurricane blows by Britain's Imperial Forces which by their speed and almost instantaneous effect wherever they were delivered made the miracle of Jericho seem almost common-place. The stucco front of Fascist imperialism, raised by rhetorical frothings from balconies in Rome, collapsed at the first real British onslaught, to reveal the hollow sham which had been masquerading as a responsible governing force.'

4 April 1941, George Whitelaw, *Daily Herald*

Easter Egg

As reported in the *Daily Record*: 'According to Nazi officials, Berlin's State Opera House, on Unter den Linden, was burned out in one of the fires caused during a three-hour raid by the R.A.F.. Aircraft of the Bomber Command made the long flight to Berlin on a clear night and under a moon that was almost full. The result of the attack on Berlin provides an infamous example of the methods of the British Air Force," squealed German Radio. "The attack was aimed at the cultural centre of the city, such as the State Opera House, State Library and the Unter den Linden, which were deliberately attacked. Two hospitals were also bombed, a part of one building being destroyed." Air Chief Marshall Charles Portal advocated strategic area bombing against German industrial areas, the same sort of targets that the Luftwaffe was already targeting in Britain.'

12 April 1941, Cecil Orr, *Daily Record*

According to the *News Chronicle*: 'Perhaps the bitterest pill for Mussolini and his admirers to swallow is the fact that the Fascist system which set out to make the Italians a nation of conquerors is the root cause of their military failure. Graziani's army in Libya suffered the most humiliating defeat in modern history, losing prisoners in greater numbers than the whole British attacking force, not because the Italian troops lacked courage but because of poor equipment, bad staff work, insufficient reconnaissance, slow and stupid planning, but above all political interference from Rome and most of all from the Duce in person.'

14 April 1941, Victor Weisz 'Vicky', *News Chronicle*

On the Treadmill

According to the *Daily Record*: 'Berlin resumed its fire-eating campaign yesterday after a period of comparative inactivity. A radio announcement regarding the Nazi campaign in the Balkans stated that its object was to destroy the Yugoslav Army, break the Greek and British line of resistance, drive Britain completely out of the Balkans and North Africa, and then to launch "the final great offensive against England herself."'

16 April 1941, Cecil Orr, *Daily Record*

BUT COURAGE IS NOT ENOUGH

According to the *Birmingham Mail*: An *Associated Press* correspondent from 'somewhere in Montenegro' wrote: 'I have just traversed much of Jugoslavia watching a gallant army try unsuccessfully with rifles and ox-drawn artillery to fight off the ponderous force of Hitler's Panzer and Luftwaffe legions.' A day later the same paper reported that despite having capitulated, 'Jugoslavian troops were still offering a strong resistance and that, though they are no longer fighting under one command, they are forcing the German troops to attack on a larger scale than had been expected. S.S. divisions which fought in Poland are now being sent to the spot.'

18 April 1941, George Whitelaw, *Daily Herald*

Women of twenty register for national service to-day.

According to the *Manchester Evening News*: 'Thousands of young women answering the call for war workers, are registering at Labour Exchanges throughout the country today. They were all born in 1920, and it is expected that something like 300,000 of them will sign the register. Many of them were already doing important work, but unless they were in one of the services open to women they had to sign on the dotted line.'

19 April 1941, Cecil Orr, *Daily Record*

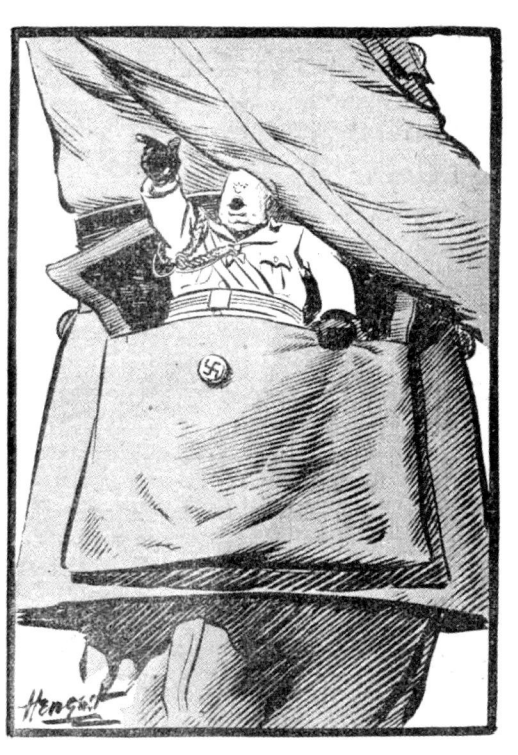

TRIUMPHAL ORATION FROM A BALCONY

According to the *Daily Herald*: 'Mussolini's Fascist state has in effect been taken over by the Nazis. It's navy, army and air force are in the charge of Germans. The Italian fleet went out to meet Admiral Cunningham's battleships under German orders; the Italian army made its disastrous counter-attacks in Albania under German orders. And the whole of the Italian Government is now as much under German control as the Governments of the Czech "Protectorates." Every Italian official and every Italian industrialist of any importance has at his elbow a German "political adviser" or "Government specialist" or "economic co-ordinator."'

21 April 1941, W. H. Woodburn 'Hengest', *Manchester Evening News*

On the Neutrality Joy-Wheel

According to the *News Chronicle*: 'Most significant diplomatic feature is the story that Stalin would welcome understanding with Britain and the United States. Feelers are being put out in Washington to see how the wind blows. Russia now fears that the logic of events will bring her in, sooner or later. It is believed that Russia and Turkey have already reached agreement on common policy, but the Kremlin would Like American co-operation as well, before deciding on a more open line. The pro-Nazi coup in Iraq has jolted Moscow. If Nazis were in Iraq, they would be ideally placed on the Russian flank. Truth is that Stalin has not made up his own mind what to do. The present spate of rumours shows how uncertain his policy is. He does not desire to join in the Balkan war, but realises he is getting more and more into a dangerous situation. He is showing his hand more as a last-minute effort to slow up the speed of Hitler's expansion.'

22 April, Cecil Orr, *Daily Record*

According to the *Western Mail*: 'While Empire Forces in Greece were consolidating their new defensive positions Australian troops and the R.A.F. in Libya have again inflicted heavy losses on both the Germans and Italians. During Monday night the Australians raiding from Tobruk captured 17 Italian officers and 430 other ranks.'

26 April 1941, Kimon Evan Marengo 'Kem', *Daily Herald*

Holding the Bag Again

According to the *Irish Weekly*: 'While the British and Anzac forces were fighting a slow retreat against odds worse than Dunkirk, the motor-cyclist vanguard of the German armoured division entered Athens, the Greek capital, at 9:30 a.m. on Sunday morning, and the Swastika flag was hoisted on the Acropolis. A great part of the British troops and equipment have been safely evacuated from Greece for service in North Africa.'

2 May 1941, Fred O. Seibel, *Richmond Times-Dispatch* (Virginia, United States)

THE PICTURE OF THE YEAR

According to the *Liverpool Evening Express*: 'American reports that additional vessels loaded with tanks, planes and ambulances for the British Middle East armies are reported to be on the way to the Red Sea and the Suez Canal. Vichy reports of the arrival at the Suez Canal of 26 merchant ships from America with full cargoes of war material are unofficially confirmed in Washington. It is also understood that several American vessels made the trip around the Cape, and others are on the way.'

5 May 1941, Wyndham Robinson, *Star*

Britain's Finest Hour 107

INSPECTION FOR BARNACLES

According to the *Evening Sentinel*: 'The war debate in the House of Commons ended with a rousing speech by Mr. Churchill which evoked such cheers as made a vote of confidence, even by 447 to three, a formality. The debate was well worthwhile if only for the Prime Minister's speech, but it was even more valuable than that. It showed Hitler and his gangsters, as well as his slaves, that here in this supposedly beleaguered country, against which the chief gangster is projecting his most violent and virulent hate, the people can debate calmly and even critically the conduct of the war, with a view to its prosecution with more vigour, thoroughness and efficiency. This is an example of the freedom of thought and expression, for which, among other things, we are fighting.'

7 May 1941, W. H. Woodburn 'Hengest', *Manchester Evening News*

THIS HOUSE IS NOT INTERESTED IN THE POSSIBILITY OF DEFEAT

German air raids on 10 and 11 May saw both the House of Commons chamber and the roof of Westminster Hall, the oldest part of the Palace of Westminster, set ablaze. Fire services decided they could not save both and focused their efforts on Westminster Hall, leaving the Commons to be totally destroyed.

13 May 1941, Clive Uptton, *Daily Sketch*

On 10 May, Deputy Führer of the Third Reich, Rudolf Hess, flew from Bavaria in a Messerschmitt Bf110 before parachuting into Scotland, on a one-man peace mission in the days leading up to Germany's invasion of Russia.

14 May 1941, Wyndham Robinson, *Star*

"HESSENTIALITY"

Albert Speer later said Hitler described Hess's departure as one of the worst blows of his life, as he considered it a personal betrayal. Hitler ordered Hess to be shot should he return to Germany and abolished the post of Deputy Führer on 12 May 1941.

20 May 1941, George Middleton, *Birmingham Gazette*

CON — CRETE

Having conquered Greece the month before, Hitler launched an airborne attack on the island of Crete on 20 May. New Zealand, British, Australian and Greek forces fought desperately to repel the huge airborne assault by German paratroopers. Despite the paratroopers suffering high casualties, the Allied forces misjudged the attack and, after an intense eight days of fighting, Crete fell to the Germans and the Allied forces withdrew.

22 May 1941, W. H. Woodburn 'Hengest', *Manchester Evening News*

Britain's Finest Hour

CASUALTIES ON THE WAY

According to the *News Chronicle*: 'Threatened with an attack by the undefeated German armies, Stalin has decided to capitulate. The 61-year-old, bull-necked "vozhd" has taken over personal leadership of the Government to make sure concessions are made without incident, and go no further than absolutely necessary. Apparently the first set of demands presented by German Junker-Ambassador Von der Schulenberg have been satisfied to the letter. It seems likely that a new Soviet-German understanding has been reached.'

26 May 1941, Victor Weisz 'Vicky', *News Chronicle*

On 24 May, HMS Hood was sunk by the German battleship Bismarck with the loss of 1,415 sailors. She was the largest Royal Navy vessel to have been sunk, causing the biggest loss of life suffered by any single British warship. Incensed by the loss of HMS Hood, three days later a large British force pursued and sank the Bismarck.

29 May 1941, Clive Uptton, *Daily Sketch*

Rommel pushed the British and allied forces eastwards towards Egypt, threatening the Suez canal. According to the *Sunday Post*: 'When Hitler launches his drive on Suez he will find distances over external lines of communication an even greater problem for him than it was for us. Tanks and heavy guns and munitions can only come by sea. Now that Abyssinia is no longer a threat to our rear, and the Red Sea open to direct U.S.A. shipments already in full swing and steady delivery — I believe the battle for Suez may offer us the same chances for handing Hitler no less smashing a blow than that our forebears handed Napoleon in exactly the same corner of the world. The struggle will be the greatest perhaps in the history of warfare. Hitler has ordered his High Command to spare neither men nor munitions to win a decision.'

8 June 1941, Percy Walmsley 'Lees', *Sunday Graphic*

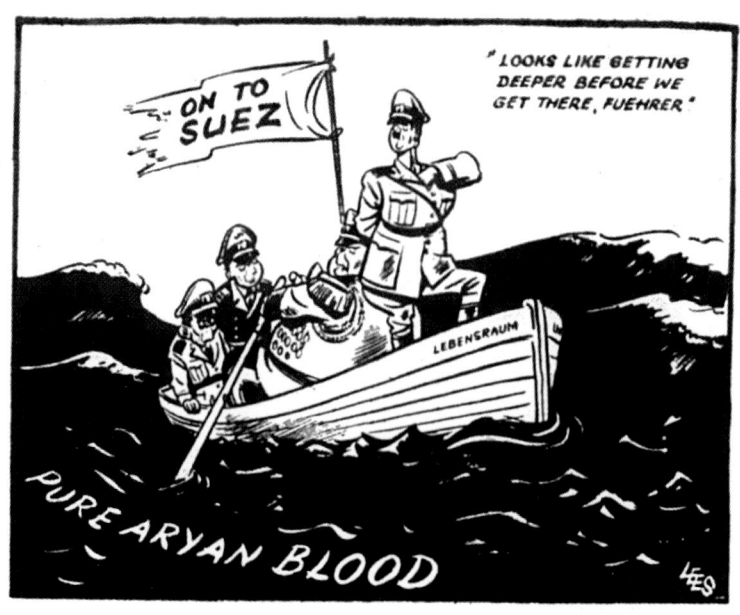

4
The World at War

TURNING IT OVER

In *Mein Kampf*, Hitler had written about his desire to acquire Lebensraum in the east so as to settle Germans in western Russia with all its resources of food and raw materials. Information on Hitler's intention to invade the Soviet Union came to Stalin from various sources, including Churchill and his own top spy, Richard Sorge. He was even informed of the exact date of the German invasion.

10 June 1941, Clive Uptton, *Daily Sketch*

"WHAT'S GOING ON BEHIND?"

Many in the Western Press wondered that If Hitler invaded the Soviet Union would Japan honour its five-year neutrality agreement, which had been signed in April, with the Russians. Although traditional enemies, the non-aggression pact allowed both the Soviet Union and Japan to free up large numbers of troops occupying disputed territory in Manchuria and Outer Mongolia, which they could then use for more pressing purposes.

19 June 1941, W. H. Woodburn 'Hengest',
Manchester Evening News

The Try-Out

According to the *Manchester Evening News*: '"If I had the Ural Mountains with their incalculable store of treasures in raw materials, Siberia with its vast forests, and the Ukraine with its tremendous wheat fields, Germany would swim in plenty." Hitler at Nuremberg in 1936. Hitler has not given up that dream of plenty, and now a full-blooded war of nerves is raging between Moscow and Berlin, with Britain, America, and Japan embroiled in one of the strangest diplomatic battles of the war.'

20 June 1941, William Furnival, *Lancashire Evening Post*

KISS OF DEATH

Despite Hitler's non-aggression pact with Stalin, Germany invaded the Soviet Union (Operation Barbarossa) on 22 June.

24 June 1941, George Aria, *Sun* (Sydney, Australia)

President Roosevelt responded to the German invasion of the Soviet Union by dispatching Harry Hopkins to Moscow to assess the Soviet military capability. The US War Department warned Roosevelt that the Russians would not last more than six weeks (a view shared by many members of the British Government), but Hopkins urged Roosevelt to provide assistance. The president agreed to extend the Lend-Lease Act to the Russians, which allowed American-built weapons and supplies to be sent to the Eastern Front.

24 June 1941, Ding Darling, *New York Herald Tribune* (United States)

THE SURPRISE GUEST

In spite of his personal feelings about Communism, and the fact that the Soviet Union had signed the Molotov–Ribbentrop Pact that had allowed Hitler to invade Poland, Churchill knew how to respond. In a broadcast he declared: "Any major state who fights against Nazism will have our aid . . . we shall give whatever help we can to Russia." On 23 June, Churchill ordered intensified bombing raids on German bases in France to take pressure off the Eastern Front and, from 27 June, shared newly decrypted military intelligence with Stalin. "If Hitler invaded Hell, I would make at least a favourable reference to the Devil in the House of Commons," Churchill said.

25 June 1941, Ray Evans, *Columbus Dispatch* (United States)

Forget Him, Jeeves!

On 28 June, humourist P. G. Wodehouse, creator of Wooster and Jeeves, made the first of five broadcasts from Berlin to the United States. Though gently mocking of his Nazi captors they landed him in deep trouble. It did not go over well in Britain, prompting the House of Commons to consider prosecuting "Britons broadcasting under enemy auspices" under the Treachery Act, which carried a death sentence. After the war George Orwell defended Wodehouse, describing him as a man trapped in the amber of the past who had no idea what he was doing.

29 June 1941, Sidney Moon, *Sunday Dispatch*

The World at War 113

SIGNATURE TUNE

Britain and the Soviet Union signed an agreement for joint action in the war against Germany. They pledged to assist one another against Hitler and agreed that neither would make peace with Germany separately. The agreement was signed with immediate effect on 12 July by diplomats Stafford Cripps and Vyacheslav Molotov.

15 July 1941, George Middleton, *Birmingham Gazette*

COMING ALONG NICELY

"In these last few weeks alone, we have thrown upon Germany about half the tonnage of bombs thrown by Germany upon our cities during the whole course of the war. This is only the beginning, and we hope by next July to multiply our deliveries manifold." — The Premier.

15 July 1941, Talbot Ellison, *Birmingham Mail*

SITTING ON THE FENCE

Japan, as a signatory of the Pact with Germany and Italy, considered denouncing the Soviet–Japanese Neutrality Pact after the German invasion of Russia, but it decided to keep the pact and instead decided to invade the European colonies in Southeast Asia. This would have a direct bearing on the battle for Moscow since the absence of a Japanese threat allowed the Soviets to move large forces from Siberia and send them to the front against the Germans.

16 July 1941, George Whitelaw, *Daily Herald*

HEAD WANTED

According to the *Daily News*: 'Referring to the proposal for Minister of Production, Mr. Churchill said: "Nothing would be easier than for me to ask one of my colleagues in the Government to become Minister of Production. But the relation between this Minister of Production with the three Supply Departments would be most unsatisfactory. He would either have to trust them and use them to execute the prescribed programme or he would have to break into these Departments and interfere with their work. These matters cannot be considered without reference to the personalities involved, and I have not been told which is to be this superman."'

23 July 1941, Arthur Potts 'Spot', *Bristol Evening World*

ANOTHER RED PLOT

According to the *News Chronicle*: 'A Berlin spokesman said last night that Russian troops had launched counter-attacks against the German advance spearheads in the Smolensk and Mogilev areas. They had been repulsed with heavy losses he claimed. Goebbels, Propaganda Minister, is apparently in two minds what to tell the German people about the Soviet Air Force, says Reuter. One radio commentator said last night the Red Air Force was still in a position to make counter-attacks.'

23 July 1941, Victor Weisz 'Vicky', *News Chronicle*

"Don't look round now, but I think we're being followed."

According to the *Daily Herald*: 'United States naval and military chiefs gave Japan two serious warnings about her aggression in Indo-China. The first came from Admiral Standley, former Chief of Naval Operations. In a broadcast he said: "Our Navy is ready and adequate to meet essential defense needs in the Pacific as well as giving the British enough support to win the Battle of the Atlantic." This warning was reinforced by General MacArthur, the newly-appointed Commander-in-Chief of all American forces in the Philippines.'

29 July 1941, George Whitelaw, *Daily Herald*

The World at War

With the heading 'Hitler's Great Miscalculation,' the *Daily News* reported: "Now there is another considerable lull for Britain. This time it is due to a serious German miscalculation. Hitler and the majority of his general staff shared the almost universal view that his Panzer divisions would go through the Russian resistance like butter" and then the intention was, within a month or six weeks, to turn West and with the full military might of Germany to strike down Britain. Thanks to the Russian armies, the first plan has failed to come off. Therefore, the second is indefinitely postponed.'

1 August 1941, W. H. Woodburn 'Hengest', *Manchester Evening News*

THE INTRUDER

According to the *Daily Mail*: 'Since the German assault on Russia began some of the old complacency seems to have returned, and no doubt the Prime Minister had this in mind when he said: "It would be madness for us to suppose that Russia or the United States are going to win this war for us. The invasion season is at hand. All the armed forces have been warned to be at concert pitch by 1 September and to maintain the utmost vigilance meanwhile. We have to reckon with a gambler's desperation." . . . Mr. Churchill knows, better than anyone, that Hitler hates his potential victims to be prepared. The inference should be our inspiration.'

3 August 1941, Sidney Moon, *Sunday Dispatch*

IN THE SWIM

According to the *Courier and Advertiser*: 'German casualties in the first two months of the war amounted to nearly 2,000,000, of which about half were killed, stated M. Lozovsky, Deputy Chief of the Soviet Information Bureau. History has never known an example of an army suffering such losses in such a short time, he declared. Against these losses, it was true, Hitler had gained some Soviet territory, but it afforded only ruined towns and villages and blown-up factories. Moreover, Hitler has to cope with guerrilla warfare and the hatred of the populations in the occupied regions.'

8 August 1941, George Whitelaw, *Daily Herald*

116   THE SECOND WORLD WAR IN CARTOONS

TURKEY'S DIRE STRAITS

According to the *Belfast Telegraph*: 'Next week is expected to be decisive in the shaping of Turkey's fate. Turkish official circles regard the situation as nearing a climax, the pressure on Turkey to come from the German side. Since the occupation of Iran, Turkey is virtually encircled in the east by Britain and Russia. In the west she is facing German troops. She is compelled geographically. therefore, to choose between one side or the other.'

19 August 1941, W. H. Woodburn 'Hengest', *Manchester Evening News*

THEY'LL LISTEN TO THIS ONE!

Goebbels's frantic efforts to stop Germans listening to our broadcasts prove that it is like trying to catch a will-o'-the-wisp.

According to the *Birmingham Gazette*: 'Certain quarters in London have indisputable evidence that there is now throughout Germany a huge new listening audience to the British service of news, comments and features not only in German, but in a whole lot of other languages. The Nazi civil population are in fact relying on Britain to give them straight unembellished news about the progress of the war — that is to say they distrust their own communiques.'

20 August 1941, George Middleton, *Birmingham Gazette*

ON THE MOVING STAIRCASE or, IT'S A LONG, LONG WAY TO VLADIVOSTOK

According to the *Western Mail*: 'Amid the uncertainties of the battles which are being fought with such relentless fury along the whole Eastern Front there is one fact which may encourage composure, namely that whatever temporary victories the Nazis may get by the wanton sacrifice of men, Russia will be able to maintain a front throughout the winter. Hitler is furiously staking everything on an effort to get Leningrad first, to achieve Baltic control, and, secondly, to encourage his people in the inevitable winter campaign. It is not the first time for Hitler to stake so much on a spectacular success. Progress is being made by the enemy, but it is slow progress, and Voroshiloff has a million men in the defence lines of Leningrad.'

21 August 1941, George Whitelaw, *Daily Herald*

The World at War

THE WRONG "DESIGN"

According to the *Press Association*: 'There are indications that the reply from Iran (Persia) to the British Note on the Nazi danger in that country is likely to be unsatisfactory. The British Note pointed out the potential dangers to Iran's neutrality inherent in the presence of some hundreds of Nazis in that country, directed the urgent attention of the Iranians to the fate which had overtaken so many other neutral countries which, prior to subjugation, permitted the presence of Nazis in their midst or turned a blind eye to insidious German infiltration.'

22 August 1941, William Furnival,
Lancashire Evening Post

"We're helping the Russians splendidly by keeping the Germans guessing where we'll invade them in 1943!"

According to the *Birmingham Gazette*: 'Mr. Harry Pollitt, British Communist leader said: "We now need the creation of a second front and despatch to Russia of as many fighter planes, guns and tanks as possible. The creation of a second front means death for thousands of British forces, but if it is not organised the result will be death for millions in the next few months. We have the chance of a lifetime, the British and Russian people, working and fighting together to wipe Fascism of the face of the earth."'

28 August 1941, Victor Weisz 'Vicky',
News Chronicle

"FINN-ISH"

Finland: With your permission, Fuehrer, I'll start flying my dove now!

According to *Reuters*: 'An order of the day was issued by Marshal Mannerheim, the Finnish Commander-In-Chief, appears to dispose of the suggestion that once Finland had reached her former frontier, she would seek peace. The Order stated: "Part of Finland that was violently torn from us without any justification for the peace of Moscow has been restored in its entirety by the heroic deeds and untiring exertions of the Finnish Army. Endurance is still demanded of the Finnish Army. The time has not yet come to turn our swords into ploughshares."'

4 September 1941, Arthur Potts 'Spot',
Bristol Evening World

118   THE SECOND WORLD WAR IN CARTOONS

According to the *Associated Press*: 'Moscow radio asked German listeners how long can Germany wage this war against the Soviet Union and Great Britain, who are supported by the United States, and how long this war will last. The Moscow broadcaster then said that Hitler was held fast on the Eastern front and he wanted Mussolini to help him, but "how can a mule pull a tank from the mud?" Hitler needed petrol. His calculations for getting hold of the oil wells in Iraq, Iran and the Caucasus had failed. Now he was speculating on another adventure in Asia Minor and he needed Mussolini's help.'

7 September 1941, Percy Walmsley 'Lees', *Sunday Graphic*

"Calling all cars! Calling all cars! Roosevelt speaking."

According to the *San Francisco Chronicle*, speculating on President Roosevelt's forthcoming radio address, asked: 'Why, if the time has come to start "eliminating" outlaw submarines, stop at one? Why not eliminate their desperado masters and their stranglehold on Europe, from which they propose to strangle the whole world, including America? Why not move to eliminate this black, reactionary Nazi revolution, which has made the whole world unsafe and keeps every peaceable inhabitant at the mercy of outlaw recklessness When rattlesnakes invade our garden, do we stop at eliminating one?'

12 September 1941, George Whitelaw, *Daily Herald*

BIG ENOUGH TO GET THROUGH

After the United States destroyer Greer was attacked by a U-boat off the coast of Iceland, Roosevelt stated in a radio address that: "From now on, if German or Italian vessels of war enter waters the protection of which is necessary for American defence, they do so at their own peril. According to the *News Chronicle*: 'The President made it clear — U.S. warships will not wait to be attacked, but will shoot first. "Our patrolling vessels and planes," he said, "will protect all merchant ships ... ships of any flag engaged in commerce in our defensive waters."' This became known as his "shoot-on-sight" order, effectively declaring naval war against Germany and Italy in the Battle of the Atlantic.

13 September 1941, Clive Uptton, *Daily Sketch*

The World at War

PRODUCING THE RABBITS

Mr. Churchill is to open the debate on aid to Russia.

In the Commons, Churchill calling for sacrifices to aid Russia stated: "I may say at once, however, that in order to enable Russia to remain indefinitely in the field as a first-class war-making power sacrifices of the most serious kind and the most extreme efforts will have to be made by the British people, and enormous new installations or conversions of their existing plants will have to be set up in the United States with all the labour, expense, and disturbance of normal life which these entail.'

30 September 1941, George Middleton, *Birmingham Gazette*

Standin' in the Need of Aid

According to the *Belfast Telegraph*: 'After a movement which the Nazis said had encircled four Soviet armies, Hitler's high command claimed last night that German troops had entered Kiev, capital of the Ukraine. Twenty-four hours previously Moscow admitted that the invader was at the city's gates and that the situation was grave.'

21 September 1941, Fred O. Seibel,
Richmond Times-Dispatch **(Virginia, United States)**

HEAR NO TRUTH, SEE NO TRUTH, SPEAK NO TRUTH!

According to *Reuters*: 'All German stations broadcast a warning by Goebbels that death remains the penalty for listening to the BBC. The warning was contained in an article of the Nazi Propaganda chief in '*Das Reich*.' "Even in Germany there are a few people who can never be taught," Goebbels declares. "Quite recently two death sentences and a number of sentences of penal servitude proved that there are people who cannot refrain from listening to the London Radio in the evening behind closed doors. The action of these people is not only criminal. but boundlessly stupid. We clearly realise the devastating effect the British lie propaganda had on our nation in the last war. We do not wish to expose our people lor a second time to this danger."'

6 October 1941, Wyndham Robinson, *Star*

120   THE SECOND WORLD WAR IN CARTOONS

KEEP THE BELT RUNNING

According to the *Irish Independent*: 'The Three-Power Conference on supply problems concluded its deliberations in Moscow. The British and American delegations reaching an agreement to place at the disposal of Russia "practically every requirement for which the soviet military and civil authorities asked." Russia, in turn, agreed to supply Britain and the United States with "large quantities of raw materials ungently required in those countries."'

7 October 1941, Clive Uptton, *Daily Sketch*

According to the *Staffordshire Advertiser*: 'The battle for Moscow has been raging for more than a week. The Germans are striving to batter their way through on the direct road from Smolensk to Moscow — Napoleon's road in 1812. They have twice been thrown back since the fighting began on the Eastern front in June, and it remains to be seen whether the Soviet High Command can hold out in this supreme hour of crisis.'

10 October 1941, William Furnival, *Lancashire Evening Post*

"GERMANS — YOUR 'LIVING ROOM'"

According to the director of the Soviet Information Bureau on Radio Moscow: 'Germany has lost over 3,000,000 men killed, wounded or taken prisoner since she invaded Russia.' The director also added 'that the Germans have lost 11,000 tanks, 13,000 guns and 9,000 aircraft.'

12 October 1941, Percy Walmsley 'Lees', *Sunday Graphic*

The World at War 121

UNCLE ADOLF

According to the *Civil and Military Gazette*: 'Referring to the protest often made by Hitler that his plans for conquest did not extend across the Atlantic Ocean, President Roosevelt declared: "I have in my possession a secret map made by Hitler's Government. It is a map of South America and part of Central America as Hitler proposes to reorganise it." The President also disclosed that the U.S. Government had in its possession another document made by Hitler's Government — a detailed plan to abolish all existing religions.'

28 October 1941, Talbot Ellison, *Birmingham Mail*

HOLDING THE BABY

According to the *News Chronicle*: 'Italy today presents a phenomenon and tragedy which are, perhaps, unique in history. She is forced out of sheer patriotism to desire her own defeat in a war which she never wanted. She must also mourn her dead with a personal sorrow, knowing that she lacks the moral strength to remedy the situation. Suffering agonies of humiliation, she can only dramatise them. Defeat is the only way to get rid of the Germans and the Government. Her eyes are fixed on England, whose victory is her only hope of liberation.'

3 November 1941, Victor Weisz 'Vicky', *News Chronicle*

"IF ONLY I'D THOUGHT OF DEFENCE REGULATION 18b"

Defence Regulation 18b was used by the British Government to intern without trial people suspected of being actively opposed to the ongoing war with Germany. Robert Liversidge, a successful Jewish businessman and therefore a highly atypical 18b internee, was interned under Regulation 18b and held without charge. He took a civil action for false imprisonment against the Home Secretary John Anderson. The action failed, but the case is remembered for Lord Atkin's dissenting speech in the House of Lords when he protested against a construction of words which would give uncontrolled power of imprisonment to a minister.

5 November 1941, W. H. Woodburn 'Hengest', *Manchester Evening News*

HON. RIGHTEOUS INDIGNATION BOILS OVER

The Japanese Foreign Office's official newspaper, *The Japan Times and Advertiser*, accused the United States of 'tottering perilously on the brink of war,' declaring that 'Washington reached across several thousand miles of land and water to intrude its mailed fist in East Asia, to ferment violence, and prevent the establishment of a mutually trustful condition amongst nations which are quite outside the American sphere of influence.'

6 November 1941, George Whitelaw, *Daily Herald*

THE WOULD-BE SWORD SWALLOWER

According to the *Aberdeen Evening Express*: 'The surprise mission to Washington from Tokyo of Mr Kurusu is of the highest importance. Reliable advices reaching London make it clear that it has been undertaken in a last-minute effort to see whether it is possible to evade Hitler's request that Japan should enter the war. Hitler's blunt reminder to Japan of her obligations under the Tripartite Pact is believed to have arisen from a Nazi recognition that the year of decision is at hand, and that Japan must play the role assigned to her under the major strategy of totalitarian combination.'

7 November 1941, William Furnival, *Lancashire Evening Post*

ON THE BOIL!

According to the *Daily Mirror*: 'Eleven Italian ships were destroyed by a small force of British warships in a brilliant action during darkness early yesterday against two convoys escorted by Italian warships twice as strong in numbers and armament. This is the Navy's biggest convoy success in the Mediterranean since Italy entered the war. Not one British warship was damaged. Not one British sailor was hurt. Once again, the Italian Navy refused to fight and left the ships they were supposed to protect to their fate.'

13 November 1941, W. H. Woodburn 'Hengest', *Manchester Evening News*

124   THE SECOND WORLD WAR IN CARTOONS

HON. NOAH SENDS OUT HON. PEACE VULTURE

According to the *Yorkshire Evening Post*: 'Japan's special envoy is in Washington offering an olive branch to America on the Pacific crisis, but simultaneously Japan's Premier in Tokyo is dictating terms on which they will keep the peace and uttering warlike threats. General Tojo makes a three-point demand on the Allies, and emulates Hitler's "patience exhausted" attitude. General Tojo stated his terms for peace in the Pacific as follows: 1. The Powers (meaning particularly Britain and the United States) to refrain from obstructing the successful conclusion of the "China affair." 2. These Powers to refrain from directly militarily menacing the Japanese Empire, cease hostile measures such as the economic blockade, and restore normal relations with Japan. 3. They must do their utmost to prevent the European war spreading to Eastern Asia.'

20 November 1941, George Whitelaw, *Daily Herald*

THE BATTLE OF THE STANDARD

According to the *News Chronicle*: 'Mr E. Shinwell, M.P. returned to his attack on the Government in a speech at Barnsley. "As a team of goalkeepers they are to be admired," he declared, "but as a scoring team they are a wash-out. The Prime Minister has declared that he will not change his Government or modify his policy. Regarding Mr. Churchill's invasion warning he said: " The repeated suggestions of invasion sound suspiciously like an attempt by the Government to justify its failure to take the initiative If the people are told what is expected of them they will rise to the occasion, but constant warnings are leading to confusion. "I must exercise great care," he added. "I have a suspicion, for what it may be worth, that the Government are watching every word I say, I beg of them not to be more afraid of me than they are of Hitler."'

21 November 1941, W. H. Woodburn 'Hengest', *Manchester Evening News*

The World at War

THE HOPEFUL JOSHUA

According to the *Daily Mirror*: 'Japan is to sign a five-year extension of the Anti-Comintern (anti-Soviet) Pact. And as Berlin announced this the Japanese Premier, General Tojo, beat the war drum in Tokio. "There is no retreat for Japan from her immutable policies," the Premier told a gathering of 60 provincial governors. Finland will join with other German vassal States, including Rumania, Slovakia, Denmark and Bulgaria, as a new signatory of the Anti-Comintern Pact. Hitler is on his way to the Berlin conference for the signing of the pact and Mussolini may be there, too, say Swiss reports.'

2 December 1941, W. H. Woodburn 'Hengest', *Manchester Evening News*

TIME TO TURN ON THE HEAT

According to the *Daily Herald*: 'Japan's military leaders are athirst for war. Only flames, it seems, can soothe their throats. Very well. We Democracies know that in any war against us the Japanese fighting machine will go down eventually to destruction.'

2 December 1941, George Whitelaw, *Daily Herald*

THE INTERMINABLE POLE SQUATTER.

According to the *News Chronicle*: 'For the last five years Japan has been making war in the Far East. Within the next few weeks, within the next few days perhaps, Japan may extend that war. The core of Japanese Imperial policy for the last quarter of a century has been the establishment by force of a Japanese sphere of influence over the whole of East Asia, which latterly she has dignified by the resounding title of "The East Asia Co-Prosperity Sphere."'

3 December 1941, Clive Uptton, *Daily Sketch*

REMOTE CONTROL

On 7 December, Japan's navy launched a surprise attack on the American naval base at Pearl Harbor, Hawaii, killing 2,400 Americans and destroying or damaging eight battleships. There were also co-ordinated attacks on British Malaya and the Dutch East Indies. On 8 December, the United States declared war on Japan. In turn, Hitler declared war on the United States on 11 December. In his 88-minute speech to the Reichstag, Hitler disparaged Roosevelt and the whole 'Anglo-Saxon Jewish-capitalist world', for their policy of 'unrestricted world domination and dictatorship'.

8 December 1941, W. H. Woodburn 'Hengest', *Manchester Evening News*

UNITED STATES

According to the *Evening Dispatch*: 'Following President Roosevelt's message to Congress and the completion of the formality of declaring war on Japan, comes further evidence of the solidarity of the United States people. Ex-Col. Lindbergh, Isolationist, has declared: "Our country has been attacked by force of arms and by force of arms we must retaliate," while John Lewis, leader of the recent coal strike, has announced support of the Government "to the day of its triumph over Japan and all other enemies."'

10 December 1941, Victor Weisz 'Vicky', *News Chronicle*

TUG OF WAR

According to the *Daily Herald*: 'Mr. Roosevelt calls for a "world-wide grand strategy against the Axis." Sir Walter Citrine says the resources of Britain, Russia and America must be employed in unison — "It is a common front." It will not be enough for any one of the Allies to plan her own performance, however brilliant it may be. Production policy, military policy, economic policy in each country must be devised and executed in accordance with a central scheme.'

11 December 1941, George Whitelaw, *Daily Herald*

MEIN KAMPF versus ATLANTIC CHARTER

On 11 December, Churchill told the House of Commons: "We can already see after six months of fighting in Russia that Hitler made one of the outstanding blunders of history, and the results so far realised constitute events of cardinal importance in the final decision of the war."

12 December 1941, George Whitelaw, *Daily Herald*

1942 OVERTURE

According to the *News Chronicle*: '"Retreat from Moscow," say the headlines. For every schoolchild throughout the Western world — and in Germany just as surely as in Russia — the words have symbolic significance. The Reichswehr's gigantic, six-months-long effort to take the Soviet capital has failed, and its troops are now in full retreat across the white wastes of snow. As our war correspondent Philip Jordan, now back in Moscow, points out, the Germans are falling back on to prepared positions which they hope to hold for the winter. This is a retreat, not a rout. But while in the military sense it may at present be orderly, in the moral sense it is a rout, a debacle, of the first magnitude.'

16 December 1941, Victor Weisz 'Vicky', *News Chronicle*

History Repeats

According to the *Sunday Dispatch*: 'Goebbels, mouthpiece of Hitler, appealed over the Berlin radio for the people of Germany to send all the warm clothing they could spare for the freezing Nazi Army on the Russian front. He also read out a message from Hitler in which the Führer admitted: "We are facing an enemy far superior in number and material." "If we have to suffer air raids, they cannot be compared with the terrible hardships which our armies endure now on the Eastern Front," said Goebbels. "The winter this year has set in much earlier than in normal times, and is much colder than was expected by our High Command."'

17 December 1941, William Summers,
***Buffalo Evening News* (New York, United States)**

A FULL SOCK FOR SOMEBODY

According to the *News Chronicle*: 'Mr. Churchill now conferring with the President at the White House, and conversations are to be held during the next few days between the President and the Premier and the respective Staffs of the two countries. They have a huge task to weld the limitless resources of the free nations of the world into a great ring of steel to crush the resistance of the Axis Powers.'

24 December 1941, Joseph Parrish,
***Chicago Tribune* (United States)**

"MOSCOW OUT OF DANGER." — Official

With the headline 'Moscow now "out of immediate Danger," the *Evening Telegraph* reported: 'The Soviet Army is continuing to roll back the Germans. "In a number of sectors our troops continued to advance and occupied a number of localities," the Soviet midnight communique stated. The two arms which the Germans attempted to throw round Moscow have now both been flung back, and the capital, as well as Tula, described as its "armoury," have been freed from immediate danger, asserts Moscow radio.'

30 December 1941, Victor Weisz 'Vicky', *News Chronicle*

According to the *News Chronicle*: 'Vital new Allied defence measures formulated in Washington, and made known here in a message from Mr. Churchill, were communicated to the Australian War Cabinet by Mr. Curtin, Australian Prime Minister, today. It is understood that the direct result of the Washington talks has been to enhance considerably the security of Australia's position and to create a greater degree of optimism than was apparent a few days ago.'

31 December 1941, W. H. Woodburn 'Hengest', *Manchester Evening News*

According to the *Washington Post*: 'While citizens of Washington discuss and endorse President Roosevelt's colossal armaments programme, assurances of co-operation pour in from industrial leaders all over the country. They pledge themselves to see the programme through, declaring "It will be done." The President's great message was what the American people — 140,000,000 of them — are ready to act on now. The staggering production totals for which it calls are its most invigorating and reassuring single feature. Stupendous as the task may be, its scale will simplify rather than aggravate the innumerable problems with which we have been fumbling in half measures and weak expedients.'

7 January 1942, Jim Berryman, *Washington Star* (Washington D.C. United States)

THE BALLOON BLOWS BACK

According to the *Daily Herald*: 'The German armies on the Moscow front are themselves now feeling what it is like to be caught and cracked between a strong pincers movement. Two big salients have been dug deep into the German lines, and the Russians are developing an offensive in the Mojaisk-Bororsk area, halfway between these two towns, which may eventually become a double pincers movement.'

7 January 1942, George Whitelaw, *Daily Herald*

AT HIS OWN GAME!

With the headline 'U.S. To Aid In Invasion Of Germany,' the *Daily Herald* reported: 'Invasion of Germany or occupied Europe has been brought nearer by many months. That is the meaning of President Roosevelt's statement in his 1942 message to Congress that "American forces will take stations in the British Isles. As our power and our resources are fully mobilised, we shall carry the attack against the enemy. We shall hit him, and hit him again, wherever and whenever we can reach him. We must keep him far from our shores, for we intend to bring this battle to him on his own home grounds. To do this and to destroy the German army in Europe, one thing is essential — air mastery over any stretch of coast on which the Allies choose to strike."'

8 January 1942, George Middleton, *Birmingham Gazette*

A STROKE — AND THE GENERAL DIED

With the headline 'Nazi General Removed By Gestapo Says Moscow,' *Reuters* reported that: 'Field Marshall Walter von Reichenau is dead. An official Nazi announcement said he was taken ill at the front in Russia and 'died as the result of a stroke while being brought back to Germany.' His death caused no surprise, in well-informed circles in Stockholm, states the correspondent of Tass, "Rumours that something must happen to Reichenau had been current for several weeks, where it became known that the heavy defeats inflicted by the Red Army on Reichenau's troops enraged Hitler and a number of generals closely connected with him. Stockholm circles, he says, "do not doubt that Reichenau was "removed by Himmler's agents."'

19 January 1942, Clive Uptton, *Daily Sketch*

The World at War   131

SOME BIRD — SOME EGGS

According to the *News Chronicle*: 'Mr. Churchill fresh from his successful visits to Washington and Ottawa, began one of the most difficult tasks of his Premiership at the weekend to assess the full weight of criticism in the country over the Far Eastern failures, and to find a means of satisfying critics of the Government. His first talks with Cabinet colleagues shortly after he had reached No. 10, Downing Street impressed him with the need for a thorough personal investigation of political feeling at home.'

19 January 1942, Victor Weisz 'Vicky', *News Chronicle*

It Couldn't Have Been Worse

According to the *Daily Herald*: 'America is gasping with amazement at the astounding revelations of the Pearl Harbour, Honolulu, disaster which put part of the American Pacific Fleet out of action and resulted in Japan's furious drive towards Australia. Roosevelt promised that the nation should have the truth. Never in the midst of a war has such a devastating document been issued. Justice Roberts and his commission of four flew to Honolulu, took over 1.800 pages of evidence. As a result. Admiral Husband Kimmel and Lieut-General Walter Short, who were in command of the defences, are charged with dereliction of duty and with errors of judgment that were the effective cause of the success of Japan's surprise attack on Pearl Harbour. Both officers were dining out the night before the attack, each assuming that the other had taken certain defence precautions, whereas neither had done so.'

27 January 1942, Fred O. Seibel, *Richmond Times-Dispatch* **(Virginia, United States)**

THE DOOR MUST HOLD

With Japanese forces only 60 miles from Singapore, Churchill told the Commons: "The battle for the Malay peninsula and the approaches to Singapore will be fought to the last inch by the British, Australian and Indian forces, which have been considerably reinforced in the last week."

27 January 1942, Sam Wells, *Melbourne Herald* (Australia)

THEY'LL STICK TO THE SHIP

The Sea-sick: Our only alternative is to get out and walk!

After two and a half years of war and without a major victory against the Germans, there were politicians from all three major political parties as well as a hostile press criticising Churchill for Britain's lack of military success.

28 January 1942, George Middleton, *Birmingham Gazette*

On 27 January, with mounting opposition, Churchill called for a vote of confidence in the House of Commons. He won the vote of confidence by 464 to one. Only James Maxton (a pacifist and member of the left-wing Independent Labour Party) voted against the government. After the result was announced, members of both sides of the House stood waving and cheering wildly.

30 January 1942, William Furnival, *Lancashire Evening Post*

The World at War

"Your Far East — But Our Near North"

With the headline 'Menace to Australia,' the *Yorkshire Evening Post* reported 'Japanese military observers are saying that the capture of the Dutch island of Amboina would give their airmen a springboard for operations as far south as Port Darwin, Australia, 600 miles away.'

3 February 1942, W. H. Woodburn 'Hengest', *Manchester Evening News*

"That's Rommel — No, sorry, it's Auchinleck — No, it's Rommel."

According to the *Daily Herald*: 'Tobruk is now threatened by the Axis drive In Libya and Rommel is throwing the full weight of his offensive along the coastal road from Derna, now in enemy hands.

Yesterday's Italian communique claimed that Axis forces had taken Tmimi and were advancing on El Gazala, about 30 miles west of Tobruk. Nazi officials said Rommel may even attack Egypt and that, with the reinforcements he has received he is strong enough to do so.'

4 February 1942, George Whitelaw, *Daily Herald*

WHAT HE IS FIGHTING FOR

According to the *Daily Herald*: 'With the Japanese claiming to be only five miles from the outskirts of Singapore city, weary Imperial troops fought back stubbornly last night against the Invaders pouring in hordes into the battle-torn island. A British communique said Japanese military bombers with fighter escort fought an unsuccessful engagement against our air force over Malaya. Heavy fighting continues in the western and northern sectors. In the north of the island enemy activity has been intensified.'

11 February 1942, George Whitelaw, *Daily Herald*

134 THE SECOND WORLD WAR IN CARTOONS

ONCE MORE!

Singapore was the foremost British military base and economic port in South-East Asia and had been of great importance to British interwar defence strategy. During the war it allowed forces to support India and Australia, as well as attack Japanese shipping.

11 February 1942, W. H. Woodburn 'Hengest', *Manchester Evening News*

OUR TROOPS EXPECT

With the headline 'Wide New Power For Lord Beaverbrook, the *Western Daily Press* reported: 'Lord Beaverbrook, as the Minister of Production, will have coordinating power over all Supply departments, and keep in close contact with his vis-a-vis in America, going to and from between the United States and Britain. The entry of America into the war and the pooling of resources created a new situation. Lord Beaverbrook, with his intimate connection with production, enjoyed the confidence and goodwill of the American President, and it followed that he should be put into a position to speak to the United States representing British war production as a whole.'

12 February 1942, J C Walker, *Western Mail*

AND ON OUR HEARTS . . .

According to the *Daily Herald*: 'The news from Singapore may move you to sorrow or anger or both. But neither of these emotions will profit our cause. Only by action can we relieve our feelings and heal our wounds. So far as the public is concerned action must take the form of aiding by every possible means the output of the weapons which our troops so urgently need. Read the story which the *Daily Herald* publishes today about the ancient biplanes in which our RAF men are competing with a powerful and up-to-date Japanese air force. Then ask yourself: Have I so far done enough towards increasing the strength of our armaments?'

12 February 1942, George Whitelaw, *Daily Herald*

The World at War

"This unworthy person must now take honourable Sir to prisoners' camp, sorry to say."

The cartoonist was under the common misconception that Japanese soldiers were inferior and only capable of fighting the Chinese. According to British intelligence at the time: 'The Japanese are badly trained, badly equipped, and physiologically unfit to fight. They are buck-toothed, slant-eyed, near-sighted, scrawny little people.' The day after this cartoon was published, Lt General Arthur Percival signed the largest surrender in British history at Singapore. The city was supposed to be a fortress, but his force of 85,000 men had been defeated by just 35,000 Japanese troops. Following the surrender, Churchill was despondent, calling it "the worst disaster and largest capitulation in British history". The Japanese treated the prisoners with brutality and contempt. Many prisoners died from neglect, abuse, or forced labour.'

14 February 1942, Bruce Bairnsfather, *John Bull*

THE TOO WILLING HORSE

Some Conservative backbenchers believed Churchill had taken on too many official roles. During the vote of confidence debate some MPs had expressed doubt that it was possible for any one man to be both Prime Minister and Minister of Defence, and that they felt Churchill was acting as a one-man government.

16 February 1942, Talbot Ellison, *Birmingham Mail*

DUCKS AND DRAKES

According to the *Lincolnshire Echo*: 'Disappointment and disquiet at the way the German battleships Scharnhorst and Gneisenau and the cruiser Prinz Eugen ran the gauntlet of the Dover Straits and escaped disaster, will intensify in the days ahead the already anxious atmosphere at Westminster, writes a Lobby correspondent. Ordinary Parliamentary business seems of little moment beside this, the ominous position at Singapore, which Mr. Clement Davies is to raise immediately, and the all-pervading impression among M.P.s that the present political unrest may be the prelude to important happenings.'

16 February 1942, J C Walker, *Western Mail*

INTO THE STORM AND THROUGH THE STORM

According to the cartoonist: 'Winston Churchill had a quality of suggesting in his square-built, durable person that no disaster was more than temporary. When Churchill spoke, calmly and earnestly, his people acquired a confidence which was not warranted by any fact. The reason for it is one of the puzzles of British character and statecraft. It may lie in the recollection that Churchill had foreseen national tragedy when he spoke out against appeasement so long ago, that he had urged arming England for years. However it was, he took his country smoothly through the loss of the oil and rubber of the East, performing a small miracle in creating a belief in a safe end to the storm.'

17 February 1942, Jerry Doyle, *Philadelphia Inquirer* (United States)

CHIP OFF THE OLD BLOCK

According to the *Coventry Evening Telegraph*: 'The Royal Australian Air Force has been ordered to use every resource to attack the Japanese now threatening Australia's mainland from New Guinea and not to go on the defensive. Revealing that the home squadrons have been strengthened, Mr. Drakeford, the Air Minister, said: "Whatever the odds our airmen will continue to hammer the enemy to the utmost. There is no lack of the offensive spirit and no retreat complex so far as our airmen are concerned."'

24 February 1942, Clive Uptton, *Daily Sketch*

The World at War

HONOURABLE SPAWN

According to the *Daily Mail*: 'Japanese atrocities against military prisoners and civil population in Hong Kong were revealed by Mr Eden in the House of Commons. Mr Eden said that the testimony of eyewitnesses established the facts of the atrocities. They were committed without distinction of race or colour, and were the same kind of barbarities which aroused horror at the time of the Nanking massacre of 1937. Mr Eden said that 50 officers and men of the British Army were bound hand and foot, and then bayoneted to death. Women, both Asiatic and European, were raped and murdered, and one entire Chinese district was declared a brothel, regardless of the status of the inhabitants.'

12 March 1942, J C Walker, *Western Mail*

'Ah, Take the Cash, and Let the Credit Go'

By early March, Japanese troops were on the Indian border. The threat of invasion by the Japanese led Churchill to send Sir Richard Stafford Cripps, Lord Privy Seal and leader of the House of Commons, to India to try to secure the support of Indian leaders for the British war effort in return for a promise to give India dominion status. The Cripps proposals were rejected.

13 March 1942, Fred O. Seibel, *Richmond Times-Dispatch* (Virginia, United States)

THE GOOD EARTH

According to the *News Chronicle*: 'In the Ukraine Timoshenko has pushed his way into the outskirts of Kharkov, the great Russian industrial city which, in German hands for five months, has so far withstood every attack launched against it. Guerillas actually inside the city have been of immense value in cooperating with a daring assault from east and south, which has now reached the stage of hand-to-hand fighting beneath the very walls of the city. Heavy artillery and large tanks are backing the shock troops who stormed their way through machine-gun nests and pillboxes under the cover of smoke screens.'

17 March 1942, Victor Weisz 'Vicky', *News Chronicle*

"SO WE MEET AGAIN, YELLOW RAT!"

According to the *Melbourne Argus*: 'News that Gen. Douglas MacArthur, the gallant defender and hero of the Philippines, had arrived in Australia to take over as Supreme Commander of Allied Forces in the South-West Pacific, including the Philippines, was received with enthusiasm throughout Australia yesterday. The appointment was made by arrangement between the US and Australian Governments.'

18 March 1942, W. H. Woodburn 'Hengest', *Manchester Evening News*

PAINFUL — BUT IT'S TRUE

By the end of March, the Japanese had conquered Malaya, the Netherlands East Indies, most of the islands to the north and east of Papua New Guinea, and occupied the main coastal centres of Lae and Madang on the New Guinea mainland.

18 March 1942, J C Walker, *Western Mail*

The World at War

PUTTING THE STOPS IN

"Our visitors speak like us, think like us and fight like us." — Mr Curtin.

Australia swiftly became a base for American forces, and in March General Douglas MacArthur arrived in Australia to become the Supreme Commander of Allied forces in the South-West Pacific Area. He was to direct almost all of Australia's war effort in the coming years, loyally supported by the Prime Minister, John Curtin.

19 March 1942, Sam Wells, *Herald* (Melbourne, Australia)

TRUNK CALL

On the day this cartoon was published, the Indian Congress Working Committee rejected Stafford Cripps's proposals for India to be given Dominion status after the war. The failure of the Cripps Mission led to Gandhi calling for voluntary British withdrawal from India. This developed into the Quit India Movement which called for India's immediate independence and for British withdrawal from the subcontinent.

7 April 1942, J C Walker, *Western Mail*

POSITION TO BE HELD!

By April, Rommel had forced Allied forces to retreat all the way back to the Egyptian border, except for the garrison of Tobruk, which was being defended by the 9th Australian Division. In the east, British-Indian troops fought a long running battle against advancing Japanese forces in Burma.

10 April 1942, W. H. Woodburn 'Hengest', *Manchester Evening News*

According to the *Scotsman*: 'Pierre Laval, new Chief (Premier) of the Vichy Government, is observing great secrecy about his future plans and trying to create the impression that his policy will not entail handing over the destiny of France to the Germans. Reports from New York suggest that Laval will go further than Darlan had hitherto done in the matter of allowing the Germans transport facilities for supplies and even reinforcements to Rommel in North Africa.'

18 April 1942, Clive Uptton, *Daily Sketch*

. . . THINGS THAT GO 'BUMP' IN THE NICHT . . .

A raid by Royal Navy and Army Commando units succeeded in destroying the heavily defended and biggest dry dock in occupied Europe at St. Nazaire in occupied France. Despite heavy casualties, it was judged to be highly successful as the dock was severely damaged and remained unusable until 1947. The raid on St. Nazaire so enraged Hitler that he issued his infamous 'Commando Order' which allowed the summary execution of any captured commando.

24 April 1942, W. H. Woodburn 'Hengest', *Manchester Evening News*

IF HE ASKS FOR IT

In a broadcast on 10 May, Churchill told the nation that the Soviet government had expressed fear that the Germans would use poison gas against the Russian people. Churchill explained that the British would 'treat the unprovoked use of poison gas against our Russian ally exactly as if it were used against ourselves . . . [we will] carry gas warfare on the largest possible scale far and wide against military objectives in Germany. It is thus for Hitler to choose whether he wishes to add this additional horror to aerial warfare.' The German press, however, reported that Churchill, 'mad with desperation', had been the first to threaten use of chemical weapons.

11 May 1942, William Furnival, *Lancashire Evening Post*

"RETRIBUTIVE JUSTICE" – Mr. Churchill

According to the *Daily Herald*: 'Hitler warns us solemnly that if we go on smashing up the German cities, his war factories and bases, he will retaliate against our cathedrals and historic monuments. Herr Hitler has even called into question the humanity of these grim developments of war. What a pity this conversion did not take place before he bombed Warsaw or massacred 20.000 Dutch folk in defenceless Rotterdam. or wreaked his cruel vengeance upon Belgrade. But now it is the other way round. We are in a position to carry into Germany many times the tonnage of high explosives which he can send here.'

12 May 1942, J C Walker, *Western Mail*

According to the *Manchester Evening News*: 'Timoshenko's full-scale offensive against Kharkov has carried the Soviet troops across the Donets River and seven miles westwards towards Kharkov. The breach forced in the German lines is being steadily widened. At least 150 German tanks have been smashed in two days' fighting. Many Germans have been captured and much war material has fallen into the hands of the advancing Red Army. Although in the Kerch Peninsula the Russians have been driven back, the Germans have not won the great victory they claimed. The Russians are inflicting heavy casualties, and it does not look as if the Germans have taken Kerch.'

18 May 1942, W. H. Woodburn 'Hengest', *Manchester Evening News*

"YOUR LEADERS ARE TOILING FOR YOU" — Goering

According to Hannen Swaffer in *The People*: 'Goering made a speech to Berlin arms-makers so grim and awesome that Goebbels has since had to go to extraordinary lengths to suppress it: "If you workers despair at being separated from your families and are toiling to exhaustion," he said, "think of the suffering of your brothers at the front. We have nothing to celebrate today. You must make a stand like soldiers. I pray to Providence that each of you grows tougher and tougher, prepared to laugh the war last, no matter how long the war lasts. Do not believe what people say. War regulations must be obeyed. Your leaders are toiling for you. The Fuehrer has stamped out weakness." Covered with medals, Goering ended: "Do you really believe that Providence would let the Fuehrer raise the people so high only to throw them into the abyss?"'

22 May 1942, Victor Weisz 'Vicky', *News Chronicle*

THE WOUNDED SPIRIT

Intuition: Himmel, I'm hit!
Adolf: Which front?
Intuition: In the back.

According to the *Daily Record*: 'Hitler has been asked by his Generals to give up his position as Supreme Commander of the German Army according to a Stockholm report. He has left Berlin urgently for his Headquarters at the front to confer with the Army Commanders. Hitler's reply, adds the message, will be to tell the Generals that he proposes to keep the Supreme Command, in his hands, and that no opposition to his direction of operations will be tolerated.'

28 May 1942, George Middleton,
Birmingham Gazette

EAU DE COLOGNE

On the night of 30 May over a thousand planes raided Cologne.

Accepting that precision bombing had proved impossible, the War Cabinet sanctioned 'area bombing' — the targeting of whole cities to destroy both factories and their workers. On 30 May, 890 bombers reached Cologne causing massive damage. According to German figures, 469 people were killed and 45,000 made homeless. Only 41 aircraft were lost. Harris followed through with a second raid two nights later, fielding 956 bombers against the industrial town of Essen.

1 June 1942, Talbot Ellison, *Birmingham Mail*

RIGHT ON THE CHIN

With the headline 'Why Germans Howl for Revenge,' the *Yorkshire Evening Post* reported: 'The damage at Rostock, after the four R.A.F. raids on the Baltic port, is worse than at Lubeck. All sources are agreed on this. No casualty figures or details of damage are available, but the correspondents talk of tens of thousands of people being homeless, and say that smouldering ruins are all that the R.A.F. has left of the city. Howls for vengeance are still going up from the Nazis. All pretence that the German "reprisal" raids are directed against military objectives has now been dropped. The German Press openly admits that they are directed against residential districts and historical monuments.'

2 June 1942, George Whitelaw, *Daily Herald*

"It Has Happened Here!"

On 1 June, under the cover of darkness, a group of Japanese midget submarines secretly cruised into Sydney harbour and launched an attack that would bring the war to the city's doorstep. 21 Australian and British sailors were killed when a converted ferry, the HMAS Kuttabul, was sunk by a torpedo in the surprise naval offensive that shocked Sydney. Left shattered was the belief held by many Sydneysiders they were safe and protected from the conflict being played out across other parts of the world.

2 June 1942, Ian Gall, *Courier-Mail* (Australia)

ON POINT DUTY — OVER GERMANY

In 1942, the RAF introduced into service the Lancaster bomber, which made a major contribution to Bomber Command's night offensive on Germany. Targeting German cities to destroy both factories and their workers, this was seen by many as retribution for the Luftwaffe's earlier bombing of British and European historic towns and cities.

3 June 1942, Clive Uptton, *Daily Sketch*

A BIG HAND IN THE NEXT PAGE

Congratulating us on the history-making Cologne raid (since followed by Essen), Lieut.-General Arnold, of the U.S.A., said they would soon be joining us in such raids.

According to the *Evening News*: 'An indication that American air forces hope soon to be helping the R.A.F. in their attacks on Germany was given by Lieut-General Arnold, commanding the U.S. Air Force. In a message to Air Marshal Harris, General Arnold says the Cologne raid "was bold in conception and superlative in execution." Extending his congratulations to the crews engaged he asked Air Marshal Harris to say "that our air forces hope very soon to fly and fight beside them in these decisive blows against our common enemy. It is obvious that no offensive against Nazi-occupied Europe can succeed without air superiority, and we mean to have it. My visit has, hastened the day when our air arms shall join in an air offensive against the enemy which he cannot meet, defeat, or survive."'

3 June 1942, George Middleton, *Birmingham Gazette*

ALLES ÜBER DEUTSCHLAND

According to the *Evening News*: 'From dawn today the BBC told Germany and the occupied countries the full story of the Cologne raid. Interspersed in the European service giving the story were verbatim quotations of Goering's promise to the German people that no bombs would fall on them, and of Hitler's speeches conveying similar assurances. Emphasis was laid on Mr Churchill's phrase — "This proof of the growing power of the British bomber force is also the herald of what Germany will receive, city by city, from now on."'

3 June 1942, Victor Weisz 'Vicky',
News Chronicle

THE FUNERAL MARCH

On 26 May, Reinhard Heydrich, Deputy-Protector of Bohemia and Moravia, second-in-command to Himmler as head of the Gestapo, was mortally wounded when a bomb was thrown and bullets fired at him by two Czech resistance fighters while he was riding in an open top car through the suburbs of Prague. Berlin officially announced on 4 June that he had died the previous day. Thousands of people were waiting for the funeral, including many Czechs, who had not yet realised what awaited them from the Germans, who had already begun actions to avenge Heydrich's death before the ceremony. In retaliation over 7,000 Czechs were arrested, of which almost 1,500 were sentenced to death. A further 4,000 were sent to concentration camps, prisons and extermination camps. After Heydrich's death, Himmler ordered the acceleration of the extermination of the Jewish people. The action was codenamed "Reinhardt," in honour of Reinhard Heydrich.

6 June 1942, Clive Uptton, *Daily Sketch*

CAUGHT MIDWAY

On the morning of 4 June, after sending planes to attack the U.S. base at Midway, three Japanese carriers were fatally damaged by American dive bombers. Later that day, the USS Yorktown was abandoned after bomb and torpedo hits by planes from Japanese carrier Hiryu. The latter was, in turn, hit by U.S. carrier planes. Compelled by their losses to abandon their plans to capture Midway, the Japanese retired westward. The battle was a decisive win for the United States and continued with the American Navy pursuing the rest of the Japanese fleet.

8 June 1942, William Furnival, *Lancashire Evening Post*

THE MASSACRE OF LIDICE

On the 10 June, Nazis entered the mining village of Lidice, shot 173 men, removed all the women and children and razed the village to the ground. The atrocity took place in retaliation for the assassination of Reinhard Heydrich, 'The Butcher of Prague', by British-trained Czech resistance fighters.

11 June 1942, Wyndham Robinson, *Star*

PEACE IS INDIVISIBLE

With the headline '"Smash Anglo-Russian links at all costs!" — Hitler's Order,' *The People* reported: 'The impotent fury shown by the Nazis to the Grand Alliance between Russia and the Democracies is its own admission of their dismay. A clarion call to the United Nations, a tocsin to the Axis, it has wiped out many months of high-pressure Nazi-Fascist efforts to split the will of the free peoples to destroy Hitlerism. Now the people of Central Europe can see the future they are up against and how worthless are the promises of the Fuehrer to remove the Allies.'

13 June 1942, Clive Uptton, *Daily Sketch*

IT'S A SMALL WORLD

Churchill returned to America to decide with Roosevelt over whether to attempt an invasion of Europe in 1942 or stage a peripheral attack in North Africa. Molotov, the Soviet Union's foreign minister, had just left Washington after talks with Roosevelt in regard to a Second Front in 1942. According to the *Daily Mail*: 'Mr Churchill's arrival has led to speculations that the talks may be broadened to include the leaders of other countries, says an Ottawa message. It is pointed out that Queen Wilhelmina is shortly going to Washington, and that also on this side of the Atlantic are the Prime Minister of Norway and the King of Greece, and that King Peter of Yugoslavia is known to be coming.'

20 June 1942, S J Ray, *Kansas City Star* (United States)

THE OVERSHADOWED GLOAT

With the headline 'Churchill And Roosevelt Plan 1942 Offensive,' the *Daily Mail* reported: 'American opinion holds firmly to the view that the immediate purpose of the talks is the opening of the second front in Europe, and there are growing hopes that, so rapid has been the multiplication of Allied power and munitions of war, that the Free Nations will be in a position to abandon their defensive role and turn to a general offensive this year.'

20 June 1942, George Middleton, *Birmingham Gazette*

EIGHTH PLAGUE?

On 21 June, the Axis forces captured the port of Tobruk, Libya — which was of great strategic value due its deep-water port — and took more than 30,000 Allied prisoners. The defeat also allowed Axis forces under Rommel to advance towards Egypt. Churchill later wrote of the incident: 'Defeat is one thing; disgrace is another.''

24 June 1942, W. H. Woodburn 'Hengest', *Manchester Evening News*

THE PENALTY OF FAME

The fall of Tobruk prompted a surge of resentment across Britain. Churchill's critics forced a vote of censure against him in the House of Commons. Churchill won the vote easily, but the Labour MP Aneurin Bevan reflected a widespread feeling when he declared: 'The Prime Minister wins debate after debate and loses battle after battle.'

27 June 1942, J C Walker, *Western Mail*

HOMECOMING

Churchill returned to the Commons in a fighting mood to answer his critics. On the second day of the debate, he said: "Everything that could be thought of or raked up has been used to weaken confidence in the Government . . . to represent the Government as a set of nonentities over whom the Prime Minister towers, and then to undermine him in his own heart and, if possible, before the eyes of the nation. All this poured out by cables and radio to all parts of the world, to the distress of all our friends and to the delight of all our foes . . . If democracy and Parliamentary institutions are to triumph in this war, it is absolutely necessary that Governments resting upon them shall be able to act and dare, that the servants of the Crown shall not be harassed by nagging and snarling, that enemy propaganda shall not be fed needlessly out of our own hands . . . I am your servant, and you have the right to dismiss me when you please. What you have no right to do is to ask me to bear responsibilities without the power of effective action."'

29 June 1942, Victor Weisz 'Vicky', *News Chronicle*

The World at War   149

GLITTERING PRIZES

According to the *Daily Herald*: 'Hitler, back at his headquarters on the Russian front, is beginning to put his "summer offensive" into operation. In a vast pincer movement aimed ultimately at the Caucasus oilfields, he is driving all out for Egypt and Intensifying his pressure in Southern Russia. It is likely to aim first at clearing the bend of the Don between Rostov, at Its mouth, and Stalingrad, 250 miles to the north-east. Then — if this task Is achieved — it will swing south to the Caucasus.'

1 July 1942, George Whitelaw, *Daily Herald*

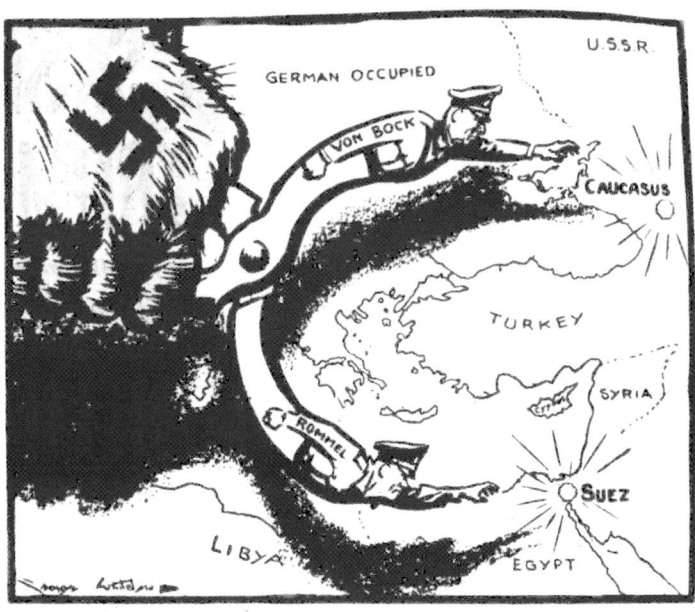

An Island born of dreams

The cartoonist highlights both Luftwaffe air attacks on British historic cities and Allied shipping losses which had both peaked in the previous month.

3 July 1942, Joseph Nyary, *Lustige Blätter* (Berlin, Germany)

OUTLOOK STORMY

According to the *News Chronicle*: 'The Battle of Egypt will be lost or won on the approaches to El Alamein. Whether the battle moves east or west, the final issue depends on the timely arrival of reinforcements. From the many accounts of the operations derived from Cairo it is evident that substantial reinforcement in the form of men and material are reaching General Auchinleck.'

6 July 1942, William Furnival, *Lancashire Evening Post*

TOUGH NUTS

According to the *Lancashire Evening Post*: 'The gallant stand by the depleted Eighth Army has stopped Rommel in his dash to Alexandria, and the time gained has meant that Auchinleck has been able to get up reinforcements in both men and material. The enemy has not only been held, but has suffered a reverse — if only a minor one — and lost guns and men. That is likely to have a depressing effect on the enemy forces while heartening our own men to hang on until still further reinforcements are able to reach Auchinleck. It is far too early to hope that Auchinleck may yet be able to turn the tables on Rommel.'

10 July 1942, J C Walker, *Western Mail*

The Road To Hell Is Paved With Good Intentions

Despite the threat of a Japanese invasion, Gandhi called for a voluntary British withdrawal from India. On 14 July, the Congress Working Committee authorised him to take charge of the non-violent mass movement. The Resolution, generally referred to as the 'Quit India' resolution, was to be approved by the All India Congress Committee meeting in Bombay in August.

22 July 1942, Clive Uptton, *Daily Sketch*

"And they said I was a savage!"

According to the *Sydney Morning Herald*: 'Almost incredible revelations of Japanese atrocities in New Guinea are contained in a statement issued officially to-day. Details of the atrocities have been given by three Australian servicemen who are the sole survivors of a party of 10 officers and about 50 men who were trapped while escaping. They had picked up leaflets dropped from Japanese planes stating that those who surrendered would be well treated, and that those who did not would be killed. They were captured by a landing party from a Japanese destroyer. They were lined up and their hands were tied behind their backs. They were then either shot or bayoneted to death.'

29 July 1942, George Whitelaw, *Daily Herald*

The World at War   151

SERENADE TO A 'PACIFIST'

According to the *Daily Mirror*: 'Riots have broken out in Bombay, Allahabad, and other cities following the arrest of Mahatma Gandhi. A Government communique states that the police were forced to open fire on the rioters on five occasions and to use tear gas. Demonstrators stoned the police and police stations and stoned buses. A message reputedly left by Gandhi before his arrest said: "Every man is free to go the fullest length under civil disobedience to cause complete deadlocks by strikes and all other possible methods. Karenge ja marenge (Do unto death)."'

12 August 1942, Clive Uptton, *Daily Sketch*

CONCRETE

On 12 August, Churchill arrived in Moscow to meet Stalin for the first time — alongside Roosevelt's representative, Averell Harriman — to cement the ties between the nations. Though the two leaders did not seem to get along well personally and disagreed about the opening of a second front, the meeting, Stalin remarked, was 'of very great value'. In a frantic desire to put a negative spin on Churchill's first visit to the Kremlin, Goebbels claimed that the Prime Minister's trip was 'a symptom of a crisis of the first magnitude.'

18 August 1942, Victor Weisz 'Vicky', *News Chronicle*

152 THE SECOND WORLD WAR IN CARTOONS

WINSTON SMASHED ANOTHER RECORD

According to the *Leicester Mercury*: 'Goebbels is driving himself frantic in his desire to explain that Mr. Churchill and Stalin quarrelled. A Wilhelmstrasse spokesman stated today: "All reports from the enemy side support the opinion, formed some days ago in German political circles, that Churchill's visit was an act of desperation, which he decided on under pressure of military and political developments in the Soviet Union."'

19 August 1942, George Middleton, *Birmingham Gazette*

SOME GENTLEMEN HAVE CALLED

On 19 August, the Allies attacked the German occupied port of Dieppe. Despite the wishful thinking behind this cartoon, the raid was a disaster. No major objectives were accomplished. 3,623 of the 6,086 men who made it ashore were killed, wounded, or captured. The Allied air forces failed to lure the Luftwaffe into open battle, and lost 119 planes, while the Royal Navy suffered 555 casualties. The Germans claimed that the operation was an attempted full-scale invasion, which was repulsed with heavy Allied losses. The catastrophe at Dieppe later influenced Allied preparations for Operation Torch and Operation Overlord.

23 August 1942, Stuart Peterson, *Sun* (Sydney, Australia)

"ONE FOR THE ROAD."

"Between 25 and 30 toasts were drunk at the Stalin-Churchill banquet, the Russians drinking a full glass each time. Stalin proposed half a dozen toasts."

On 12 August, Churchill flew to Moscow to see Stalin, for the first time, a mission that Churchill's wife, Clementine, had described to him as a "visit to the Ogre in his Den." With the headline 'Stalin Toasts' the *Newcastle Journal* reported: 'Stalin, according to one distinguished guest, was "in great good humour." Maximum friendliness and minimum formality were the features of this historic dinner. Stalin himself proposed half-a-dozen of the 25 toasts. Others were proposed by Harriman, Sir Archibald Clark-Kerr, and Admiral Standley. Dinner, served with traditional Russian hospitality, went on to well after midnight.'

26 August 1942, Norman Lindsay, *Sydney Bulletin* (Australia)

The World at War

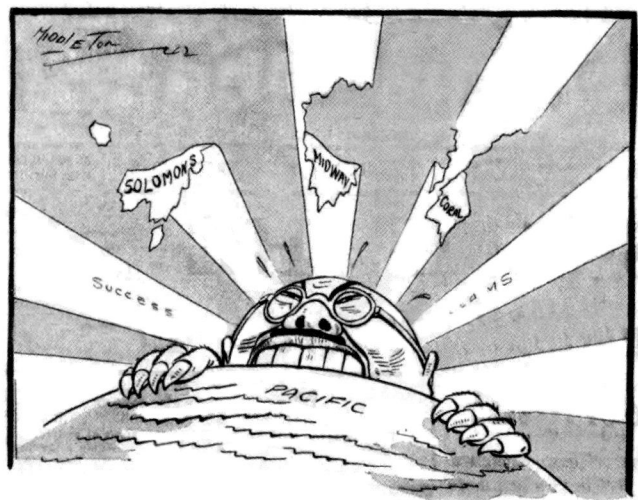

SPOILING THE HON. RAYS

According to the *Courier and Advertiser*: 'The account by the U.S. Navy Department of the recapture of six of the Solomon Islands shows that an extremely difficult operation was carried out with signal success. Within two days of the first landing by U.S. marines five of the islands were completely and the sixth partly in American hands. The complete occupation followed. Since then, several landings of fresh troops have been made by the enemy, but every Jap soldier has been killed or captured. Allied air-sea-land co-operation has dealt a heavy blow to Japan's Pacific hopes. It has been done by a combination of well-planned strategy and the magnificent courage of U.S. marines in grim fighting.'

1 September 1942, George Middleton, *Birmingham Gazette*

MAROONED!

According to the *Bradford Observer*: 'A previous attempt to dislodge the Americans from the Solomons was made on 20 August, when 700 Japanese attempted to land near United States marines positions from speed-boats. Severe hand-to-hand fighting followed, the Japanese being completely wiped out without gaining their objective. Over 600 of them were killed and the rest taken prisoner.'

2 September 1942, Stuart Peterson, *Sun* (Sydney, Australia)

According to the *Lancashire Evening Post*: 'The Russians continue to show heroic sacrifice, incredible powers of endurance and grim determination in their stubborn defence of Stalingrad and of other vital places on their long front. Many violent enemy attacks have been repulsed and heavy toll is being exacted from Bock's reinforced armies by the gallant defenders of Stalingrad. This great battle for the Volga city has now continued for almost four weeks and there is no doubt that the Germans, by incessant bombing and heavy assaults by masses of men and tanks, fully expected to have achieved its capture long before this.'

10 September 1942, Ian Gall, *Courier-Mail* (Brisbane, Australia)

THE PROFITEER

According to Hannen Swaffer in *The People*: 'Stalingrad, the city of the man of steel! Never, surely, in all history has a town been so fittingly named. So called because Stalin, named the man of steel by Lenin, had saved it from the White Russians in the early days of the Bolshevik Revolution. Not even against Moscow was such might hurled. Yet, day after day, Stalingrad has held out, piling up the German dead in its outskirts, blunting the weapon that the Nazis intend, when winter comes to hurl against us, achieving what seemed impossible.'

16 September 1942, Clive Uptton, *Daily Sketch*

HELD

According to the *Rochdale Observer*: 'The Soviet communique reveals that a German attempt to achieve a major breakthrough into Stalingrad had been held up. The Germans reached the suburbs, but were driven out by a powerful counter-attack which restored the position.'

18 September 1942, William Furnival, *Lancashire Evening Post*

AUSTERITY IN EUROPE

According to the *Northern Whig*: 'Lord Woolton said food shortages in Europe this winter would cause privations that would awaken the people to a realisation of the folly of sacrificing the lives of their menfolk and the future health of the children to the devilish ambitions for over-mastering power of today's leaders of Germany and Italy. Those who continued to accept the yoke of servitude to those wicked men were the enemies of all men of good will. Their punishment was near. They would be hungry and sad and bereaved in their tens of thousands before the winter finished. But Europe need not starve. Desperate men could make superhuman efforts to achieve freedom. When they did, food would be nearby.'

24 September 1942, Stuart Peterson, *Sun* (Sydney, Australia)

The World at War

DIVERSION

British officials describe German claims to have sunk three troop transports in the Atlantic as "quite untrue."

With the headline 'Goebbels Biggest Lie Nailed Down' the *Gloucester Citizen* reported: 'The enemy claim to have sunk troop transports in the Atlantic is quite untrue the Ministry of Information announced today. The *Press Association* says the German claim was evidently put out in an effort to "fish for Information," but the official disclaimer not only gives the lie to their claim but denies them any information they may be seeking.'

1 October 1942, George Whitelaw, *Daily Herald*

MORE "NEW ORDER"

Nine hundred Guernsey men have been forced to work in Germany. More are expected to be conscripted from Jersey.

According to the *Aberdeen Press and Journal*: 'The Nazis are deporting hundreds of families from the Channel Islands for forced labour in Germany. All male civilians not born in the Channel Islands, between the ages of 16 and 70, have been deported to Germany, together with their families. This deportation took place last week and 900 men were conscripted from Guernsey. Four hundred are still to go. and it is expected that there will be more from Jersey than there will be from Guernsey.'

8 October 1942, Talbot Ellison, *Birmingham Mail*

Sweeping Broom . . .: Hitler is pushing. Churchill is watching. Solemn promise to open the Second Front in Europe in 1942".

During this period, Efimov regularly ridiculed Churchill's reluctance to open a second front in Europe as an example of British cowardice. The road sign reads: 'To Soviet-German front.' The sea reads: 'The English Channel.'

18 October 1942, Boris Efimov, *Izvestia* (Soviet Union)

THERE'S SMUTS ON YER NOSE!

The Prime Minister of South Africa, Field Marshal Jan Smuts, visited Britain to address both Houses of Parliament. Smuts said that the moment for a great Allied attack was approaching and that the defensive phase of the Allied strategy had now ended. "Once the time has come to take the offensive and strike while the iron is hot," he said, "it would be folly to delay, to overprepare and perhaps miss our opportunity." It was reported that Smuts was in Britain for secret talks about the opening up of a second front in North Africa.

23 October 1942, J C Walker, *Western Mail*

PASSPORT TO SLAVERY

American Secretary for State Cordell Hull condemned Laval for his pro-Hitler acts and stated that Laval's demand that French men should work for Germany was the same as asking them to become slaves: "Such workers might just as well be prisoners of war in Germany" he said. "In some ways it is worse than imposing forced service on war workers, and I am glad to see that the French people are waking up to the conditions Laval is attempting to impose on them."

25 October 1942, Will Hope, *Sunday Chronicle*

The World at War

OH HULL

According to the *News Chronicle*: 'By one vote Hull Watch Committee refused to approve as a wartime measure the appointment of a woman to take charge of a cinema. It was contended that the difficulties caused by the black-out made it necessary for a man to be in charge. The Chief Constable, Mr. Wells, offered no objection, pointing out that the candidate was suitable and that women had done exceptionally good work during the war.'

28 October 1942, Wyndham Robinson, *Star*

PINCER MOVEMENT

According to the *Liverpool Echo*: 'Hitler is no longer dictating the course of the war, and he must now shape his plans to counter the growing strength of the Allies. The fighting in the East will relieve the pressure on Russia and intensify the strain on the German air forces. We are approaching the climax of the war, and much will happen before this year has run its course.'

1 November 1942, Will Hope, *Sunday Chronicle*

According to the *Yorkshire Observer*: 'After a night-long barrage, which almost rivalled the "Somme" gunfire with which the Allied offensive was ushered in, the Eighth Army scored new gains — and consolidated them in spite of fierce opposition.' A middle east joint war communiqué read: — The Axis forces in the Western Desert, after twelve days and nights of ceaseless attacks by our land and air force, are now in full retreat. Their disordered columns are being relentlessly attacked by our land forces and by the Allied air forces by day and night.'

4 November 1942, Wyndham Robinson, *Star*

ENOUGH ROPE

According to the *Liverpool Daily Post*: 'The Eighth Army's success breaching the Axis lines west of El Alamein has forced on Rommel a general withdrawal from all his forward positions right down to the Qattara Depression, forty miles from the Mediterranean. That is the most striking result so far of the great infantry and tank battle still raging in and beyond the gap which Highland and Empire troops have torn through the depth of the Axis mine-fields, gun positions, and tank traps.'

6 November 1942, Will Mahony, *Daily Telegraph* (Sydney, Australia)

THE EIGHTH PLAGUE OF EGYPT

According to the Newcastle *Sunday Sun*: 'The Eighth Army last night was going all out to trap Rommel's panzers for a final "kill," and, more than 120 miles from the starting point of their offensive, our forces are hard on the heels of the retreating enemy, with mobile columns in the open desert sweeping towards the coast from south of Mersa Matruh in an effort to force a decisive battle.'

6 November 1942, William Furnival, *Lancashire Evening Post*

ALL LINES LEAD TO BERLIN

"Listen, you boys — ain't I got troubles of my own?"

Military defeats at Stalingrad and at the Second Battle of El Alamein led to the tide turning in favour of the Allies over the Axis.

6 November 1942, Arthur Potts 'Spot', *Hull Daily Mail*

RING IN THE NEW PHASE

Churchill marked the victory at El Alamein by authorising the mass ringing of church bells throughout the country, not heard since 1940, and declared: "Now this is not the end. It is not even the beginning of the end. But it is perhaps, the end of the beginning."

14 November 1942, David Ghilchik, *Daily Sketch*

160 THE SECOND WORLD WAR IN CARTOONS

5
The Tide Turns

According to the *Queensland Times*: '"A momentous event," was the description given by the Minister for the Navy to the American naval victory in the Solomons. Mr. Makin said the victory would give Australia "much needed relief from the possibility of enemy invasion." In gratitude towards the Americans, Australian Prime Minister Curtin stated: "I often wonder to what extent the Australian people are grateful for these intervening forces which so far have stood between the enemy and our cities."'

18 November 1942, George Finey, *Daily Telegraph* (Sydney, Australia)

"There's nothing like having good seconds."

Thanks to American Lend-Lease, which supplied large quantities of material aid to the Soviet Union, the Red Army continued to survive the ongoing onslaught of the German Wehrmacht. In all, the United States shipped $11.3 billion to the Soviet Union providing it with more than 400,000 jeeps and trucks, 14,000 aircraft, 8,000 tractors and construction vehicles, and 13,000 battle tanks. In addition, much of the $31 billion worth of aid sent to Britain was also passed on to the Soviet Union via convoys through the Barents Sea to Murmansk.

22 Nov 1942, Tom Carlisle, *The St. Louis Globe-Democrat* (United States)

DER FUEHRER IS ALWAYS RIGHT

According to a reporter with the Eighth Army, the *Sunday Dispatch* reported: 'We occupied Benghazi without a shot being fired after Rommel had abandoned the port to get most of his forces away before we reached the coast road to the south. Now defying wind and rainstorms which are sweeping the desert, the Eighth Army are pushing relentlessly forward to get to grips with the Axis forces regrouped at Agheila. Montgomery's advanced groups are hitting hard at Rommel's rearguard. Some of the German transport has been cut off in the Benghazi bulge.'

23 November 1942, Victor Weisz 'Vicky', *News Chronicle*

"HE'S SOLD US A PUP!"

According to the *News Chronicle*: '"The Hitlerite army has now become considerably weaker," declared Stalin on 7 November. "We can and must clear the invaders from Soviet soil. The day is not far distant when the enemy will feel the force of new blows of the Red Army." Hitler will have to do some hard thinking. The Reich with Its vassal States now stands ringed about by enemies; it is vulnerable, not on two fronts, but on half a dozen. The Soviet advance is part of a gigantic stranglehold which must presently reduce Germany to submission.'

25 November 1942, Victor Weisz 'Vicky', *News Chronicle*

THE PLUMBER'S WATERLOO

According to the *Falkirk Herald*: 'All the cunning ingenuity and light regard for truth for which Dr Goebbels is notorious are being summoned to explain to the German people the reverses in Russia and North Africa. Doubtless the now popular phrase, "elasticity in defence," came from his fertile brain. It would be likely to occur to a man of such elastic morals, and if recent pronouncements by Hitler, and that lesser Nazi deity, Rommel, are to be covered up, the stretching of the piece of propaganda elastic which he handles will have to be manipulated with extra adroitness for the Germans on the home front.'

28 November 1942, George Middleton, *Birmingham Gazette*

THE DEUCE!

In a radio broadcast on 30 November, Churchill stated: "Mussolini could not resist the temptation of stabbing prostrate France, and what he thought was helpless Britain, in the back. Mad dreams of Imperial glory, the lust of conquest and of booty, the arrogance of long unbridled tyranny led him to his fatal shameful act. In vain I warned him. He would not harken. On deaf ears and a stony heart fell the wise far-seeing appeals of the American President The hyena in his nature broke all bounds of decency and even common-sense. Today his Empire is gone."

1 December 1942, Thomas Arthur Challen 'Tac', *Daily Mirror* **(Sydney, Australia)**

REWARD FOR CO-OPERATION

In a radio broadcast on 30 November, Churchill stated: "We have over 100 Italian generals and nearly 300,000 of his soldiers in our hands as prisoners of war. Agony grips the fair land of Italy. This is only the beginning, and what is there to show for it? A brief promenade, by German permission, along the Riviera; A flying visit to Corsica, a bloody struggle with the heroic patriots of Yugoslavia, a deed of undying shame in Greece; the ruins of Genoa, Turin, Milan. And this is only a foretaste."

1 December 1942, J C Walker, *Western Mail*

He's beginning to lose his grip

According to the *Gloucester Citizen*: 'Before the war can be won, the Allies must close with the huge body of the German octopus. It is not enough to hack off the tips of encircling tentacles. This octopus has a tougher hide than any monster ever had, but there, where the body bulges towards the south-east, the hide is flabbier than it is elsewhere. And close behind this vulnerable patch the monster's heart is situated.'

4 December 1942, Matthew Sandford 'Matt', *Daily Sketch*

The Tide Turns

ALL SET FOR BIG DRIVE

According to the *Manchester Evening News*: 'Front door to Italy, though but 120 miles from Tunis, and possibly very prominently in General Eisenhower's mind, Sardinia probably quakes in spirit today as much as Mount Etna has at various periods in the past physically shaken its companion Isle of Sicily, another of the stepping stones for the invasion and conquest of Mussolini's pitiful, stab-in-the-back State.'

8 December 1942, J C Walker, *Western Mail*

STORY WITHOUT WORDS

According to the *Evening Sentinel*: 'The House of Commons today went into secret session to debate developments in North Africa, including the position of Admiral Darlan. Mr. Churchill made a statement opening the debate. Earlier, Mr. Eden, Foreign Secretary — when pressed by Mr. Aneurin Bevan — had declined to give an undertaking that the country should be given a statement as to the attitude of the House on the question of Admiral Darlan. Mr. Bevan asked if the Government would consider before the Christmas recess some way in which the House could put on record its attitude regarding Admiral Darlan, so as to reassure opinion in the country, which was "very uneasy about the whole situation."'

10 December 1942, George Middleton, *Birmingham Gazette*

GETTING TOGETHER

British General Kenneth Anderson was chosen to command the invasion of Tunisia from the west with the Allied 1st Army attacking the recently reinforced German garrison in Tunisia under the command of General Walther Nehring. In the east, General Montgomery and the Eighth Army were chasing General Rommel's Africa Korps back towards Tripoli.

16 December 1942, George Whitelaw, *Daily Herald*

CHRISTMAS WITH GANGSTERS
THE SCARY UNCLE

The cartoonist mocks Britain's perceived military weakness as Canada and especially Australia now looked to America to defend them. The previous year, Australian Prime Minister John Curtin had stated that Australia "looks to America, free of any pangs to our traditional links or kinship with the United Kingdom." Curtin's message was a public acknowledgement that Australia faced an imminent crisis to which Britain was unable to respond and the nation now depended on the US for its security.

20 December 1942, Arthur Johnson, *Kladderadatsch* (Germany)

THAT'S CAIRO — THAT WAS!

Due to shortages of fuel, ammunition and equipment, Rommel had decided to withdraw rather than stand and fight. What followed was a staggering 1,400 miles retreat by the Afrika Korps across Libya and into Tunisia. The 8th Army chased him all the way. During its retreat, the Afrika Korps lost 130 tanks and 1,000 artillery guns. Heavy rains limited the ability of the Royal Air Force Desert Air Force to fully harass the retreating Germans. But with retreat, the Axis left behind airfields. Each airfield captured added to the RAF's ability to support ground forces, drop in supplies, and attack the Germans.

20 December 1942, Will Hope, *Sunday Chronicle*

STIRRING DAYS

According to the *Daily Mirror*: 'The United Nations have no reason to complain of the contents of their Christmas stocking. In it they have found many pleasant, comforting, and exciting gifts. The biggest gift of all comes from Father Stalin's lovely Don Basin crammed, with good things: with territory, with prisoners; with booty, all nicely mixed with optimism and the feeling that there is more to come. A grand and most significant gift, this, from the snow-clad lands of Russia.'

23 December 1942, Will Mahony, *Daily Telegraph* (Sydney, Australia)

The Tide Turns

The Woolton Victory Way — Forward To 1943

Minister of Food, Lord Woolton, enlisted the support of the country's leading cartoonists in order to encourage the public to eat more potatoes and to discourage food wastage. Woolton felt that the 'public was either going to laugh or to cry about food rationing, and that it was better for them that they should laugh even if it was only a somewhat wry smile.' According to *Daily Express* cartoonist Sidney Strube: "When Lord Woolton wanted us to eat more potatoes and less bread, what did he do? He called in the cartoonists who helped his campaign by pointing out, with much fun, the value of the potato in the war effort. With a smile, the country ate more potatoes!"

28 December 1942, David Ghilchik, *Daily Sketch*

HAVING A PLUNDERFUL TIME

According to the *Aberdeen Press and Journal*: 'Nazi looting of art treasures in Europe has been organised on military lines. Ribbentrop has formed a corps of art experts in uniform who have come to be known as "Ribbentrop's Own." They consist of experts in the plastic and graphic arts architecture and literature. They have been following in the wake of the German occupying armies to give expert advice on the seizure of treasures. The best are sent to Germany, either for Hitler's or Goering's collections or for the museums.'

7 January 1943, George Whitelaw, *Daily Herald*

"The remaining strong-points of Stalingrad are not worth a second Verdun — Hitler, November 8, 1942

As the weather worsened, thousands of wounded, starving German infantrymen in Stalingrad froze to death amid subzero temperatures. General Paulus pleaded with Hitler to let the remnants of Sixth Army attempt a breakout but Hitler insisted Stalingrad be held at all costs. The Russians, having assembled seven armies, offered a last-minute ultimatum to avoid the onslaught. This was turned down by Paulus, acting on Hitler's direct order. As a result, the Russians blasted the remaining Germans with five thousand artillery guns followed a week later by a massive infantry assault.

18 January 1943, Victor Weisz 'Vicky', *News Chronicle*

IT JUST CAME TO PIECES IN MY HANDS

According to the *Lincolnshire Echo*: 'Very soon now the Eighth Army is likely to reap the fruits of its long and victorious advance of over 1,000 miles and Mussolini will see the last remnants of his African Empire disappear as a dream.' While the *Edinburgh Evening News* reported: 'It will be a great moment when the Eighth Army formally enters Tripoli, where, after the trying conditions of the desert, they will be able to enjoy the comforts of modern city — a town Mussolini made the "show place" of his African Empire. How Britain has, step by step, fulfilled the promise made to Mussolini by Mr Churchill at Christmas, 1940, to "tear your Africa Empire to shreds and tatters."'

22 January 1943, Wyndham Robinson, *Star*

CHURCHILL'S NIGHTMARE

The cartoonist mocks Churchill's baby like appearance. In fact, Churchill would later say: "All babies look like me. But then, I look like all babies."

24 January 1943, Oscar Garvens, *Kladderadatsch* (Berlin, Germany)

According to the *Aberdeen Evening Express*: 'Goebbels wrote recently that the Germans were having to pay a very high price for everything "with interest and compound interest." Moscow radio commented: "It is not the only thing they are being taught on the Soviet-German front. They are getting a lesson in fractions and decimals too. Hitler's patchwork army is being decimated. His allies — the Rumanians Hungarians and Italians — provide very good examples for a lesson in arithmetic."'

26 January 1943, David Ghilchik, *Daily Sketch*

The Tide Turns

Roosevelt and Churchill agreed at the Casablanca conference that Britain and the US would continue in the war until they had secured the 'unconditional surrender' of both Germany and Japan. In a press conference, Roosevelt explained that they meant 'no harm to the common people of the Axis nations', but they did intend to 'impose punishment and retribution upon their guilty, barbaric leaders'.

27 January 1943, Eric Godal, *PM* (New York, United States)

A TALE OF TWO CARPETS

After meeting Roosevelt in Casablanca, Churchill flew to Cairo and then onto a two-day conference with Turkish President İnönü. On his return flight to Egypt, he was escorted part of the way by Hurricane aircraft delivered to the Turkish Air Force only a few days previously. Hitler's famous rages earned him the nickname Teppichfresser which translates to 'carpeteater'. Historians are undecided about whether Hitler really did chew on carpets in fits of anger. It is commonly believed that the nickname was taken too literally.

3 February 1943, David Ghilchik, *Daily Sketch*

BLINKERS

According to the *Daily Herald*: 'Rear-Admiral Land, United States War Shipping Administrator, disclosed in Washington that Germany was reported to be producing a submarine a day. "This rate," he said, "is faster than our past record of submarine sinkings. We are meeting this danger with every means at our command — by utilising our naval, air and patrol forces to the utmost and by new techniques in defence."'

4 February 1943, George Whitelaw, *Daily Herald*

FOR WHOM THE BELL TOLLS...

Three days' mourning has been ordered in Germany for the loss of Stalingrad

According to the *News Chronicle*: 'Earlier the German High Command issued a special announcement stating: "The fight for Stalingrad is finished." This was at once followed by an order for mourning for the German Sixth Army, closing cinemas, theatres and other places of entertainment.'

5 February 1943, Victor Weisz 'Vicky', *News Chronicle*

THE CRIME AGAINST EUROPE

On 2 February the frozen, starving and encircled German forces at Stalingrad surrendered, cementing one of the greatest Soviet victories of the war. After the German humiliation, Goebbels launched a propaganda campaign against 'Jewish Bolshevism'. Roosevelt, Churchill (who had now become ineffectual and subordinate to the Americans in German eyes) and de Gaulle were 'to be presented as accomplices and toadies of Bolshevism, which is the most radical expression of the Jewish drive for world domination'.

7 February 1943, Oskar Garvens, *Kladderadatsch* (Berlin, Germany)

The Tide Turns 169

IN THE CORNER POCKET

With the headline 'Nazis Lose Caucasus Stronghold,' the *Daily Herald* reported: 'Krasnoarmelsk, main stronghold of the Germans trapped on the Tasman bridgehead, is in Russian hands again. By seizing Krasnoarmelsk the Russians have cut Stalingrad's communications to the west and further Imperilled the Germans' large forces in the Donets Basin. Despite continued heavy opposition, the Russians are still pressing this encircling advance.'

8 February 1943, Rube Goldberg, *New York Sun* **(United States)**

Grand Tourist

According to the *Daily Herald*: 'Winston is home again. He arrived at Paddington after the most dramatic of his global wanderings just as most people were sitting down to their lunch. And he was in such a hurry to get to his desk in Downing Street that the "welcome home" ceremony was over in less than ten minutes. There was no red carpet. No fuss. Then, with the famous cigar well in evidence, and an even broader smile than usual, he was on the platform in the middle of a surge of handshakes and a roar of laughter. In the uniform of an air commodore, he looked fitter than he had done for months.'

8 February 1943, David Ghilchik, *Daily Sketch*

According to the *Lincolnshire Echo*: 'Hitler's winter defence line, slashed by the Red Army's capture of the Kursk bastion, is today in danger of crumbling piecemeal under the Soviet armies' incessant hammer-blows. Soviet shock troops, pushing through the Kursk gap, are fanning out behind the German strong points on the blizzard-swept Russian plains. Meanwhile, General Vatutin's Army, swinging South from the Donetz to snare the German armies in the Don-basin, have made a fresh breakthrough.'

9 February 1943, Wyndham Robinson, *Star*

"DON'T THROW THAT THING — IT'LL UNDERMINE HIS CHARACTER"

According to the *Manchester Evening News*: 'Approach of the three-day Commons debate on the Beveridge report has brought not only a flood of direct opposition from vested interests, but also a spate of attempts to discredit the report by drawing red herrings across the trail. One of the most remarkable of these is the suggestion that certain "cautious" Conservatives would like to know why, although all manner of people — including trade unionists, it is asserted — sat on the committee, only Sir William Beveridge signed the report.'

15 February 1943, W. H. Woodburn 'Hengest', *Manchester Evening News*

"Help! Help! the barbarians are destroying our culture!"

According to the *Yorkshire Evening Post*: 'While Goebbels in a fit of fear is "warning" Britain and America of danger to Western culture should the "Bolshevist barbarians" overrun Europe, the Nazi regime continues to show the world who are the real barbarians. When they talk of saving Europe, they mean the keeping of Europe under German domination, which at its mildest means economic exploitation and servitude for "second-class" races and at its worst is terror without precedent in scale and savagery. Europe under the Nazis is a bestial, revolting scene of calculated crime which it is to be feared will grow worse as doom closes upon the criminals.'

15 February 1843, Victor Weisz 'Vicky', *News Chronicle*

The Tide Turns

ON THE AIR

With the headline 'Non-Stop Bombing, the *Daily Record* reported: 'During all February there were only three nights and three days with no bombing attacks on Germany or German-occupied Europe. The effects on the enemy of this continuous bombing of widely-separated points are not hard to discern. It is gratifying to know that our losses in the air are adjudged small in comparison with the results achieved.'

2 March 1943, David Ghilchik, *Daily Sketch*

TONGUE-TIED

The truth about Hitler's continued silence

According to the *Edinburgh Evening News*: 'Harold Balfour, Parliamentary Under Secretary for Air, stated that: "During all this we do not seem to hear much of Hitler. We are told that he is busy 'in conference' with his staff. There is an American interpretation that what is really meant by 'in conference' is out, don't know where the fellow's run to. Wherever he may be, we do get news of his series of hysterical decrees crying out threat and defiance, pitched in the tones of a megalomaniac who is suffering from severe spasms of self-inflicted glory."'

4 March 1943, George Middleton, *Birmingham Gazette*

GOING FLAT-OUT

According to the *Aberdeen Evening Express*: 'Rommel's attacks from the Mareth Line were shattered by the Eighth Army in one of the most brilliant actions of the Tunisian campaign. After the two initial attacks failed, Rommel threw four more attacks at our positions. General Montgomery opened up a terrific artillery, fire, pinning the enemy to the ground and smashing his drive. As darkness came, the enemy retired west towards the hills. The enemy attempt had aimed at capturing the high ground south and east of the Mareth Line, obtaining a commanding position and splitting our farces. In all objectives he failed completely.'

9 March 1943, David Ghilchik, *Daily Sketch*

ANOTHER MARCH ON ROME

With the headline 'Italians Routed By Red Army,' the *Newcastle Evening Chronicle* reported 'During the retreat in Russia the Italian Alpine regiments looked like some disorderly rabble. Officers and men fled in panic. "We used to march for 18 hours at a time. We could not get out of the Red Army pincers and had to abandon lorries, guns. and food supplies. It was a terrible catastrophe." This description at the sufferings of the Italian Eighth Army which has just returned from Russia has been given by Captain Raoul Francesco, an Italian Divisional Commander. The second Italian Alpine Division lost 10,000 men in killed and prisoners, the third Alpine Division lost 10,700 men, the fourth Alpine Division 13,200 men.'

14 March 1943, Stuart Peterson, *Sun* **(Sydney, Australia)**

FORCEFUL REMINDER

According to the *News Chronicle*: 'The news from North Africa is disappointing. It appears that a successful counter-attack has been launched against those units of the Eighth Army which forced the Mareth bridgehead and that our troops have been driven back to their original positions. As Mr. Churchill says, we have no reason to fear the final outcome of the battle. In modern warfare, which is not unlike warfare at sea, territory quickly gained can be as quickly lost and gained again. But it Is clear that there is no room for optimistic expectation of an easily won victory.'

26 March 1943, J C Walker, *Western Mail*

"The panzer divisions in particular are remarkably mauled and enfeebled." — MR. CHURCHILL

With the headline 'Panzers Enfeebled,' the *Yorkshire Evening Post* reported: 'Mr. Churchill gave the great news in reply to a question by Mr. Arthur Greenwood. He said: "Since I informed the House last week of the check on the Mareth front, the situation has turned very much in our favour. General Montgomery's decision to throw his weight on to the turning movement, instead of persisting on the frontal attack, has been crowned with success. Another severe defeat has been inflicted by the Desert Army on the Axis forces they have so long pursued. The enemy losses in men and materials have, of course, been serious to him, and the panzer divisions in particular are remarkably mauled and enfeebled."'

31 March 1943, Victor Weisz 'Vicky', *News Chronicle*

The Tide Turns 173

OFF WE GO AGAIN!

According to the *Belfast Post*: 'As General Montgomery, maintaining pressure on the Mareth Line, launched a big new frontal attack on the Line, south-west of Mareth, taking ground and prisoners, and at the same time pushed his huge outflanking armoured column to the outskirts of El Hamma, in the rear of the Line, Rommel's position worsened rapidly at the week-end.'

31 March 1943, W. H. Woodburn 'Hengest', *Manchester Evening News*

In the House of Commons, Churchill asked for a measure of confidence in the U-Boat campaign. When referring to a motion asking the Government to relieve anxiety about the campaign, an MP asked whether opportunity would be taken to inform the House of the great improvements recently effected. Churchill replied: "I deprecate discussion on this matter. It would be quite impossible, in public, and even in secret session I should feel very much hampered in stating the full case. I must ask for a full measure of confidence."'

3 April 1943, Charles Werner, *Chicago Sun* (United States)

According to the *Birmingham Daily Gazette*: 'Rommel's new line in Southern Tunisia is under fire from British artillery as Gen. Montgomery prepares to launch a new assault against the retreating Axis forces, stated Algiers radio last night. "The Eighth Army," stated the radio, "is assembling fresh forces among them shock troops. In the meantime, retreating Axis columns are being continuously attacked from the air by Allied aircraft. The Germans have mined the road to Sfax and numerous anti-tank obstacles have been placed at the side of the road to slow down the Allied advance."'

7 April 1943, Wyndham Robinson, *Star*

174   THE SECOND WORLD WAR IN CARTOONS

P.S. — HEIL HITLER!

According to the *Liverpool Daily Post*: 'An American broadcaster from Algiers radio gave this warning to Rommel's soldiers last night: "To be drowned is not a very nice death. It may well be that the ships which might have to evacuate you in the very near future will meet with the same fate as Axis ships accounted for in the Mediterranean during last week. Save your lives by following the example of Paulus, his 23 generals and 2,500 officers by laying down arms just as they did at Stalingrad. There is no other way out of the African trap."'

14 April 1943, George Whitelaw, *Daily Herald*

WE MUST HAVE PATIENCE

With the headline: 'Montgomery Massing Powerful Forces,' the *Daily Mail* reported: 'General Sir Harold Alexander's forces are jockeying for position preparatory to their final assault on the Axis armies boxed in behind the formidable mountain ranges protecting Bizerta and Tunis. A Berlin military spokesman, quoted by Vichy radio, said: "The British and American forces are concentrating powerful forces, and are bringing up a large number of guns. There are also other indications which tend to confirm that a new offensive by General Montgomery is forthcoming."'

19 April 1943, J C Walker, *Western Mail*

According to the *Bristol Mirror*: 'Women between 18 and 65 are now eligible for nomination as auxiliaries with the Home Guard to perform non-combatant duties such as clerical work, cooking and driving. Sir James Grigg, Secretary for War, who made this announcement in the House of Commons, told Dr. Edith Summerskill (Lab., Fulham W.) that instructions had been issued to Home Guard battalion commanders to give preference to those over 45 or to women not eligible for direction to other work. Women nominated would wear a badge brooch, but no uniforms would be issued. Dr. Summerskill, on behalf of these women who are helping the Home Guard, asked Sir James to accept their thanks for this official recognition of the work they were doing. It was an appropriate birthday message to Hitler.'

21 April 1943, Wyndham Robinson, *Star*

DER SCHPLITS

According to the *Daily Herald*: 'Half the population of Germany was sent scurrying to shelter as Hitler's birthday celebrations were ending — the Royal Air Force and the Red Air Force were out in strength. By far the heaviest attack was on Stettin, largest Baltic port and a U-boat building centre. There Lancasters, Stirlings and Halifaxes dropped more than 130 four-thousand pound blockbusters, hundreds of other high-explosive bombs, tens of thousands of incendiaries all in 40 minutes. 300 miles to the east the Russians were heavily raiding Tilsit, while 80 miles to the west Stirlings were blitzing Rostock. 60 miles away from Stettin. and about 100 miles from Rostock, Mosquitoes were bombing Berlin.'

22 April 1943, George Whitelaw, *Daily Herald*

The Fiend That We Are Fighting

According to the *Daily Herald*: 'President Roosevelt announced that the Japanese had executed some of the United States airmen who bombed Tokyo last year. "This Government has vigorously condemned this act of barbarity," said a White House statement. "We have informed the Japanese that the American Government will hold all officers of the Japanese Government who participated in them personally responsible for these diabolical crimes, and will in due course bring them to justice." It was not disclosed how many men have been executed, but the United States War Department said eight members of the expedition were probably captured.'

23 April 1943, William Summers, *Buffalo Evening News* (New York, United States)

EASTER PROBLEM

During the British Army's evacuation from Dunkirk in 1940, French Generals had told their Prime Minister that "In three weeks England will have her neck wrung like a chicken." Eighteen months later, Churchill repeated the story to the Canadian Parliament adding: "Some chicken! Some neck!"

26 April 1943, J C Walker, *Western Mail*

THE WITCH DOKTOR

With the headline 'Falling For Goebbels,' the *News Chronicle* reported: 'It is serious news that Russia has broken off relations with Poland. The Polish Government certainly acted in the most reprehensible manner in calling for a Red Cross investigation into the German claim to have discovered at Smolensk — suddenly, after 18 months' occupation! — the "mass graves" of several thousand Polish officers "executed" by the Russians in 1940. This is falling for Nazi propaganda with a vengeance. It is exactly what Goebbels hoped for when he gave out his fantastic story: and the Polish Government and its Press seized upon it so readily as to suggest that they welcomed the chance to asperse the Soviet Union and to discredit her with her principal Allies.'

28 April 1943, Victor Weisz 'Vicky',
News Chronicle

A Poor Place For An Argument

In April, the German army had uncovered the mass graves of Polish army officers in the Katyn Forest. Despite British press reports to the contrary at the time, it turned out that the murders had actually been carried out by the NKVD on the orders of Stalin. Goebbels had deliberately embarked upon a cynical publicity campaign, albeit correctly blaming the Russians in order to create disunity amongst the Allies.

2 May 1943, Tom Carlisle, *Des Moines Register* (United States)

ALLIES THROUGH THE LOOKING-GLASS

After Admiral Darlan, commander-in-chief of all French Armed Forces, and High Commissioner of French North Africa, was assassinated in December the previous year, his US-nominated replacement, General Henri Giraud, began a period of uneasy coexistence with the British approved leader of the Free French forces, General Charles de Gaulle. Relations between Giraud and de Gaulle were strained. De Gaulle wanted neither to share any power with Giraud, nor to give any impression of collaborating with Vichy, with whom Giraud had dealt. Giraud and de Gaulle would later become co-presidents of the French Committee of National Liberation.

5 May 1943, David Ghilchik, *Daily Sketch*

According to the *News Chronicle*: 'For once, Dr. Goebbels subtle and intensive propaganda to disrupt the unity of Germany's enemies has scored a major success. Whatever may be the rights and wrongs of the present dispute, the overriding consideration must be that of securing Germany's total defeat in the shortest possible time. It would be unwise to underestimate the seriousness of the possible consequences of the Soviet-Polish rupture, and even more unwise to underrate the harm that German propaganda is capable of doing.'

6 May 1943, W. H. Woodburn 'Hengest', *Manchester Evening News*

GEE! — IT'S GRAND NEWS!

According to the *Yorkshire Post*: 'Mr. Stalin has cabled the following message to Mr. Churchill: "I congratulate you and the gallant British and American forces on, the brilliant victory which has led to the liberation of Bizerta and Tunis from Hitlerite tyranny. I wish you continued successes."'

10 May 1943, J C Walker, *Western Mail*

FASCIST SPECTATOR'S APPEAL

According to the *Birmingham Mail*: 'Franco said that the world war had reached a point where neither belligerent had the power to destroy its opponent. There might be more victories at the cost of great sacrifices, but sooner or later the deadlock would force the belligerents to listen to the voices calling for peace, like those of Spain and the Vatican, to which so far they had turned deaf ears. "Therefore," he said, "those of us who witness the struggle serenely, consider it senseless to delay peace."'

13 May 1943, J C Walker, *Western Mail*

"It shouldn't be long, old chap!"

According to the *Yorkshire Post*: 'The invasion of Europe now comes into the forefront. Allied plans were set on a time schedule of which Tunisia was a part. Our occupation of the naval base at Bizerta and our holding of the anchorage in the Gulf of Tunis have made crossing to Europe a practical proposition. The Axis no longer has a port or base on the African shore. The enemy's air strength in North Africa is confined to insignificant bases on Cape Bon peninsula, and these will not last long now.'

16 May 1943, Stephen Roth, *Sunday Pictorial*

IT WON'T BE LONG NOW

With the headline 'Mussolini Rumour,' the *Daily Mail* reported: 'Algiers radio says that the wildest rumours are current in Italy, one to the effect that the King had asked Mussolini for the resignation of his Cabinet, which was refused. It is also said that Marshal Badoglio and the former Ambassador to England, Grandi, were recalled by the King to participate in a Privy Council.'

17 May 1943, Will Mahony, *Daily Telegraph* (Sydney, Australia)

THE MAN WHO DIDN'T WANT TO HEAR IT

According to *Reuters*: 'Mr. Churchill's speech to the U.S. Congress has been hailed as one of the most masterly and important of his career. All over Moscow crowds gathered round windows, displaying the first brief Soviet Press report of Mr. Churchill's speech. The point which most struck the interested readers was Mr. Churchill's opinion that Hitler will attempt a third offensive on the Russian front. Another phrase particularly noted was: "We must do everything in our power that is sensible and practicable to take more of the weight off Russia in 1943."'

20 May 1943, George Middleton, *Birmingham Gazette*

'Where shall we go first?'

According to the *New York Times*: 'June promises to be fateful for a world at war, for it now appears inevitable that this month will see the beginning of the Allied invasion of the European continent. It will be, without doubt, the most ambitious and the most difficult military undertaking in history. Sweden's expectation of an invasion in June is reflected in today's newspaper headings, including: "Biggest naval operation in history imminent" — "Invasion fleet ready" — and "Air raids paralyse German industry."'

30 May 1943, Stephen Roth, *Sunday Pictorial*

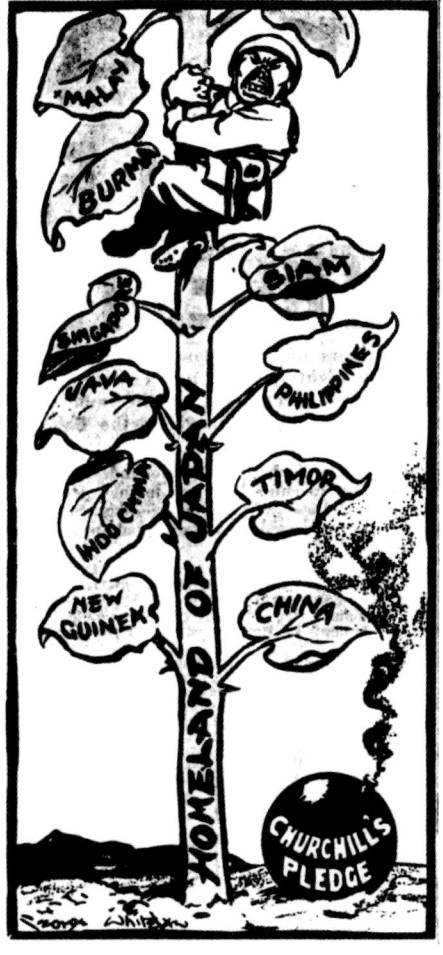

Jap and the Beanstalk

According to *Reuters*: 'Mr. Churchill's pledge that Britain will fight Japan until she has been beaten is regarded by Americans as particularly timely, because it dispels misapprehension from the recent hint of partial British demobilisation after the defeat of Hitler.'

21 May 1943, George Whitelaw, *Daily Herald*

CAUSE FOR ANXIETY

According to the *Portsmouth Evening News*: 'Big developments are expected to follow closely upon the conclusion of the talks between Mr. Churchill and President Roosevelt and the combined British and American staffs in Washington. According to well informed observers in Washington, the developments are likely to follow the following lines: 1. A Churchill-Roosevelt-Stalin meeting. 2. The opening of a Second Front very soon. 3. Intensified action against Japan.'

31 May 1943, David Ghilchik, *Daily Sketch*

The Tide Turns

NOT YOU, BENNY — SIT DOWN!

According to the *Daily Mirror*: 'The RAF have scattered the leaflets of a last warning over Italian cities. Rome is not outside the area of that destruction to which, as the leaflets proclaim, the Italian people are doomed. If Germany, with her strong ground defences, suffers immense damage, what about weakly defended Italy? The Italian people must judge and answer. How can they answer? How can they express themselves? "We know the people want peace. But wanting peace is not enough." The people must demonstrate. The people must "clamour" for peace. In fairness to the people of Italy it must be said that the means of demonstration are nowadays scanty under a regime of thugs.'

1 June 1943, W. H. Woodburn 'Hengest', *Manchester Evening News*

THAT'S NEWS

According to the *Leicester Evening Mail*: 'It was officially confirmed that the French naval squadron at Alexandria has come over to the Allies of its own free will. The squadron joined the Allies after negotiations with General Giraud. The allegation by Vichy that the squadron was starved into submission — that supplies of food were cut off — is quite untrue. The German News Agency had stated earlier that the French Government had announced that the French Fleet at Alexandria had yielded to Anglo-American pressure. "According to a telegram from British sources, the crews have announced that they are joining up," the report added.'

1 June 1943, Will Mahony, *Daily Telegraph* (Sydney, Australia)

"The first week of June . . . is the best ever." — Mr. Churchill

With the headline 'U-Boats Worst Pounding,' the *Aberdeen Press and Journal* reported: 'May, it can now be said, was the most disastrous month for U-boats in this war. Probably one U-boat out of every three which leave their bases to prey on Atlantic shipping is now being attacked damaged or sunk by Coastal Command. This is apart from the great numbers of U-boats which are located and hunted by the Royal Navy. New methods of attack and new weapons are being employed.'

9 June 1943, Victor Weisz 'Vicky', *News Chronicle*

Back To The Man Who Threw It

'The New Pepys' in *Truth* wrote a jingle on the German outcry for the abolition of Blitz bombing except on the battlefield, on grounds of its inhumanity:

    They blitzed us and gloated;
    We blitz them, they squeal,
    Sheer murder they vote it,
    The work of the de'il,
    Even old Nick makes merry,
    Laughs again and again,
    To hear his friend Jerry,
    Assume the humane!

11 June 1943, Ding Darling, *Des Moines Register* (United States)

ZERO!

With the headline 'Japanese Air Rout in Solomons,' the *Sydney Morning Herald* reported: 'In an air battle over Guadalcanal (Solomons), the Japanese lost 77 machines — 32 bombers and 45 fighters — out of a force of 120. Only six U.S. planes were lost. The raiders did only minor damage. An American military writer suggests that offensive operations — by the Allies — are pending in the South Pacific.'

19 June 1943, George Finey, *Daily Telegraph* (Sydney, Australia)

The Tide Turns

WHERE THE "HEADLINES" GOT TO

With the headline 'Allies Now Have Hitler Guessing,' the *Gloucestershire Echo* reported that: 'Elmer Davis, U.S. Director of War Information stated: "It looks as if the German commanders do not dare commit themselves to any serious action in Russia until they have seen where the British and Americans are going to strike in Western Europe — where and when and how hard."'

19 June 1943, George Middleton, *Birmingham Gazette*

ALLONS, ENFANTS DE LA PATRIE

According to the *Daily Mirror*: 'The United Nations have intervened in the dispute between Giraud and de Gaulle. The two generals met, but were unable to reach an agreement on military control and the part the Free French are to play in the war against the Axis. The Allied intervention is a final effort to bring all Free France under one flag. The rival generals have probably been told that with the large number of Allied troops in North Africa, command of the French Forces should be regarded as a military and not a political affair. When the generals had their first differences the French troops and civilians in North Africa regarded them as no more than a storm in a teacup. Now rumours and counter-rumours have spread to such an extent that there is a danger of two separate camps being formed to support the rival leaders.'

24 June 1943, Victor Weisz 'Vicky', *News Chronicle*

AERIAL RECONNAISSANCE SHOWS...

According to the *Daily Mail*: 'The R.A.F. are now operating a bombing shuttle service between this country and North Africa, bombing German and Italian targets on the run. Last night Lancaster bombers caused havoc at the Italian naval base of Spezia on their return run from North Africa, where they landed after bombing the Zeppelin and motor engine works at Friedrichshafen two nights before. Both attacks were made without loss.'

25 June 1943, George Whitelaw, *Daily Herald*

ANY TIME NOW

According to the *Aberdeen Press and Journal*: 'All the larger towns in Southern Italy have now been evacuated in preparation for an imminent Allied landing, reported German correspondents in Rome. According to the Rome correspondent of the *Rheinisch Westfälische Zeitung*, "the Italians are now braced for the Allied Second Front, which they believe is imminent. Italian propaganda is now entirely devoted to preparing the people for the second phase of the Allied offensive — the invasion of the islands and even the mainland."'

30 June 1943, Burt Thomas, *Detroit News* (United States)

HITLER GETS A FREEDOM, TOO

According to the *Scotsman*: 'Why doesn't the Führer visit the Ruhr? His continued absence is an intriguing phenomenon. We have reason to believe that Hitler believes that the unity and cohesion of Nazi Germany are almost entirely due to a mystical attachment to his person. We also know from Hitler's own statements that he is prepared to go where the danger is greatest, and to share the agonies and anxieties of his people. Well, even. German propaganda admits that the fiercest battles are now being fought over the Ruhr. Think what a few words from their Führer could do to the inhabitants of the Ruhr. At the magic of his voice their tears and worries would vanish, At the sight of his heroic person their spirit would surge within them. Hitler, why don't you go to the Ruhr?'

4 July 1943, Sidney Moon, *Sunday Dispatch*

WE COME TO BURY CAESAR

According to the *Evening News*: 'A moonlight invasion of Sicily was made by Allied soldiers early today, following a tremendous bombardment by air and naval forces on the "Pantellaria model" The drive is going "according to plan," say reports reaching Washington. Axis sources say that a landing was made on the south-east coast of this largest island of the Mediterranean while a Washington message gives the rocky western tip as the scene of fighting. Admitting the invasion, the Italian communique this afternoon reported that parachutists were being used.'

12 July 1943, Victor Weisz 'Vicky', *News Chronicle*

Going Down For The Third Time

On 16 July, Churchill and Roosevelt made a radio broadcast to the Italian people, calling on them not to die for Hitler and Mussolini but to "live for civilisation". On the same day, the Italian Fascist leaders opposed to Mussolini began to agitate for his removal.

24 July 1943, Tom Carlisle, *Des Moines Register* **(United States)**

". . . And what a game Mussolini is playing in defence! Cool, calculating . . . he's got Montgomery on the run."

According to the *Dundee Courier*: 'General Montgomery has declared himself very satisfied with the progress in Sicily. "Sicily is fed up with the Fascists and the Nazis," he said. "Now the Sicilian population is working for us, both on the railways and elsewhere, and is pleased to do so." The situation on the whole front is complicated by developments in Italy itself. Italian morale, already shaken by the speed of the Allied campaign, now has to face the further shock of Mussolini's dismissal.'

25 July 1943, Stephen Roth, *Sunday Pictorial*

DROPPING THE PILOT-1943 VARIANT

With the headline 'Marshal Badoglio Clears Out All Fascists,' the *News Chronicle* reported: 'Marshal Badoglio, new Premier of Italy, announced his Cabinet, 24 hours after he had ousted Mussolini. Only a few hours before he had decreed martial law throughout the country; imposed a dusk-to-dawn curfew and threatened to quell all demonstrations, if need be by force of arms, Marshal Badoglio's new Cabinet sweeps away all men who were intimately associated with the Fascist regime.'

27 July 1943, David Ghilchik, *Daily Sketch*

186 THE SECOND WORLD WAR IN CARTOONS

Italy's Pathway To Peace

According to the *Liverpool Daily Post*: 'Hitler's great concern today is to keep Italy in the war, as if she breaks away it involves the loss of Sardinia. The way would then be opened to the South of France via Corsica. Italy's fall would weaken the Balkan position by the loss of the Italian Army there. More than ever, must Hitler curse the Russians, who made it impossible for a German army group of adequate size to occupy the lynch-pin territory of the Mediterranean formed by the Italian peninsula.'

4 August 1943, Ding Darling,
***Des Moines Register* (United States)**

HOW DOES IT FEEL TO BE A REFUGEE?

With the headline 'Panic Stories From Berlin', the *Dundee Courier* reported: 'Berlin is in a state of panic and the authorities are at their wits' end to control a mass stampede from the city. Thousands of Hamburg refugees arriving without official permit and spreading stories of fantastic casualties in the raids, have been arrested in an effort to control the situation. R.A.F. planes have dropped leaflets on Berlin, warning the citizens they must await the same fate as Hamburg. Panic broke out and the population rushed to the stations or streamed out of the city on bicycles or on foot.'

4 August 1943, Victor Weisz 'Vicky', *News Chronicle*

The Tide Turns 187

"SMOKE GETS IN HIS EYES"

According to the *Portsmouth Evening News*: 'Lord Halifax, British Ambassador at Washington, has travelled more than 50,000 miles and visited more than half the States in the Union. "The production of all vital munitions is enormous, and no reflection comes more sharply to my mind when I visit American war industries and shipyards than a wish that the German and Japanese Dictators could share my experience and see what is coming to them," he said in an interview in London today.'

6 August 1943, Sam Wells, *Herald* (Melbourne, Australia)

HARE HITLER

According to the *Liverpool Echo*: 'Marshal Stalin's victorious armies, smashing forward in the twin drive which has already gained Orel and Byelgorod (also spelled Belgorod), have today the initiative along a 250-mile front. They are menacing the German lifeline linking Ukraine with Central Russia, the Bryansk-Kharkov railway.'

10 August 1943, George Frederick Shilling, *Daily Herald*

Point of Interest

Churchill flew to Quebec to meet Roosevelt and Canadian Prime Minister Mackenzie King for a high-level military conference. They agreed to increase the bombing offensive against Germany and continue the build-up of American forces in Britain prior to an invasion of Northern France.

12 August 1943, William Summers, *Buffalo Evening News* (New York, United States)

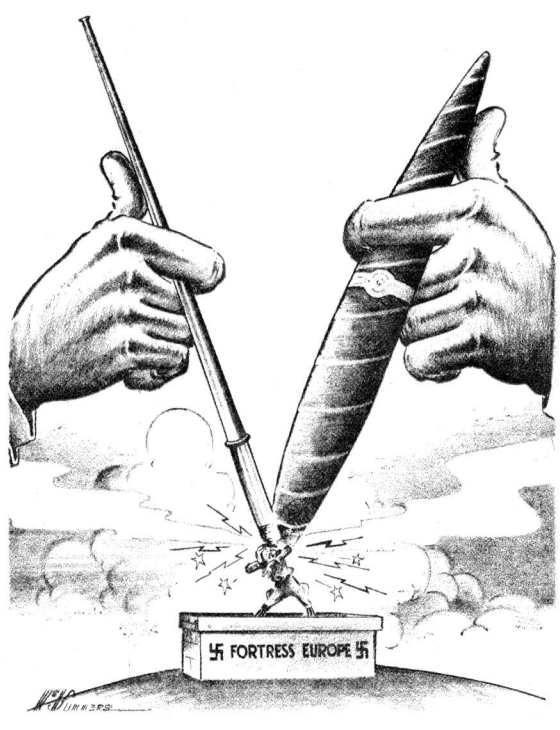

MUSIC WHILE THEY WORK

According to the *Halifax Daily Courier*: 'In addition to the Soviet two-fold offensive on the central front, which, according to Reuter from Stockholm is not only developing towards Bryansk but is breaking through the German hedgehog defences protecting the south-eastern gateway of Smolensk, the great attack on Kharkov is making more progress, with fierce street battles taking place in the suburbs, and the Germans themselves report yet another Red Army onslaught, south of Lake Ladoga, in the sector east of Leningrad.'

13 August 1943, George Middleton, *Birmingham Gazette*

'Boo-hoo! They have all the outings now.'

At the Quebec conference, the Allied leaders reiterated their intention to prioritise a cross-Channel landing in May 1944 and from there 'strike at the heart of Germany and destroy her military forces'. They also agreed the details of the invasion of Italy, which would not go much further north than Rome to conserve supplies for the invasion of France.

15 August 1943, Stephen Roth, *Sunday Pictorial*

"WHAT, AT THIS MOMENT, COMRADES?"

According to the *Yorkshire Evening Post*: 'An official of the Transport General Workers' union said that the dockers strike at Liverpool "is entirely unofficial and our officers at Liverpool are advising men to return to work immediately. We have received an undertaking from the divisional port director that the men's complaints will be investigated, and they have been told this investigation will start immediately work is resumed." The strike is a protest against the suspension of 35 dockers for refusing to work overtime.'

18 August 1943, Victor Weisz 'Vicky', *News Chronicle*

The Tide Turns

HITLER'S BACK-ROOM BOYS

According to the *Skegness News*: 'There are now over twelve million foreign workers in Germany. A few may have gone there willingly, lured by the prospect of higher wages or better food than they could get at home, but for the main part this is a vast slave population, recruited by force. In short, into the fortress of Germany a Trojan horse has been introduced. In order to allow the German workers to become soldiers to march out and invade other countries, and yet to keep the wheels of industry moving at home, Hitler was forced to conscript this slave army. It remains in his midst, an unorganised incoherent mass, yet an alien growth and a potential danger.'

23 August 1943, David Ghilchik, *Daily Sketch*

Unity Against Nazi Gangsters

According to the *Belfast Newsletter*: 'Mr. Churchill declared at the conclusion of the great Allied War Conference in Quebec, that Britain and America are now in a position to bring the whole of their weight to bear against the Axis. To a Press conference assembled to hear a joint statement from himself and President Roosevelt, the Prime Minister said that he looked forward to great steps being taken to beat down the enemies of the United Nations one after the other.'

27 August 1943, Burt Thomas, *Detroit News* **(United States)**

'All Pull Together, Boys — NOW'

According to the *Belfast Newsletter*: 'Mr. Churchill declared at the conclusion of the great Allied War Conference in Quebec, that Britain and America are now in a position to bring the whole of their weight to bear against the Axis. After referring to the superiority which Allied arms had obtained in equipment and munitions, and the growing successes against the submarine menace in the Atlantic, he predicted that Britain and the U.S. would be able to bring their whole weight to bear on the foe-blows to accompany what he termed "the superb operations of our Ally, Russia."'

29 August 1943, Stephen Roth, *Sunday Pictorial*

Heil Himmler!

According to the *Belfast Newsletter*: 'Germany is now completely in the grip of the Gestapo. Sweeping changes were made known in Berlin yesterday under which Heinrich Himmler, chief of the Gestapo and the Nazi Black Guard, takes over the vital Ministry of the Interior.'

29 August 1943, Will Hope, *Sunday Chronicle*

WHAT'S ROTTEN IN DENMARK

On 29 August, after a wave of strikes and sabotage actions across most of Denmark forced its government to cease functioning. This marked the official end of the policy of collaboration with the German occupation forces that had been in force since 9 April 1940. The Germans declared Denmark "enemy territory" and martial law was imposed. As a consequence, German security police tactics became more brutal and widespread.

2 September 1943, Anne Mergen, *Dayton Daily News* (Ohio, United States)

"WE THANK OUR LEADER" (Now and as it was in Berlin four years ago)

According to the *Evening Chronicle*: 'One thousand tons of high explosives and incendiary bombs were dropped on Berlin last night in a highly concentrated attack lasting 20 minutes. A strong force of Lancasters carried out the attack. "The attack was more concentrated than the last raid on the city," said one airman. Parts of the target area appeared like an inferno as "cookies" — 4,000 pounders and incendiaries crashed down in tons by the hundred.'

3 September 1943, Victor Weisz 'Vicky', News Chronicle

"Sorry, old man, but they've got all the grub across the road."

According to the *Civil and Military Gazette*: 'Marshal Badoglio informed the British Government in the middle of August that he was prepared to join the Allies as soon as they landed in Italy. It was this spontaneous declaration by Marshal Badoglio which led to the conclusion of the Armistice.'

12 September 1943, Stephen Roth, Sunday Pictorial

"I want some more bars on my window!"

On 12 September, a German commando raid liberated Benito Mussolini from the hotel in the Italian mountains where he was being held captive. Mussolini was not exactly overjoyed at his 'rescue' as he had grown world weary, having been deeply affected by the betrayal of his party colleagues in July.

14 September 1943, Victor Weisz 'Vicky', News Chronicle

Mein Dummy

According to the *Birmingham Post*: 'The absorption into the "Greater Reich" of the three Italian provinces of Bolzano, Trento and Belluno, in the Southern Tyrol, whose puppet prefects will be compelled to pledge loyalty to Hitler and not to Mussolini, was reported in a Berne despatch to Stockholm.

17 September 1943, William Summers, *Buffalo Evening News* **(New York, United States)**

"Protector" of the Vatican

According to the *Sunday Sun*: 'With unparalleled impudence, his voice emerging from the silence of months, Adolf Hitler, renegade from his Christian loyalty, has declared his soldiery as the protectors of the Vatican. Simultaneously, German guns and bombs were turned against Rome, so recently declared by Italy, and loudly echoed in Berlin broadcasts, as an "open city." Rome has not been sacked since the Huns stormed through its ancient streets putting the population to the sword and pillaging the palaces. It has been left to Adolf Hitler and his Nazi soldiers to consummate this grisly nightmare and to do by stealth, after a peaceful penetration of the country, what their barbarous forebears accomplished at least as a feat of arms.'

19 September 1943, Bill Falconer 'Con', *Sunday Chronicle*

CHILDREN OF THE EMPIRE

With the headline 'Bengal Famine "Man-Made",' the *Daily Herald* reported: 'Bitter comment on the Bengal famine was made by the British-owned "Statesman" of Calcutta. "The present sickening catastrophe is man-made," it declares. "The most outstanding factor has been the lack of foresight and planning capacity by India's own civil governments, central and provincial. The famine constitutes the worst and most reprehensible administrative breakdown since the political disorders of 1930 and 1931." The newspaper suggested a truce in local politics, a broader-based Ministry and far stiffer powers for the Central Government in dealing with food problems.'

21 September 1943, Victor Weisz 'Vicky', *News Chronicle*

The Tide Turns

HIS MASTER'S VOICE

According to the *Halifax Daily Courier*: 'Detailed plans for the mass invasion of Europe from the west," referred to by Mr. Churchill yesterday, have already been submitted to Marshal Stalin and have received his full approval, states Robert Vivian, Reuter's special correspondent in Washington. The statement that operations in the Mediterranean are only the essential preliminaries to this main attack on Germany from the west is by far the most important of the points Mr. Churchill made according to the *New York Times*.'

22 September 1943, George Frederick Shilling, *Daily Herald*

ALL GOD'S CHILLUN. It was stated in the House of Commons yesterday that a girl had been rejected for service with the Women's Land Army because she was coloured.

According to the *Newcastle Journal*: 'Miss Amelia King (26), coloured London girl, whose rejection for service in the Women's Land Army was questioned in the House of Commons yesterday, told a *Newcastle Journal* representative that the colour question was raised when she went for an interview at a Women's Land Army office. An official said it would be the farmers who would object, and then the billeting people. "I said I did not think it was fair. I had a brother in the Navy and my father was at sea, and I thought we were fighting for freedom," went on Miss King. The official replied "I have had trouble with other girls coming like you, and I suppose if I went to your country the position would be the same."'

24 September 1943, Victor Weisz 'Vicky', *News Chronicle*

'THAT'S JOE'S DEPT. — <u>YOU</u> WATCH OUT FOR THE SMILERS'

With the headline 'Defeatism', the *Belfast Newsletter* reported: 'Another spokesman at the meeting was Himmler, the Gestapo Chief and Minister of the Interior, who declared that "defeatism is non-existent in Germany." but none the less deemed it necessary to echo Goebbels's recent "off with their heads" threat to "traitors." Hitler said: "In this world-historic struggle not only the power of arms but also the will. power and perseverance of those who bear them are of decisive importance for victory. "Whatever the war situation may be, the determination and the unswerving perseverance in the pursuit of our aims must always remain the same."'

29 September 1943, W. H. Woodburn 'Hengest', *Manchester Evening News*

"It is expected that it will be a month before rationing in Calcutta is working." — Mr. Amery, in the House of Commons, 23 September 1943

According to the *News Chronicle*: '"I cannot shake off the haunting memory of skeletons of men and women feeding on jungle leaves and roots, and women in rags hunting for morsels of bread," said Balchandra Sharma, secretary of the Marwari Relief Society after a visit to Midnapore. He appealed to every country to aid the starving people. "The Calcutta Press severely criticises Mr. Amery's statement in Parliament. A columnist in the Hindustan Standard writes that the death toll is mounting and that Mr. Amery's invisible help is matched only by the invisible stocks of rice in Bengal."'

4 October September 1943, Victor Weisz 'Vicky', *News Chronicle*

The Tide Turns

A FOOL AND HIS ARMIES

According to the *Evening Telegraph*: 'Russian forces are streaming along the railways and roads heading from Smolensk, beating off counter-attacks, striking at the Germans on the flanks, and inflicting heavy losses. Across a 400-mile stretch of the Dnieper thousands of guns are snarling in a cross-river duel. Day and night bombers of the Red Air Force are showering terrific bomb loads on the enemy's western bank defences and are systematically bombing the immediate rear of Kiev, Cherkassy, and Dnepro-petrovsk.' The Squander Bug was created by the British National Savings Committee to discourage wasteful spending.

6 October 1943, George Whitelaw, *Daily Herald*

Phone Service Open To Moscow

In October, senior diplomats from the US, Britain and the Soviet Union gathered for talks at the Kremlin. They discussed co-operation in the war effort and agreed to create a new world organisation. The participants then issued the Moscow Declarations, which set out how their goals were to be achieved. Later in November, the leaders of the 'Big Three' countries — Roosevelt, Churchill and Stalin — met for the first time, at a conference held at the Soviet embassy in Tehran. The three leaders also spoke about the post-war world order, including the need for a United Nations organisation and the division of Germany into smaller states.

7 October 1943, Reg Manning, *Evening Outlook* (Santa Monica, United States)

Remember When They Had Us Believing The Versailles Treaty Was Too Rough On Germany?

With the headline 'Mass Murder In Italian Town,' a *Reuters* correspondent reported, 'from Cajazzo, Italy, that before the Germans were thrown out of the town they shot 25 men, women and children. In a barn near the town were the bodies of children aged 3, 7, 10 and 11, and their mother and father. The parish priest described how the Germans worked themselves into a fury of brutality as they saw their military position worsening. "The brutality, arrogance, and licentiousness of the officers and N.C.O.s gave a lead to the German soldiers," he said. One citizen said that he saw his sister shot dead by a German because she refused to go out with him. American soldiers who saw the mangled corpses have been restrained with difficulty by their officers from allowing the Italians to take revenge on Germans captured with Italian aid.'

21 October 1943, Ding Darling, *Des Moines Register* (United States)

THE RUSSIAN "ROLLER" — Or the lengthening bill

According to *Truth*: 'The powerful offensive which Stalin is conducting is steadily shattering the power of the Wehrmacht. The German armies in Russia have not yet collapsed, but they are being bled white. So terribly weakened are those armies that their power of resistance is weakening visibly. The Russian rate of progress, considering the powerful and desperate resistance with which the Huns have opposed them, has been rapid.'

28 October 1943, George Middleton, *Birmingham Gazette*

"I'D PREFER SOMETHING FUTURISTIC"

According to the *Daily Mail*: 'Mr. Churchill, moving a resolution in the Commons for the setting up of a Select Committee to consider and report upon plans for the rebuilding of the House of Commons, said: "We shape our buildings and afterwards the buildings shape us (laughter). Having dwelt and served for more than 40 years in the old chamber, and having derived very great pleasure therefrom, I naturally would like to see it restored in all essentials, and in all the old form. H.M. Government are most anxious and are resolved to ask the House to adhere most strongly to the structure of the House of Commons as we have known it."'

30 October 1943, W. H. Woodburn 'Hengest', *Manchester Evening News*

WASHED UP

According to the *Western Daily Press*: 'Striking proof of Mr Churchill's assurance at the Mansion House that we have broken the back of the U-boat war was given in the monthly statement of U-boat losses issued in Washington and London. It stated that we have been able to cope successfully with new tactics and weapons and that "the battle continues in full vigour." Approximately 60 U-boats were destroyed in August, September and October, which exceeds the total number of Allied merchant ships lost by U-boat action. More than 150 U-boats have been destroyed during the past six months out of the total of between 700 and 800 since the beginning of the war.'

11 November 1943, George Whitelaw, *Daily Herald*

HESS (reading the news): "I'm not feeling so good myself-perhaps I'll be next."

According to the *Daily Mail*: 'Sir Oswald and Lady Mosley were released from Holloway Prison, soon after 7 o'clock this morning. Sir Oswald had been detained under Defence Regulation 18B since May 1940, and his wife since June of that year. After the announcement that they were to be released many protests were made by workers and other organisations. It was on Thursday that it was announced that Mr. Herbert Morrison, the Home Secretary and Minister of Home Security, had decided on medical grounds to suspend the order of detention.'

21 November 1943, Stephen Roth, *Sunday Pictorial*

DOKTOR JEKYLL AND MR. HYDE

According to the *Belfast Telegraph*: 'Germany believed in bombing. She believed in the bombing of Warsaw, in the bombing of the defenceless Rotterdam, in the bombing of Belgrade, and Coventry, London and Belfast. She does not believe in the bombing of Berlin. Attempting to explain away the strangely illogical attitude which can view the bombing of Rotterdam as military expediency and the bombing of Berlin as calculated terror, the Nazi propaganda machine alleges that bombing was "forced upon" Germany's long suffering and infinitely patient High Command.'

30 November 1943, George Middleton, *Birmingham Gazette*

"My object all sublime I shall achieve in time — To make the punishment fit the crime — the punishment fit the crime:"

According to the *News Chronicle*: 'The meeting between President Roosevelt, Mr. Churchill and Generalissimo Chiang Kai-shek will rank in retrospect as one of the outstanding events of the Second World War. Its strategic implications are significant: Its political implications of greater significance still. In effect, this meeting has, at long last, pronounced sentence upon Japan for the misdeeds of half a century. The upstart nation which has for so long played havoc with the peace of Asia, in furtherance of its own selfish interests, is to be stripped to the bone of its ill-gotten gains and must make a fresh start within the framework of a new world order.'

2 December 1943, Victor Weisz 'Vicky', *News Chronicle*

"Don't listen do them, they're leading you into the abyss!"

With the headline 'Goebbels Is Worried Over The Talks,' the *News Chronicle* reported: 'Berlin radio, stating that "the conference between Stalin, Churchill and Roosevelt was concluded in the Soviet-occupied area of Persia," claimed that "the communique to be issued after the meeting will contain an appeal to the German people asking them to overthrow the Nazi Government and surrender unconditionally to the Allies." Whether or not these German statements prove to be true, it is very evident that the German propagandists fear deeply the psychological impact on the German people. The enormous volume of comment and speculation on the meetings on the German radio and in the German Press, all of which is directed towards attempting to minimise in advance the effect of any declaration which may be made by the Allied leaders, is clear proof of this fear.'

6 December 1943, Victor Weisz 'Vicky', *News Chronicle*

THIS UMBRELLA OPENS

According to the *News Chronicle*: 'Moscow radio announced that a treaty "of amity, mutual aid and collaboration after the war" between Soviet Russia and Czechoslovakia was signed in the Kremlin yesterday. Stalin and President Kalinin were present at the signing. President Benes after the ceremony, said the treaty represented a return to the policy which the two countries were carrying out before the war. "It emphasises what all the great Allied Powers have emphasised so often been before, namely that the German Drang nach Osten — Drive to the East — must be brought to an end and the present gangster policy of Germany never repeated again," he declared.'

14 December 1943, Victor Weisz 'Vicky', *News Chronicle*

Sacked Nazi Generals: How about sacking the corporal?

According to the *Nottingham Journal*: 'Hitler, who told the Germans in his New Year message that there would be no more retreating than "absolutely necessary," has sent General Jodl, Chief of German Supreme Command, to Manstein's H.Q. with power to sack any general who retreats without Supreme Command orders. With Jodl, said Moscow radio giving this news last night, is General Zeitler, Chief of Staff. Both have been given extensive powers, including that to prosecute generals who move in the wrong direction.'

2 January 1944, Alexander Saroukhan, *Akher Sa'a* **(Cairo, Egypt)**

The Tide Turns 199

A NEW ONE ON 'EM

According to the *Scotsman*: 'A jet-propelled fighter aircraft which flies propeller-less at extreme speed at great altitudes will shortly be in production for the British and American Air Forces. This revolutionary development in the air war was announced in 'a joint statement by the R.A.F. and U.S. Army Air Force. Hundreds of highly successful flights have already been made, both in Britain and in the United States. There has not been a single mishap. The greatest credit should be given to Captain Whittle for this fine performance, for it was his genius and energy that made this possible.'

7 January 1944, Talbot Ellison, *Birmingham Mail*

According to the *Scotsman*: 'The capture of over 80 places, including large towns and railway stations, in the steady advance by Soviet troops from Zhitomir and Berdichev to the Odessa-Lvov railway, was announced in last night's official communiqué from Moscow. The first official news was also given of the Red Army's advance across the Polish border by the announcement of the capture of Rokitno, a small town west of the line on the Korosten-Sarny railway.'

9 January 1944, Sidney Moon, *Sunday Dispatch*

COLLECTING DIVIDENDS — AND HOW!

Reporting to Congress on Lend-Lease aid to the Allies, President Roosevelt replied to critics by emphasising that it was saving American lives and shortening the war: "Neither Lend-Lease statistics nor dollar figures of any kind can measure relative contributions toward winning the war. Each of the United Nations is giving what it can, in fighting manpower and war production. The real measure of the aid we and the other United Nations have received from the Soviet people is to be found at Stalingrad, Kharkov and Kiev, and in the millions of Nazi soldiers killed, wounded or captured on Russian soil, who will not be there to oppose our forces in Western Europe."

12 January 1944, Anne Mergen, *Dayton Daily News* (Ohio, United States)

According to *The People*: 'After a year of almost constant reverses on the Eastern Front, the Nazis are compelled, in their desperate anxiety to get the last ounce of effort out of the German Home Front, to resort to the one weapon they have ignored so long — the truth. The fact that Berlin newspapers now stress the gravity of the situation facing Manstein, and emphasise that the Russians are hoping to achieve decisive victory, indicates that the German propaganda machine is paving the way for more bad news — possibly withdrawal not only from the whole of Russia, but from the Baltic States and the Southern Balkans as well. Truth today may be Goebbels' best line. By fostering deliberately in the hearts of the German people fear of Russian victory he hopes to make war production capital out of their desperation. But the Doctor cannot hope to allay the feeling that the German nation in the past few weeks has been tricked by the Nazi propagandists.'

16 January 1944, George Frederick Shilling, *The People*

ANOTHER OF THOSE STRATEGIC WITHDRAWALS

With the headline 'Leningrad Completely Freed of Blockade,' the *Western Morning News* reported: 'Leningrad, the cradle of the Soviet régime, has now thrown off the last vestige of the German blockade which von Leeb first fastened on the city in the middle of August, 1941. The siege, lasting two years and five months, was the longest of modern times. Last night 324 of Leningrad's guns thundered forth in a 24-salvoed salute and all Russia rejoiced in the news given in an exultant Order of the Day addressed by Gen. Govorov, commander of the front, to his Red Army men and Baltic sailors and to the city's "brave and steady" people.'

28 January 1944, Anne Mergen, *Dayton Daily News* **(Ohio, United States)**

BROTHERS IN CRIME

According to the *Scotsman*: 'An indictment of the "unspeakable savagery" of the Japanese towards prisoners of war and interned civilians was made in the House of Commons by Mr Eden (Foreign Secretary.) Quoting evidence of torture, flogging, and bayoneting, he warned the Japanese Government that the record of their military authorities would not be forgotten. An official report on Japanese atrocities against American prisoners of war, based on sworn statements by escaped officers, was also published by the U.S. Army authorities in Washington.'

29 January 1944, Talbot Ellison, *Birmingham Mail*

As the P.M. sees it.

According to the *Scotsman*: 'Mr Churchill is accepted by the whole country as its war leader. There is no one who wishes to depose him, but at one by-election after another an attempt is made to undermine his authority as leader of the nation. The Prime Minister is not the most patient of men, but he has kept back the bitter words that must sometimes have risen to his lips when independent candidates claimed that they were his supporters. In his message to the Government candidate at Brighton he has cast away this studied restraint, and has openly denounced independents who claim to be standing "in full support of the Prime Minister and the Cabinet."'

4 February 1944, George Middleton, *Birmingham Gazette*

According to the *Daily Mirror*: 'American forces have landed on the Kurile Islands, Japanese home territory. Washington emphasised that this attack was part of the ever-increasing offensive against the Japs — not a propaganda measure. Yesterday a Tokyo newspaper forecast a landing on the Kurile Islands. "By such an attack the enemy is hoping to reach Japan quicker than by way of Rabaul and the Marshal Islands."'

13 February 1944, George Frederick Shilling, *The People*

MONK OF CASSINO

According to the *Courier and Advertiser*: 'News that the Allies have at last bombed and shelled the historic monastery of Monte Cassino will be received with approval and relief by the vast majority of the people in this country. It has long been known that the Germans had established observation posts and gun positions in the building on its commanding hill overlooking the town of Cassino. There Allied troops have for weeks been engaged in bitter fighting, street by street and house by house. That they should be exposed to needless danger and loss of life through allowing the enemy to turn the monastery into a fortress safe from attack was becoming intolerable.'

14 February 1944, Talbot Ellison, *Birmingham Mail*

"BARBARIANS!"

According to the *Courier and Advertiser*: 'Goebbels was already proclaiming the previous day that Allied shelling had been going on ceaselessly. The truth was that the shells were harmless messengers of warning to the monks and Italian refugees in the building — leaflets dropped in canisters telling them it could be spared no longer, and that they must leave at once. After four years in which the German Army has pillaged the art treasures of a continent and wantonly desecrated, burned, and destroyed cathedrals and palaces in a dozen countries, the use Nazi propaganda can make of Monte Cassino's destruction will be recognised for the sickening hypocrisy it is.'

18 February 1944, George Butterworth, *Daily Dispatch*

According to *Reuters*: 'Goebbels is now putting out the story that, on Mr. Churchill's orders, parts of London have been cordoned off so as to conceal the "devastation" caused by recent German raids. German-controlled Paris radio say: "Churchill has now personally issued the strictest instructions to the British censors to prevent the leakage abroad of any news of the effect of the German bombing of London."'

20 February 1944, George Frederick Shilling, *The People*

The Tide Turns

THE LOST LEGION

According to the *Evening Telegraph*: 'Stalin's armistice terms are reasonable enough to melt even distrust of the Finns into early acceptance. The six main points demand no more than the 1940 territorial settlement. But the terms do call for the internment of General Dietl's army in Lapland. At Finland's request, but not otherwise, the Red Army would enter Finland if the Finnish Army found itself unable alone to carry out the internment. This point crystallises the question that for months past has puzzled Allied diplomats and military experts alike — are the Finns not in fact helpless in the Nazi trap? If they defy Hitler and sign an armistice, will Finland not find herself where Italy was landed after Badoglio's capitulation — out of the war on paper but still a battlefield?'

3 March 1944, W. H. Woodburn 'Hengest', *Manchester Evening News*

INTERRUPTED

According to the *Herald Express*: 'Loss of production as a result of the widespread coal miners' strike in South Wales is now estimated at about 60,000 tons a day. Approximately 70,000 men out of a total of 100,000 in the coalfield are now idle. Individual miners' lodges rejected the advice of their executive to return to work. It is apparent that the strike will continue until Saturday, when a delegate conference will discuss developments over the removal of anomalies in the Porter Award, over which the dispute has arisen.'

10 March 1944, William Furnival, *Lancashire Daily Post*

"MURDERERS!"

According to the *Mearns Leader*: 'Pierre Pucheu, the former Minister of the Interior, was shot at dawn on Monday. He was a traitor to his country, her people and her freedoms. He is the first of many who will one day pay a similar price for their treasonable collaboration with the enemy of their country and for the part they have played in the cold-blooded mass murder of innocent "hostages." The pity is that the chief villain of the piece is meanwhile beyond the reach of the realists in Algiers; but if there is one thing more certain than another in this uncertain world, it is that the day will come when Pierre Laval will pay in full measure for his infamy, either by an assassin's bullet or at the hands of national justice.'

21 March 1944, Victor Weisz 'Vicky', *News Chronicle*

"THE GUTS OF THE GERMAN ARMY ARE BEING TORN OUT" — CHURCHILL

In a radio broadcast, Churchill paid a tribute to Stalin: "Our tasks are difficult and different, but the British and American peoples are filled with genuine admiration for the military triumphs of the Russian people. I have paid repeated tributes to their splendid deeds, and now I must tell you that the advance of their armies from Stalingrad to the Dniester River — a distance of 900 miles — accomplished in a single year, constitutes the greatest cause of Hitler's undoing. Since I spoke to you last, not only have the Hun invaders been driven from the land that they had ravaged but the guts of the German Army have been largely torn out by Russian valour and generalship."

28 March 1944, J C Walker, *Western Mail*

The Way It Must Look To Stalin

Stalin had been demanding since 1941 that his Allies open a Second Front in German-occupied Western Europe. Vague promises were made in 1942 by Roosevelt, and repeated in 1943. Churchill had been far from enthusiastic and tried to persuade Stalin that the RAF bombing campaign against Germany virtually amounted to a Second Front by diverting German military resources to the defence of the Reich. He hoped that Stalin would also see the invasion of Sicily and Italy in summer of 1943 as, in effect, another front. Stalin remained unimpressed.

29 March 1944, Ding Darling, *Des Moines Register* (United States)

The Tide Turns   205

According to the *Edinburgh Evening News*: 'Russian forces are in sight of the northern Rumanian frontier, have the great Polish oil centre of Stanislavov within gun range, and are rapidly approaching the Tartar Pass through the Carpathians to Hungary. Pressing on in all sectors with terrific weight and power, the Russians are liberating towns and villages at an astonishing rate. "It is a general soviet flood to the west and south," says one frontline dispatch, to Moscow. "The German strongpoints are being overwhelmed."'

2 April 1944, George Frederick Shilling, *The People*

CURLING THE MO

According to the *Edinburgh Evening News*: 'The Red Army was reported to have got considerable number of tanks across the River Pruth, to have gone miles into Rumania, and to have got a firm hold on the highway leading to Jassy, formerly von Manstein's headquarters. Earlier messages stated that Marshall Konev's men were within six miles of Jassy. Marshal Zhukov, in a new offensive deep inside pre-war Poland, threatens completely to cut off Brody and outflank Lvov. General Malinovsky's third Ukrainian army is moving on Odessa in the face of stiffening resistance.'

4 April 1944, Will Mahony, *Daily Telegraph* (Sydney, Australia)

HOME STUDY

According to the *Dundee Courier*: 'It happens the Führer's birthday coincides with a fever of German speculation and suspense over the impending invasion of Western Europe. Nazi spokesmen who only a few months ago derided the idea that British or American armies could ever set foot on the Continent are now at pains to explain the probability that the Allied invaders will succeed in establishing bridgeheads at several points. It is evident that "second front nerves" are now an anxious preoccupation of the Nazi authorities. We must reckon on that spirit of the wounded beast at bay. But the dread of defeat is already there, corroding German nerves.'

21 April 1944, George Whitelaw, *Daily Herald*

With the headline 'Goering Air Plan Wrecked,' the *Daily Herald* reported: 'With hundreds of Allied medium and light bombers were streaming across the Channel yesterday to smash targets in Northern France, nearly 700 Flying Fortresses and Liberators flew from Italy to pound aircraft factories in Austria. The Luftwaffe is losing more fighter planes than German aircraft factories can replace. Its fighter reserves are a mere trickle. Its frontline strength is weary while its serviceability sags.'

30 April 1944, George Frederick Shilling, *The People*

"YOU SURE YOU FASTENED ALL THE WINDOWS?!?"

With the headline 'Hitler Places His Three Anti-Invasion Generals,' the *Daily Herald* reported: 'The German High Command has completed Its anti-invasion plan. The generals have been chosen. The troops have been sent to their stations, and have got their last orders. Now only one thing is awaited — D-DAY. And here are the men who will command these armies, and the roles they have been given: Occupation Troops which have been under the command of Field Marshall Gerd von Rundstedt for over a year have been distributed all over Western Europe.'

8 May 1944, W. H. Woodburn 'Hengest', *Manchester Evening News*

'On Hearing The First Cuckoo In Spring'

According to the *Daily Herald*: 'The pre-invasion bombing plan of the Anglo-American air forces aims at dislocating completely the railway traffic in the Northern France zone, especially around Paris and towards the Channel and Atlantic coasts. It is made somewhat easier by the fact that the French railway system is highly centralised. Nearly all main lines lead to Paris, where they end in a few large stations and marshalling yards after a series of essential bottlenecks. The RAF and the USAAF have been dealing mainly in the past fortnight with the bottlenecks. Now they are tackling the Paris marshalling yards.'

15 May 1944, Will Mahony, *Daily Telegraph* (Sydney, Australia)

DANCE, LITTLE FUEHRER!

According to the *Daily Herald*: 'From distant parts of the earth these men have gathered to stake their lives against Hitler's claim to rule the earth. Most of them have experienced the rigours and griefs of the winter campaign in Italy. Particularly the French, with their Colonial troops sharing the burden, have shown by impressive advances that the resistance of their country to Nazism is still potent; that their internal dissensions do not sterilise their hatred of the main enemy.'

17 May 1944, George Whitelaw, *Daily Herald*

ALEXANDER: And you'll lose the next Cassino gamble, too!

According to the *Daily Herald*: 'General Alexander's new drive in Italy goes well. Our men have made important penetrations into the deep defences of the Gustav Line. Fresh troops move into the widening bridgehead. Some of the best regiments of Hitler's army have been battered and thrust aside. For once Allied utterances about a new push have been commendably cautious. Frankly assessing the task still before our armies, they enable the public to feel sober satisfaction at the good beginning.'

21 May 1944, Stephen Roth, *Sunday Pictorial*

General Dwight Eisenhower was named supreme commander for D-Day. By late May, over 2,876,000 Allied troops were amassed in southern England. The largest armada in history, made up of more than 4,000 American, British, and Canadian ships, lay in wait. More than 1,200 planes stood ready to deliver airborne troops behind enemy lines, to silence German ground resistance. Against a tense backdrop of uncertain weather forecasts, and related timing dilemmas based on the need for optimal tidal conditions, Eisenhower originally decided that Operation Overlord should take place on 5 June.

27 May 1944, Cyril Price 'Kim', *Daily Sketch*

"Sunny. Cooler, owing to strong breeze."

According to the *Washington Post*: 'With highly diplomatic restraint, President Roosevelt in his comments, made it clear that he does not share Mr. Churchill's tender feeling for the Government in Spain. "He had no desire," he said, "to have an international incident made of his unkind words about Generalissimo Franco. These words, however, will serve a notice on Mr. Churchill that the United States does not propose to go along with him in buttering the Spanish dictatorship.'

1 June 1944, George Middleton, *Birmingham Gazette*

In advance of D-Day, the French Resistance assisted in the gathering of intelligence, as well as in the destruction of German logistical and communications capabilities such as railroads and telephone lines.

4 June 1944, George Frederick Shilling, *The People*

6
From the Normandy Beaches to Victory in Berlin

Crusaders

Before the Allies embarked for the invasion of Normandy each man was handed an Order of the Day from General Eisenhower. It read: 'You are about to embark upon the great crusade towards which we have striven these many months. The eyes of the world are upon you. The hopes and prayers of liberty-loving people everywhere march with you. In company with our brave Allies and brothers in arms on other fronts, you will bring about the destruction of the German war machine, the elimination of Nazi tyranny over the oppressed peoples of Europe, and security for ourselves in the free world.'

7 June 1944, Ian Gall, *Courier-Mail* (Brisbane, Australia)

BERNARD THE CONQUEROR — 1944

On 6 June, General Montgomery commanded the Allied forces on D-Day. Nearly 160,000 Allied troops landed along a 50-mile stretch of heavily-fortified beaches in Normandy. More than 5,000 ships and 13,000 aircraft supported the D-Day invasion, and by the day's end, the Allies had gained a foot-hold in Continental Europe.

7 June 1944, W. H. Woodburn 'Hengest', *Manchester Evening News*

DETENTION AT No. 10

While updating the Commons on 8 June on the Normandy landings, Churchill declined to reveal whether he intended to visit Allied troops in France. In fact, he had wanted to be present on the bridge of HMS Belfast on D-Day, much to the annoyance of Eisenhower. He was only dissuaded when King George VI said to him: "Well, as long as you feel that it is desirable to go along, I think it is my duty to go along with you!" It was not until six days after D-Day that Churchill visited Normandy, and four days later the King followed him. Churchill travelled on board HMS Kelvin and made sure that the ship fired on German positions while he was on the bridge.

9 June 1944, J C Walker, *Western Mail*

FILLING IN

According to the *Belfast Newsletter*: 'The Allied beachhead — if the term is still appropriate — in Normandy continues to expand and deepen. Capture of the town of Montebourg (only 16 miles from the big port of Cherbourg), after two days of hard fighting by American troops, constitutes the most important strategic achievement so far. And as progress has been made at other points, the enemy have cause to fear that the Allies, pushing across the peninsula, will soon have cut off the Cherbourg harbour area, and that their warships will aid in its reduction.'

9 June 1944, Will Mahony, *Daily Telegraph* (Sydney, Australia)

NORMAN CONQUEST IN REVERSE

According to the *Daily Herald*: 'Bayeux is in Allied hands. It is the first town to be captured since the landing. The fall of this vital communication centre, seven miles from the coast, and 18 miles from Caen, was announced from SHAEF today. Allied troops, it was also stated, have crossed at several points the Bayeux-Caen road. The capture of Bayeux and the cutting of the Caen road mean that the Cherbourg Peninsula has lost its most direct line of communication with the valley of the Seine and the French capital. Bayeux is the most important railway station between Caen and Cherbourg.'

9 June 1944, George Middleton, *Birmingham Gazette*

According to the *Daily Herald*: 'Half a million French patriots are reported to be attacking German military strong points in various parts of France. Their activities have assumed the proportions of a general rising all over the country, causing the Germans to use against them military units urgently needed elsewhere. They have been fighting pitched battles with German troops and the Vichy militia using arms dropped by parachute from Allied planes, say frontier reports reaching Madrid.'

11 June 1944, George Frederick Shilling, *The People*

According to the *Daily Express*: 'Three days after smashing the Finnish Karelian Line, General Govorov is reported to have struck again in the far north on the Petsamo front and also in Estonia. On the Karellan Isthmus the Russians are now only 35 miles from Villuri and 25 miles from the 1939 Mannerheim line. Tonight's Soviet communique says that the advance continues today and that several enemy strong-points were taken. Said Moscow radio: "The Finns are retreating so rapidly that they are abandoning the towns and countryside intact."'

14 June 1944, W. H. Woodburn 'Hengest', *Manchester Evening News*

From the Normandy Beaches to Victory in Berlin

Ach: If only I had Montgomery's army, too!

According to the *Liverpool Daily Post*: 'General Dwight Eisenhower, Supreme Allied Commander, in a statement to all Allied invasion forces, said: "Your accomplishments in the first seven days of this campaign have exceeded my brightest hopes." The statement was addressed to General Bernard Montgomery, Commander of Allied Assault Forces: Admiral, Sir Bertram Ramsay. Naval Commander; Air Chief Marshal Sir Trafford Leigh-Mallory, Air Chief Marshal Sir Arthur Harris; Lieutenant General Carl Spaatz, and soldiers, and all airmen of the Allied Expeditionary Forces.'

18 June 1944, Stephen Roth, *Sunday Pictorial*

"LARGE PORT, PLEASE"

According to the *Sunday Post*: 'German radio admitted last night the possibility of losing the Cherbourg Peninsula. The announcer said: The port of Cherbourg has now only a relative importance for the defence plans of the German command. Should the Allies reach the Atlantic in their drive westwards and thus cut off Cherbourg and the northern towns of the Cotentin Peninsula, German forces are now sufficiently numerous to seal it off and render the peninsula useless to them.'

19 June 1944, W. H. Woodburn 'Hengest', *Manchester Evening News*

NOW FOR ANOTHER GREAT DRIVE

With the headline 'Big Battle For Caen,' the *Scotsman* reported: 'General Montgomery's forces on the Calvados front were reported to be making good progress. Driving on more than two miles on a gradually broadening front from the now firmly held bridgehead over the River Odon, they were last night about two miles from the River Orne. Pressure is increasing on Caen, the pivot of the Germans' Normandy defence, and heavy battles are reported from north and north-east of the town. German Panzer reserves have been thrown in.'

29 June 1944, J C Walker, *Western Mail*

Hitler ordered General Dietrich von Choltitz, the military governor of Paris, to burn Paris to the ground before the Allies retook the city. Choltitz ignored Hitler's instructions and later asserted his affection for the French Capital. He also later claimed that he disobeyed the Fuehrer in the belief that he had gone insane.

2 July 1944, George Frederick Shilling, *The People*

WHAT'S ON THE RAILS?

According to the *Evening Chronicle*: 'If the German front cracks before the weight of Stalin's onslaught, it will inevitably crumble to ruins on every other front. The more greatly we menace the German Army in France and Italy, the less manpower and materials they have with which to hold up the Russian drive on the road to Berlin.'

3 July 1944, Will Mahony, *Daily Telegraph* (Sydney, Australia)

THE VOICE THAT NEEDS NO MIKE

With the headline 'Russia Changes Goebbels's Tune,' the *Belfast Post* reported: 'German propaganda about the success of the flying bomb has apparently been unexpectedly successful. The glowing and gloating stories of destruction in the south of England seem to have convinced the German people that "revenge weapon No. 1" is a war winner. To a people buoyed up with the belief that the War is as good as won the news from Russia must be a heart-stopping cold douche. With Minsk fallen and Polotsk carried by assault, Goebbels must change his flying-bomb tune. While he could hope to convince his credulous listeners that the War is being won in the West, he could not at the same time ignore the shadow in the East, where a great German army is being liquidated.'

5 July 1944, George Middleton, *Birmingham Gazette*

From the Normandy Beaches to Victory in Berlin 215

THE SUPER-SUPER "BOMBSITE"

According to the *Lincolnshire Echo*: 'Dealing with what he described as "the most absurd claims about the results of the first use of the secret weapon," Mr. Churchill said between 100 and 150 flying bombs are being discharged daily, and have been discharged over the last fortnight or so from France. Up to 6 a.m. today about 2,750 flying bombs have been discharged from the French coast. A very large proportion of these have, however, failed to cross the Channel or have been shot down and destroyed by various methods. The House would be favourably surprised to learn that the total number of flying bombs launched have killed almost exactly one person per bomb."'

12 July 1944, George Middleton, *Birmingham Gazette*

The New Evacuees

According to the *Liverpool Echo*: 'Russian forces yesterday made new progress on the road to East Prussia. North and south of Olita they expanded their bridgehead on the western bank of the Niemen and occupied over 20 towns and villages. This was the only mention of the East Prussian front in last night's Soviet communique. But agency messages from Moscow said advanced elements were believed to be already fighting on the frontier approaches! The Red Army therefore by now is likely to be fighting what is probably the last battle before Reich territory is reached.'

16 July 1944, Sidney Moon, *Sunday Dispatch*

With the headline '"An Extremely Good Day" Says Montgomery,' the *Civil & Military Gazette* reported: 'A big tank battle is raging today south-east of Caen where Rommel has thrown in armoured formations to meet the British and Canadian tanks which have broken through the German lines. Intense street fighting is going on in Faubourg de Vaucelles, where about half the suburb has been cleared of the Germans. The Germans have thrown in everything they can grab to try to heal the breach in their lines south of Caen.'

20 July 1944, Cyril Price 'Kim', *Daily Sketch*

On 20 July, an attempt was made to kill Adolf Hitler and implement Operation Valkyrie by German military leaders. The assassination attempt was carried out by Lieutenant Colonel von Stauffenberg at Hitler's Wolf's Lair field headquarters near Rastenburg, East Prussia. Stauffenberg placed a bomb housed in a briefcase under the conference room table. Hitler survived after the blast was deflected by the conference room table leg.

23 July 1944, George Frederick Shilling, *The People*

"Himmel! we're not plotting, we're planning the next war!"

According to the *Scotsman*: 'Hitler — For the third time an attempt on my life has been planned and carried out. A very small clique of ambitious, irresponsible, and at the same time senseless and criminally stupid officers have formed a plot to eliminate me, and the German Wehrmacht Command. Suddenly, at a moment when the German Army are engaged in a bitter struggle a small group emerged in Germany, as in Italy, in the belief that they could repeat the 1918 'stab in the back.' they have made a bad mistake.'

24 July 1944, Victor Weisz 'Vicky', *News Chronicle*

According to the *Civil & Military Gazette*: 'The German Radio broadcast on Wednesday a speech by Dr. Goebbels, the newly-appointed Reich Trustee for total mobilisation for war, in which he declared: "Providence had stretched out its hand to protect the Fuehrer and had enabled him to continue his work. Above a devilish plan, fate is at work. It gives a pointer that this work must, can, and will, be completed."'

30 July 1944, George Frederick Shilling, *The People*

From the Normandy Beaches to Victory in Berlin

THE LAST TIME I'LL SEE PARIS

With the headline 'Nearer To Paris,' the *Liverpool Echo* reported: 'Robert de Beauplan, Paris radio commentator, said: "The war is getting nearer to Paris. The Allies are sweeping forward towards the capital, and they may capture it. It cannot be denied that the fall of the city would be a tremendous event, but it would not mean that the war was over. Fighting would continue and every inch of ground would be bitterly contested. For the Allies, Paris presents mainly strategical advantages."'

8 August 1944, Victor Weisz 'Vicky', *News Chronicle*

HEIL HITLER

According to the *Derry Journal*: 'Berlin broadcast a new decree issued by Hitler, ordering the total mobilisation of Germany and Occupied Territories. Goebbels will be responsible for the mobilisation. "The war situation makes absolutely necessary the greatest use of all resources for the armed forces and armaments." says the decree, which designates Goering to adapt the whole public life to the requirements of total war in every respect. He will appoint a Reich plenipotentiary for total war, and Goebbels will see that everything is done to further total war and that no manpower is kept from the armed forces or the making of arms.'

2 August 1944, Anne Mergen, *Dayton Daily News* (Ohio, United States)

CHOKING FEELING

According to the *Birmingham Gazette*: 'Field-Marshal von Witzleben and seven other high German officers charged with conspiring to kill Hitler and surrender Germany to the Allies were sentenced to hang by the German "People's Court". The sentences were carried out two hours after the end of the trial. The generals had no chance to defend themselves. The trial was carried out in the typical purge manner, all of them fully admitting conspiring as long ago as June 1943, and their counsel stressing unanimously that "all the accused are fully aware what punishment to expect," and that "the examination of all charges has proved the correctness of the proceedings of the People's Court."'

10 August 1944, Will Mahony, *Daily Telegraph* (Sydney, Australia)

LIKE A "PIECE OF CAKE"

According to the *Daily Express*: 'Battlefront reports last night said that von Kluge's retreat by daylight has been blitzed nearly to a standstill. Only a trickle of German units is getting through the Falaise gap, and that trickle is under non-stop air attacks. The Canadians, launching a major new offensive southwards to Falaise, reached points three or four miles from the town They also drove to within three miles of the Falaise-Lisieux road — the last main escape route for the Germans — by an attack neat Sassy, north-east of Falaise. Official summing-up was: "The offensive has gone better than according to plan."'

15 August 1944, George Middleton, *Birmingham Gazette*

"AW, WHAT'S THE USE?"

According to the *Essex Herald*: 'The headline in *The Times* is, "Blow after blow rained on the German Army." It is like a glorious dream. The defeat of the German army means the defeat of Hitlerism. And there is no question but that it will bring the end of the war very much nearer. For enclosed in that bag at Falaise, having blow after blow rained on it, is the cream of the German armed forces, the bullies of Europe, the supermen, who once thought they were going to stamp on our necks. They have worshipped Hitler: let Hitler save them.'

17 August 1944, Will Mahony, *Daily Telegraph* **(Sydney, Australia)**

La Marseillaise!

According to the *Birmingham Gazette*: 'The people of Paris have reasserted the true spirit of the French nation in an uneven battle against the armed invader. The restoration of the capital of France will send a thrill of hope and expectation through the ranks of the underground movements in all the invaded countries and should strike a note of fear and alarm in the hearts of the German armies of occupation, no longer able to rely on the instruments of terror.'

24 August 1944, W. H. Woodburn 'Hengest', *Manchester Evening News*

STICKY ENDING?

According to the *Press and Journal*: 'For weeks Londoners and the people of the Southern English counties have been saying: "The only thing to stop the flying bomb is an attack on the Pas de Calais." They had, however, one reservation; "The main attack must not be diverted for our sakes." The news of the Allied drive towards the Pas de Calais has lifted their hearts high. Amongst the attacking forces are many men who know what flying bombs have done to their families and homes. They need no urging into battle. Those Nazis who, by the pressing of a button, released death and destruction on the London back streets and defenceless hospitals may well blench at the coming of the avengers.'

24 August 1944, George Middleton, *Birmingham Gazette*

In Joe's Pipe

According to the *Scotsman*: 'An Order of the Day from Marshal Stalin announced the capture of the Black Sea port of Constanta. The Germans had earlier admitted the cutting of the Ploesti-Constanta oil pipeline. The Order, which was addressed to Marshal Tolbukhin and Admiral Oktyabrsky, said: "Troops of the Third Ukrainian Front, as a result of a swift attack by tank and motorised forces in combination with ships and landing parties of the Black Sea Fleet, today captured the most important Black Sea port of Constanta, which had served for three years as the main naval base for the German invaders."'

25 August 1944, Reg Manning, *Arizona Republic* **(United States)**

PIN-UP BOY

According to the *Leicester Evening Mail*: 'Desperate hopes in Hitler's "V" weapons are keeping the German Army going — in the opinion of both Allied and Axis radio commentators. A US broadcaster from Normandy said: "The past week as witnessed some of the most brutal destruction that one army has inflicted on another. Why does Germany continue to hold out? I think the answer to that is the weapon of weapons which Hitler says he has got up his sleeve — V2. The German people must have a terrific faith in what V2 will do for them if they believe that it will swing the war from the present prospects of defeat to an uncompromising victory for Germany.'

30 August 1944, George Middleton, *Birmingham Gazette*

Present Owner Has No Further Use For Same

After General Patton had slapped and verbally abused two of his soldiers, he was passed over as commander of the First United States Army which was forming in England to prepare for D-Day. As a result, he was not directly involved in the initial beach landings, but played a crucial role in the deception strategy by commanding a 'phantom army' designed to mislead the Germans into believing the main attack would be at the Pas de Calais instead of Normandy. After D-Day, Patton finally took command of the Third U.S. Army and led a successful breakout from Normandy, spearheading the Allied advance across France.

31 August 1944, Dorman Smith,
***Grand Island Independent* (Nebraska, United States)**

PRESIDENT-ELECT OF THE SPEED CLUB

According to the *Scotsman*: 'General Patton's hard-driving armoured columns, after an advance of approximately 35 miles in the past 24 hours, are scourging bedraggled and fleeing German remnants in the vicinity of Reims. Now they are pushing on without slackening speed. The new advance to the Reims area brings the Third Army to a point less than 50 miles from the Belgian border. These miraculously self-contained tank columns of General Patten, which seem to run on for miles without waiting for supplies, are pouring across the Marne.'

31 August 1944, W. H. Woodburn 'Hengest', *Manchester Evening News*

WATCH OUT ON THE RHINE

According to the *Coventry Evening Telegraph*: 'Allied paratroopers and glider forces were still landing in Holland late last night, according to Berlin reports. Some of them came down in the area at the mouth of the Rhine. This extended the area in the south-eastern corner of Holland already named by the Germans — Nijmegen, last bridge crossing the Rhine, Eindhoven, communications centre ten miles north of the Belgian frontier, and Wilburg, on the main line to Flushing.'

19 September 1944, Will Mahony, *Daily Telegraph* **(Sydney, Australia**

According to the *Belfast Newsletter*: 'Conflict between the Polish emigre Government in London and the Soviet-supported Committee of National Liberation in Poland took a new turn with the latter's denunciation of General Bor as "the criminal responsible for the premature uprising in Warsaw." General Bor, actually General Komorowski, has just been nominated by the Polish President, Raczkiewicz, as successor to General Sosnkowski. "If General Bor comes into the hands of the Polish Committee of National Liberation he will be tried and punished." Mr. Morawski, president of the committee, stated at a Moscow Press Conference.'

4 October 1944, W. H. Woodburn 'Hengest', *Manchester Evening News*

JOINING THE IMMORTALS

In order to shorten the war, the Allies launched a daring airborne operation to secure the River Rhine crossings so they could advance into northern Germany. On the 17 September, 10,000 British paratroopers landed near the town of Arnhem. Their objective was to capture a vital road bridge deep behind German enemy lines and await relief. Instead, ten days later, the injured remnants of the division finally withdrew from the battle. The operation was a costly failure and of the 10,000 men who dropped into Arnhem, only 2,000 made it back.

9 October 1944, Anne Mergen, *Dayton Daily News* (Ohio, United States)

AXIS OF COLLABORATION

According to the *Northern Whig*: 'Marshal Stalin, speaking at the luncheon given by the Soviet Government in honour of Mr. Churchill and Mr. Eden in Moscow last night, paid a generous tribute to the British and US war effort. Emphasising the importance of post-war cooperation and collaboration, he said that when the War began the peace-loving States were caught unawares and they should profit by the lesson and be prepared for peace.'

11 October 1944, George Middleton, *Birmingham Gazette*

DROPPING THE PILOT

According to the *Belfast Newsletter*: 'The Germans have apparently seized Budapest in frantic, last-minute efforts to keep Hungary in line. After Horthy's order, the Hungarian Nazis — presumably aided by German S.S. divisions rushed to Budapest — took over the radio and called for the "elimination of the cowards and betrayers." Horthy was seized by the Gestapo and taken to Germany. The Gestapo then carried out mass arrests in Budapest. In a broadcast, the Hungarian Nazi Party, headed by Ferenc Szálasi, announced that it had taken control of the country and "taken matters in hand to eliminate traitors at all costs." According to Algiers radio, a Hungarian delegation has left for Moscow to discuss armistice conditions.'

17 October 1944, George Middleton, *Birmingham Gazette*

FRIENDLY-LIKE

On 9 October Churchill visited Moscow for talks with Stalin. He wanted to discuss the future of Poland, where the Warsaw uprising had just been crushed. He had told the Commons on 28 September that he thought there was a solution in which "Russia gets the security which she is entitled to have" and "the Polish nation have restored to them national sovereignty and independence." He also wanted to discuss the future of Greece and Yugoslavia, hoping to prevent them also falling under Soviet control. While in Moscow, Churchill drew up what he later called his 'naughty document' (but became known as the 'Percentages Agreement'). This was a proposal to divide Europe into Western and Russian spheres of influence.

18 October 1944, Norman Lindsay, *Sydney Bulletin* (Australia)

TIME MARCHES ON!

According to the *Daily Mail*: 'Hitler's proclamation is that of a desperate man trying to inspire his followers to desperate efforts. All this talk of fighting every ditch, field, and bush is mere bunkum, even though there may be some fanatics prepared to try. Scythes, swords, knives, and even small arms will not prevail long against modern armaments. When Mr Churchill made his famous speech in which he declared that we would fight on the beaches, on the hills, and in the streets, it was at a time when our munition factories were in the making, and we had expectations of assistance from the vast resources of America's industrial plants.'

22 October 1944, Stephen Roth, *Sunday Pictorial*

THE ONE THAT GOT AWAY

According to the *Sunday Post*: 'Admiral Nimitz, Commander-in-Chief of U.S. Pacific Fleet, said last night the Japanese had been routed completely in the Battle of the Philippine Sea, and that the time will come when the U.S. Fleet will seek out the Japanese Fleet wherever it may be and completely destroy it. The fighting men of our Navy, he said, have inflicted the greatest defeat our foes have yet suffered in this war.' Admiral Nimitz requested the original cartoon from the cartoonist.

31 October 1944, Stuart Peterson, *Sun* (Sydney, Australia)

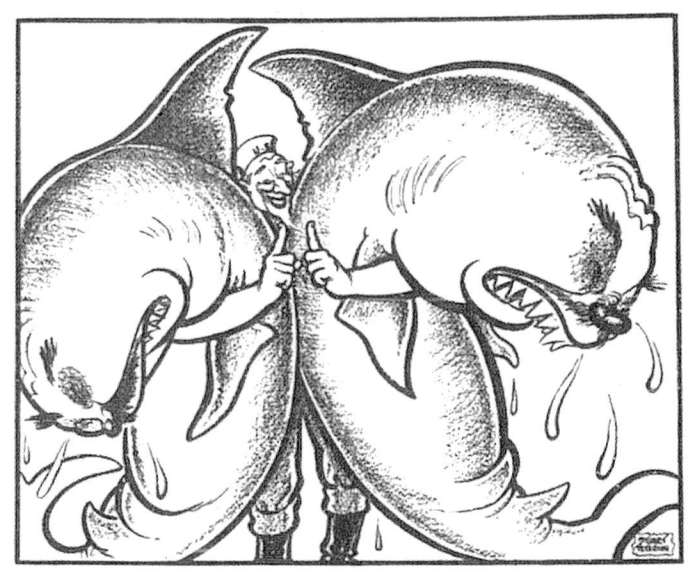

It would take more than that lot to make me laugh, Fritz

According to the *Herne Bay Press*: 'The German army is apparently poking fun at Himmler's Home Guard — the Volksturm. Lieutenant Heysing has assured them it is no laughing matter. We rather agree with him that it is rather rough on Himmler, after all the trouble he has taken to get together this bunch of human flotsam and jetsam, to eke out the dwindling national cannon fodder stock — now so sorely depleted — to have them described as "duds" and as only fit to shout "boo" at the enemy. Heysing, on Himmler's behalf, deprecates these drivellings and clownish jibes against a force which contains among its members, men who are stone deaf, the halt and the maimed, liberated convicts and goodness knows who else besides.'

5 November 1944, Stephen Roth, *Sunday Pictorial*

"I, TOO, AM AN ASIATIC" (famous utterance by J. Stalin)

According to the *Dundee Courier*: 'Marshal Stalin's blunt denunciation of Japan as an aggressor nation in his speech on the anniversary of the Russian Revolution marks a significant change in Soviet policy. Hitherto Moscow has studiously maintained the "correct" diplomatic attitude of strict neutrality towards Tokio. It can be taken as pretty certain that Marshal Stalin will at some stage take a hand in bringing Japan to final retribution. For he clearly must have an important voice in the ultimate break-up of Japan's domination on the mainland of Asia and the control to be imposed on her.'

8 November 1944, W. H. Woodburn 'Hengest', *Manchester Evening News*

IT'S THAT (WO) MAN AGAIN

With the headline 'Roosevelt's Sweeping Win,' the *Evening Post* reported: 'Franklin Delano Roosevelt is to be President of the United States for a fourth term. The re-election of President Roosevelt makes it virtually certain that he will hold an early meeting with Marshal Stalin and Mr. Churchill, says a dispatch from the Washington Bureau. Mr. Henry Wallace, the present vice-president, told Pressmen in Washington: "The election outcome is a signal for full steam ahead in the war effort."'

9 November 1944, George Middleton, *Birmingham Gazette*

THE ALSO RANS

According to the *Daily Mail*: 'Himmler has been formally appointed as Hitler's successor by order of Hitler himself, at a meeting of Party leaders at the Chancellery in Berlin two days ago, according to a neutral recently arrived from Germany. Hitler was not present, but sent Lammers, head of the Nazi party secretariat, to read the proclamation, stating: "I declare Heinrich Himmler my deputy and my successor." Those present Included Goebbels, Himmler, the head of the Nazi party executive Bormann, Admiral Doenitz, Field-Marshal Kietel and Kalten Brunner, who is Himmler's right-hand man.'

17 November 1944, Stuart Peterson, *Sun* (Sydney, Australia)

THE CRIME NO PUNISHMENT CAN FIT

The *News Chronicle* stated that overwhelming evidence had been accumulated of 'murder and bestial' tortures committed by Germans in occupied Europe: 'No retribution can be too harsh or harsh enough for the creatures who have perpetrated these infamies.'

2 December 1944, Anne Mergen, *Dayton Daily News* (Ohio, United States)

WHEN GREEK MEETS GREEK

Although Greece was liberated from German occupation, a civil war broke out between Greek Communists (ELAS), and nationalist forces (EDES). On 3 December, during a demonstration in Athens, involving more than 100,000 people, fighting broke out that led to the deaths of 28 people and 148 being injured. This signalled the beginning of the 'Dekemvriana' (the December events), a 37-day period of full-scale fighting in Athens between ELAS and EDES. The British tried to stay neutral, but when the battle escalated, they intervened to try to stop the rival combatants from causing further bloodshed.

10 December 1944, Stuart Peterson, *Sun* (Sydney, Australia)

'HIT HIM NOW, BROTHER, AND HE'S FINISHED!'

On 16 December with the onset of winter, the German army launched a massive counteroffensive that was intended to cut through the Allied line in a manner that would turn the tide of the war in Hitler's favour. The Germans attacked through the Ardennes Forest, as they had done so against the French in May 1940. They achieved initial success, pushing westwards through the middle of the American line and creating the 'bulge' that would give the battle its name.

21 December 1944, W. H. Woodburn 'Hengest', *Manchester Evening News*

From the Normandy Beaches to Victory in Berlin

THE DYING EMBERS

With the headline 'Rundstedt's Position Deteriorating,' the *Yorkshire Post* reported: 'German divisions within the Belgian salient are drifting into a bad position. Rundstedt's bulge is being compressed into a cramped area. This portends heavy losses, if not destruction for the enemy. A general German retreat may alone rectify a dangerous situation resulting from American pressure into the salient. Rundstedt has lost the first phase of the battle for the Meuse and appears to be falling back on the defensive German spearheads reached to within four miles of the Meuse.'

2 January 1945, Anne Mergen, *Dayton Daily News* (Ohio, United States)

ANOTHER RUNDSTEDT OFFENSIVE

According to the *Manchester Evening News*: 'Having driven more than three miles beyond Bastogne in his northerly attack on Rundstedt's salient, General Patten has turned east, and today the recapture of Remagen and Wardin (taken by the Germans on Saturday) was announced. All Rundstedt's attacks against the Bastogne corridor have been flung back with heavy losses, and the Third Army has also captured Heumont and Chenogne and is engaged in a stiff battle for Wiltz and Nothum about 12 miles south-east of Bastogne.'

3 January 1945, W. H. Woodburn 'Hengest', *Manchester Evening News*

CLOSED

According to the *Daily Mail*: 'Montgomery is rolling back Rundstedt's line on a 25-miles' front, says Doon Campbell from the Field Marshal's H.Q. "It does not necessarily mean that the whole thing is collapsing yet," a headquarters spokesman said, "but Rundstedt is recoiling to the weight of our hammer blows." Rundstedt was today officially stated to be "on the defensive all the way along the northern front of the Ardennes salient."'

8 January 1945, William Furnival, *Lancashire Daily Post*

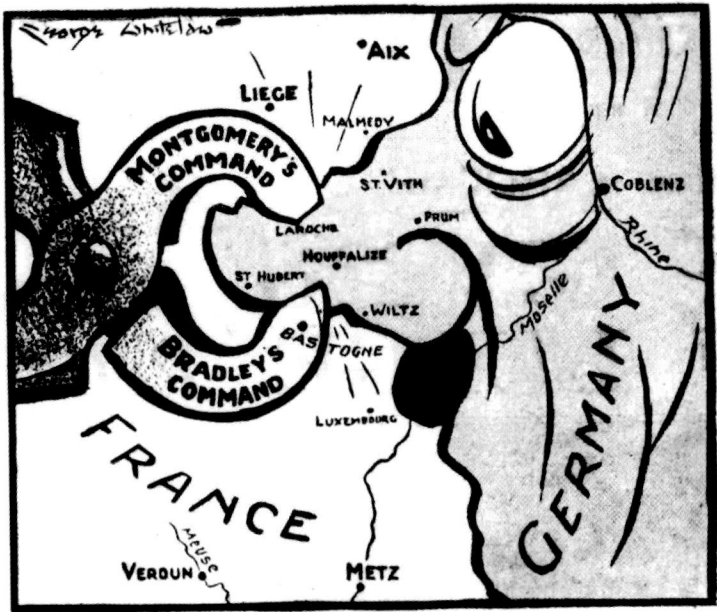

That's what you get for sticking your nose out.

According to the Sunday Mercury: 'Starting a pincer move in the Ardennes — Field Marshal Montgomery in the north of the "bulge" and General Bradley in the south — the Allies are forcing the Germans to retreat on a "Normandy scale." The new thrust by the American First Army under Montgomery is designed to trap a section of the Germans in the salient or force them back to their original Siegfried Line positions.'

11 January 1945, George Whitelaw, Daily Herald

TRUNK CALLS

According to the Halifax Courier: '"The seething cauldron which has arisen between the Carpathians and the Memel, a distance of 400 miles, is boiling over at many points," the German Overseas News Agency said today. "A flood of 155 Russian infantry divisions, about 22 tank corps and numerous artillery units and air squadrons has now been pouring over the Eastern Front for five days. This mass onslaught has naturally overrun German positions at many places, owing to the numerical superiority of the enemy."'

15 January 1945, William Furnival, Lancashire Daily Post

PARCELLING DEPARTMENT

According to the Daily Herald: 'News came from both East and West that Hitler is hurrying troops from other fronts to buttress his tottering defences. The Russians have already taken prisoners in Silesia from the Second Panzer Division and the 712th Infantry Division, who had been fighting British troops in Holland only a week ago. Others are following in their wake. Western Front pilots saw German material streaming East beginning the long trek across the Reich to the other threatened borders. Two divisions were rushed from Norway to the Prussian front between Frankfurt and Poznan, and others went back across the Alps from Italy.'

16 January 1945, George Butterworth, Daily Dispatch

From the Normandy Beaches to Victory in Berlin

AN OLD SHOE

According to the *Sunday Express*: 'Jap resistance is crumbling on the left flank of the American front on Luzon Island, General MacArthur's headquarters announced. Japs suffered heavily in making "uncoordinated counter-attacks" with armour and artillery between Rosario and Urdaneta, along the Manila highway stretching into the Benguet Mountains.'

17 January 1945, Rube Goldberg, *New York Sun* (United States)

THE REVENGE

With the headline 'Crowning Irony,' the *Liverpool Echo* reported: 'The home of Junkerdom, the cradle of the ruthless barons, the high altar of the military caste, is cut into like cheese by the armies of the brilliant young Jew, Chernyakovsky and the smiling Rokossovsky. They laugh at the legend of Tannenburg as Hitler orders the casque holding the remains of Hindenburg to be hurried to safety, and the great monument erected to him, opened with such pomp, is blown to bits before the maw of battle could grind it to powder.'

20 January 1945, Alexander Saroukhan, *Akher Sa'a* (Cairo, Egypt)

IT'S THAT MAN AGAIN!

According to the *Evening Telegraph*: 'Marshal Stalin simply poured out over the whole weekend orders of the day celebrating Russian victories in the tremendous battles now raging on the approaches to Germany and within the territory of the Reich. Even more impressive has been the rate of the Russian advance over the Polish plain where a third of the distance between Warsaw and Berlin has been covered in four days and our Ally now stands, or stood yesterday, only 200 miles from the capital of the Reich.'

21 January 1945, George Frederick Shilling, *The People*

RECOGNISED

The Polish Home Army, a non-Communist underground resistance movement, initiated the Warsaw uprising to liberate the city from the German occupation and reclaim Polish independence. The impetus for the military action was the ongoing retreat of the German forces from Poland. Although the Soviet army was within easy sight of the city, the uprising was ruthlessly crushed, reducing Warsaw to ruins in the process. On 19 January, after the Soviet forces had cleared most of Poland of the Wehrmacht, what was left of the Polish Home Army was disbanded.

24 January 1945, Richards, *Daily Worker*

According to the *Aberdeen Press*: 'There is no doubt of the Russian purpose to stop nowhere short of Berlin. With their purpose goes an ability to achieve it which must be staggering to the enemy. Stalin has the men and munitions; he has also the generals of great capacity in strategic planning, in tactical movement, and in flexibility of organisation. So far, nothing the Germans have done has been able to delay the march on Berlin.'

28 January 1945, George Frederick Shilling, *The People*

A QUICK ONE

According to the *Daily Herald*: 'Hitler, in a 16-minute broadcast last night to the German people in the midst of their greatest crisis since 1918, offered no hope of a Wehrmacht comeback — but only the prospect of greater miseries yet. It was his gloomiest and shortest speech.'

31 January 1945, George Butterworth, *Daily Dispatch*

From the Normandy Beaches to Victory in Berlin

HIMMEL, STAB IN THE BACK!

According to the *Daily Dispatch*: 'With the bulk of the German assault army which broke into Belgium last month now returned to the cover of the Siegfried Line, the Western Front Allied offensive has shown signs of starting again. Rundstedt's adventure has cost the Germans 46,302 prisoners, apart from the dead and missing, it was revealed yesterday. Six Allied armies are now pushing forward in limited advances on six sectors of the 400-miles front between the North Sea and the Alps. The threat to the Ruhr and the Sear is looming.'

1 February 1945, W. H. Woodburn 'Hengest', *Manchester Evening News*

THOSE RUSSIAN "STEPPES"

With the headline 'Berlin Hears Russian Guns,' the *Winford Chronicle* reported: 'It was announced at midday that the people of Berlin could hear the dull rumble of approaching Russian guns. General Zhukov's troops were reported to be only 65 miles from the capital. The German Command are making desperate efforts to hold the Russian advance, and 5,000 of their troops died in Wednesday's attempts. Over 3.000 Germans have been taken prisoner in 24 hours.'

2 February 1945, William Furnival, *Lancashire Daily Post*

Mr. Ernest Bevin, Minister of Labour, told a Norwich audience yesterday: "It distressed me to have to send the Bevin Boys to get coal — but coal had to be got, like other things."

At the beginning of the war the Government, underestimating the value of strong younger coal miners, conscripted them into the armed forces. By mid-1943 the coal mines had lost 36,000 workers. So young men, known as Bevin Boys, were conscripted to work in the coal mines. Nearly 48,000 of them performed vital and dangerous, but largely unrecognised service. The programme was named after Ernest Bevin who was Minister of Labour and National Service in the wartime coalition government.

5 February 1945, Talbot Wilfred Ellison, *Birmingham Mail*

WHAT'S COOKING

According to the *Lancashire Daily Post*: 'The Big Three are meeting. However, the place where this vital conference is taking place remains a well-kept secret. Broadcasts from Ankara, mainly based on reports of American correspondents, say that Churchill, Roosevelt and Stalin are meeting on board a British warship off the coast of the Crimea. Roosevelt and Churchill obliged Stalin by going to a place within the boundaries of the Soviet Union, thus "making it possible for Stalin to remain in direct touch with his headquarters, from which he directs, as supreme commander, the offensive on German soil.'

5 February 1945, William Furnival, *Lancashire Daily Post*

PROMISE FULFILLED

According to the *Bradford Observer*: 'Late last night, General MacArthur the Allied Commander-in-Chief in the South-West Pacific, announced that his troops, after a 115-mile advance in 26 days, had entered Manila, the capital of the Philippines, three years and a month after its fall. Thus, the man who made history in neighbouring Bataan and Corregidor has kept his promise, "I will return."'

6 February 1945, Ian Gall, *Courier-Mail* (Brisbane, Australia)

"We are balancing on a tight-rope." — Dittmar

According to the *Daily Herald*: 'Speaking for the High Command, General Dittmar combined the gravest warning yet given to Germany with an admission that fighting inside the Reich is affecting the army's morale. "We are balancing on a tight rope." he said. "We must at every step be conscious of the peril of falling into the abyss which yawns on both sides. Every false or hesitating or ill-conceived step can bring about the fall. We must not forget that fighting in one's own country may awaken strong impulses, but may also have serious repercussions."'

8 February 1945, George Whitelaw, *Daily Herald*

From the Normandy Beaches to Victory in Berlin

"Send Some More Chains!"

It was revealed that Churchill, Roosevelt and Stalin had met at Yalta in the Crimea region of the Soviet Union, to decide what to do with Germany once it had been defeated. The 'Big Three' also agreed to the setting up of the United Nations, an organisation that Roosevelt hoped would be dedicated to international cooperation and the prevention of future wars.

9 February 1945, George Whitelaw, *Daily Herald*

THREE FACES EAST

According to the *Daily Herald*: 'First communiqué on the meeting of the Big Three announces that plans for the knock-out blow to Germany have been agreed, and that talks about world organisation for peace have begun. Their purpose is to concert plans for completing the defeat of the common enemy and for building with their Allies, firm foundations for a lasting peace. There is complete agreement for joint military operations in the final phase of the war against Nazi Germans.'

11 February 1945, Ed Marcus, *New York Times* (United States)

SPRING SUITINGS

With the headline 'Where Can Hitler Run To?' the *Press and Journal* reported: 'The net which is inexorably closing round Germany east and west must be causing Himmler, Goering, Goebbels and company to see which escape plan they must adopt for their Führer and themselves. Already they see the coming retribution. It may be taken for certain that they have planned for the future with typical Teutonic thoroughness.'

11 February 1945, William Timyn 'Tim', *Daily Sketch*

TAKING A SEASONABLE TOSS

With the headline '1,100 West Bombers Help Red Army,' the *Western Mail* reported: 'Marshal Koniev's next big target in his drive on Berlin, was attacked by more than 1,100 Liberators and Fortresses, which also attacked targets in Dresden and the synthetic oil plant near Magdeburg.'

12 February 1945, J C Walker, *Western Mail*

QUAKE!

Recognising that the war in the Pacific was likely to continue long after the defeat of Germany, one of the main talking points at Yalta was the conditions under which the Soviet Union would join Britain and the US in declaring war on Japan. It was agreed that, if Russia were to enter the war, it would be granted possession of southern Sakhalin and the Kuril Islands held by Japan, as well as a sphere of influence in Manchuria.

12 February 1945, George Butterworth, *Daily Dispatch*

THE ROCK

According to the *Daily Sketch*: 'The conference of the Big Three in the Crimea has torn to shreds Hitler' last forlorn hope. No doubt, he always had at the back of his mind, the idea that a quarrel between the Allies might set his neck free from the noose that was slowly but surely tightening around it. One sentence alone in the report from the conference must fill his mind with dismay — "There is complete agreement for joint military operations in the final phase of the war against Nazi Germany." For Hitler this is the sentence of death.'

13 February 1945, George Whitelaw, *Daily Herald*

From the Normandy Beaches to Victory in Berlin

His New Part In The Concert Of Nations

According to the *New York Times*: 'President Roosevelt discussed with Mr. Churchill and Marshal Stalin the possibility of negotiating an inter-Allied treaty to keep Germany permanently demilitarised. An American official said the report expressed the opinion that it was the possibility of American participation in such a treaty that persuaded Marshal Stalin to depart from his demand that permanent members of the World Security Council should have a veto over all questions.'

16 February 1945, Dorman Smith, *Dayton Journal* (United States)

LAST EDITION

According to the *News Chronicle*: 'Berlin announced last night that "*Der Angriff*," Goebbels's own paper, is to close down. Saturday's will be the last issue. Berlin will then have only one evening paper "*Nacht-Ausgabe*." And weekly picture journals are to be further curtailed, and reserved mainly for export. Goebbels actually founded "*Angriff*," wrote its leaders, and so schooled himself to become Hitler's propagandist. When the rest of the Berlin Press was brought under central Nazi control, Goebbels remained sole master of "*Angriff*."'

16 February 1945, William Furnival, *Lancashire Daily Post*

"No chance of escaping yet, Adolf, there just isn't room to take off."

According to the *Press and Journal*: 'Hitler's Reich Chancellery office was damaged during the U.S. 8th Air Force's 1000-bomber raid on Berlin. Reconnaissance photographs confirm that the heart of the city has been torn by a mile-and-a-half square area of destruction. Also damaged were the Tempelhof marshalling yards, the Schlesischer railway station, the Air Ministry, gasworks, Gestapo headquarters, the Treasury, the State railway directorate, the town hall, the secret archives office, and plants making turbines and torpedo equipment.'

18 February 1945, Stephen Roth, *Sunday Pictorial*

'Tell Me When To Start Scorching.'

According to the *Daily Dispatch*: 'Hitler, in an order to German commanders on the Eastern Front, has categorically demanded that all abandoned German soil is to be "Scorched." Commandos of reliable men are to be formed to carry the order into effect, Among the objects listed in the order are private and public buildings, communal undertakings, railway installations, industrial premises with their machinery and equipment, provisions. supplies and all material that cannot be evacuated. The evacuation of the Berlin population is to follow, Moscow Radio.'

18 February 1945, Sidney Moon, *Sunday Dispatch*

According to *Reuters*: 'Goebbels: "A nation resolved to use the most daring and boldest means in defence of its life can continue the war indefinitely — at least until its enemies realise that they cannot reach their goal without endangering their own existence. Here lies one of our fundamental chances which we still possess. Courage alone will win the victory in the end. We wipe the blood off our faces and look the enemy in the eye without fear and without thought of drawing back."'

22 February 1945, W. H. Woodburn 'Hengest', *Manchester Evening News*

From the Normandy Beaches to Victory in Berlin

Jumping Jima-ny

With the headline 'Double Blow At Heart Of Tokio,' the *Lancashire Evening Post* reported: 'American Marines today dominate the second airfield on battle-scarred Iwo Jima an airfield from which it is hoped fighters will soon be winging out as escorts to Super-Fortresses in their blows at Japan 750 miles away. Tokio rocked yesterday under the weight of at least 2,000 tons of bombs which rained down from carrier-based and Super-Fortress planes in raids designed to support the American invaders of Iwo Jima and to cripple the industrially important Tokio area.'

24 February 1945, Reg Manning, *Arizona Republic* (United States)

"Goodness, Mrs. R., what a naughty little boy you have!"

Throughout the war, Roosevelt had an antipathy towards de Gaulle. He called him a "cold fish" and considered him an untrustworthy nuisance. He had earlier tried to promote General Henri Giraud as a rival leader. After de Gaulle had been excluded from the Yalta conference, he released a statement stating that France would not be responsible for any decisions made there. He then refused an invitation to meet Roosevelt in Algiers. According to the *Yorkshire Post*: 'This does not mean that France does not want to co-operate with the United Nations or that she disapproves of the decisions. She is, on the contrary, most anxious to fulfil her role in the International scene, but is awaiting details of the plans and decisions taken in the Crimea.'

25 February 1945, Stephen Roth, *Sunday Pictorial*

"PERMIT ME TO INTRODUCE . . ."

According to the *Daily Mirror*: 'Replying in advance to his critics, Mr. Churchill refused to compromise with them on the Polish question when he opened a three-day debate on the Crimea conference in Parliament. He was sharply critical of the London Poles, whose failure to take our advice he blamed for much of the difficulties. Poland, though independent, must in future be friendly to Russia, he declared, insisting on the justice of the proposed frontier adjustments. He thought the Russian claim to the Curzon Line just and right and added: "If I support this Russian claim to the Curzon Line frontier, it is not because I bow to force but because it is the fairest division which can be made."'

28 February 1945, W. H. Woodburn 'Hengest', *Manchester Evening News*

One Bright Spot

According to the *Daily Herald*: 'Goebbels last night pledged himself and the other Nazi leaders to die at the head of their followers sooner than surrender. In a "Twilight of the Gods" speech, broadcast, as his native town of Rheydt was being stormed by the Americans, he declared: " We would rather die than capitulate. Life would not be worth living for myself, for my children or for all those whom I love and with whom I have fought for so many years for a better and more noble existence. I would gladly throw away such a life. We smile contemptuously at threats that our leaders will be brought to trial for their alleged crimes and be subjected to the death penalty."'

2 March 1945, George Whitelaw, *Daily Herald*

Rhine Whine

According to the *Belfast Newsletter*: 'The crossing of the Northern Rhine by British, Canadian, and American troops under Field Marshal Montgomery's command stands out as one of the most brilliantly designed and executed achievements of the war. It was not a case of taking the enemy by surprise. This particular section of the river was regarded by the German High Command as the most important of all, because it covered what was left of the industrial area of the Ruhr and the great plain leading to the heart of the Reich.'

7 March 1945, George Whitelaw, *Daily Herald*

"SPLITTING HEADACHE"

According to the *Washington Observer*: 'It is becoming clearer every hour that the Big Three grand strategy embraces the cutting of Germany in half by a meeting of Anglo-American and Russian troops along the Elbe River somewhere on the line between Cologne and Dresden. If the Germans fail to capitulate, Allied Strategy plans to apportion Russian and Anglo-American troops for cleaning up the northern half of Germany and capturing Berlin, while continuing a joint war against the guerrillas in the Bavarian and Sudetenland mountains.'

9 March 1945, William Furnival, *Lancashire Daily Post*

From the Normandy Beaches to Victory in Berlin

According to the *News Chronicle*: 'Mr. Churchill returned to London yesterday after a three-day tour of the Western front, much of it on German soil. He did these things, among others: Discussed with Allied war chiefs "a wide field of military matters" Made a speech on German soil, saying: "Soon we shall be across the Rhine. Anyone can see that one good heave all together will end the war in Europe" Said to correspondents: "No river has ever been a barrier" Chalked on a big shell, "Hitler-personally" and fired the gun.'

11 March 1945, George Frederick Shilling, *The People*

The Punishment Fits the Crime

According to the *Lancashire Daily Post*: '`The Japanese Imperial Palace in Tokio was set on fire by a great Super-Fortress raid, says a Jap communique, which adds that the flames were under control by eight o'clock. Returning crews described smoke rising to 18,000 feet, with flames visible at distances of from 50 to 80 miles. "We scarred at least 15 square miles of Tokio," declared Brig.-General T. S. Power, whose plane was one of the last to leave the area. He describes the blaze as the most spectacular he has ever seen. His wing circled over the burning city for two hours, while the last squadrons poured the final incendiaries into the black patch still remaining within the fiery target area.'

12 March 1945, William Furnival, *Lancashire Daily Post*

MARCH HAS ALWAYS BEEN MY LUCKY MONTH

On 6 March, the US Army's surprise capture of the Ludendorff Bridge over the Rhine River at Remagen, broke open Germany's defences in the west. The unexpected prize at Remagen forced the Allies to shift their strategy for invading central Germany, and more time would pass before they broke out from their new bridgehead. The crossing of the Rhine at Remagen, however, marked a decisive moment heralding the impending collapse of Germany.

12 March 1945, Victor Weisz 'Vicky', *News Chronicle*

"Don't look round now, but I think we're being SWALLOWED!"

According to the *Lancashire Daily Post*: 'Field Marshal Montgomery, making his maiden speech in French, told cheering crowds in the Town Square, Brussels, that the battle was going well. "Final victory is certain — beyond any possibility of doubt. Only one thing still in doubt is exactly when," he said, adding: "There is not a German soldier on Belgian soil and the enemy will never come back-never, never. One by one the Allies have torn away the outer defences of the Nazi stronghold, and now in the east and in the west we fight on German soil."'

13 March 1945, George Whitelaw, *Daily Herald*

"TERRIFIC POWER, SIR — AND NO CONTROLS!"

According to the *Manchester Evening News*: 'The Conservative Party Conference, which Mr. Churchill, the party leader, addressed today, has limited influence. The resolutions passed will not bind anybody to anything. Policy is not made there; it comes down from above, but the Party Conference is one of the influences brought to bear on the leadership, and at present it is a most interesting spectacle. The Tories are not at all happy about the future, and in a few months, they have to face a general election for the first time in ten years.'

16 March 1945, W. H. Woodburn 'Hengest', *Manchester Evening News*

DISHED!

According to the *Gloucestershire Echo*: 'An unverified report from S.H.A.E.F. states that the armies of Generals Patton and Patch, fighting in the Saar salient, have closed the gap between them and are converging on Kaiserslautern. This town affords the only escape route for 80,000 Germans still fighting in the pocket. Patton's troops, who have captured about 45 towns, took a record number of prisoners.'

23 March 1945, Ian Gall, *Courier-Mail* (Brisbane, Australia)

From the Normandy Beaches to Victory in Berlin

DROPPING THE PILOTS

With the headline 'Changing Horses In The Middle Of The Rhine,' the *Maitland Mercury* reported: 'Hitler has sacked Marshal von Rundstedt, German Commander-in-Chief on the western front, and replaced him with General Kesselring, Nazi chief in Italy. The BUP correspondent says that von Rundsted's dismissal had been rumoured for months, and had now finally been confirmed by prisoners, who declare that the change was made several weeks ago. The change is likely to have the worst possible effect on the German command in the west.'

25 March 1945, Sidney Moon, *Sunday Dispatch*

STRANGERS ABOUT

On 24 March, Churchill travelled into Germany to watch Montgomery's offensive across the Rhine. He insisted on driving the full length of the offensive line to watch the crossing of the 51st Highland Division. The next day, Churchill crossed the river with Montgomery and senior American officers but came within fifty yards of being hit by a German artillery shell while viewing the Ninth Army's bridgehead. 'The Rhine and all its fortresses line behind the 21st Group of Armies,' Churchill wrote in Montgomery's message book. 'A beaten army, not long ago Master of Europe, retreats before its pursuers. The goal is not long to be denied those who have come so far and fought so well. Forward on all wings of flame to final Victory.'

26 March 1945, Talbot Ellison, *Birmingham Mail*

"We Never Did Anything Real Bad to the Russians, but It Would Be Outrageous If We — a Civilized People — Should Be Treated the Same Way."

The German civilian population had no illusions on what would happen to them in the hands of the Russians. Many Germans were required to tour concentration camps and bear witness to the atrocities committed there. The Allies instructed the Germans in their guilt and made sure they all felt some sense of personal responsibility for allowing the Holocaust to happen. German civilians were even recruited to take part in body disposal.

28 March 1945, Eric Gödel, *PM* (United States)

IT'S A "MONTY"

"Give it a go, Adolf, you've still got your collar and tie!"

According to the *Daily Express*: 'With Montgomery's armies rolling on in places without opposition there was a firm belief at his H.Q. that an Allied Victory Day declaration will not be long delayed. Airmen reported that leading British elements were so close to the Germans fleeing eastwards that enemy armour could not be attacked without risking mistakes. The extent of Montgomery's advance towards the North German plain is screened for security reasons. Opposition is weakening and disorganised. The push is "going very well indeed and gaining momentum every hour."'

29 March 1945, John Frith, *Sydney Morning Herald* (Australia)

BOOMPS-A-NAZI!

According to the *News Chronicle*: 'More than 20 armoured columns, pouring forth from the Allied armies in the greatest flood of armour yet used in this war, are loose in Germany. The security silence regarding the decisive advances that are being made is still on and so is the most remarkable co-ordinated operation yet known to military history. For the rolling armour is following a master plan from the north to the south designed to grip all of Germany and strangle what is left of the Nazi military machine.'

1 April 1945, George Frederick Shilling, *The People*

OUT OF CONTROL

According to the *Scotsman*: 'All the evidence that has accumulated in the campaign of the past three weeks points in the same direction. The Wehrmacht is but a shadow of its former self and its only aim in continuing the struggle now must be to postpone the inevitable end and fulfil Hitler's scheme of a grim and terrible Wagnerian climax. Lack of reserves, lack of petrol, the certain knowledge that the war is lost — all these factors have contributed and are contributing to the decline of the once tremendous German fighting machine.'

2 April 1945, William Furnival, *Lancashire Daily Post*

From the Normandy Beaches to Victory in Berlin

HE'S DEAD, BUT HE CAN'T LIE DOWN!

With the headline 'Rooting Out Hitler's Last Divisions,' the *Daily Dispatch* reported: 'The breathless speed of events on the Western Front warps the judgment. Rout in the West may or may not end the war; but it is the rout of not more than a quarter of the remaining German Army. Not less than 100 divisions, and perhaps more, are so far unaffected by it. Consider the events of the week. On Monday, March 26, Dempsey had just cleared Rees and was over the Issel; Simpson's Ninth Army was closing on the Ruhr from the north and was fighting in Hamborn; Hodges, with his First Army, had bypassed Altenkirchen to points 35 miles east of the Rhine; Patton was fighting in Frankfurt and had crossed the Rhine at Boppard below Coblenz; and the Seventh Army was over the river at Karlsruhe.'

3 April 1945, George Butterworth, *Daily Dispatch*

The Harmony Trio Tune-Up

According to the *Scotsman*: 'A proposal by the U.S.S.R. that the Polish Provisional Government in Warsaw — formerly the Lublin National Committee should send representatives to the San Francisco Conference has been rejected by the British and U.S. Governments. Britain and America still hope the Moscow Commission set up by a Yalta decision will reach agreement upon the names of Poles from "inside and outside the country" who shall be asked to a conference at Moscow to discuss the formation of a broadly-based United Polish Provisional Government. Although the Polish Government in London is not one that, in Mr Churchill's words, the "British Government applauds," Britain has stated she will continue to recognise it until such a time as a new provisional Government of national unity can be set up in Poland.'

4 April 1945, Cy Hungerford, *Pittsburgh Post-Gazette* (United States)

"WELL HELD, SIR"!

According to the *Edinburgh Evening News*: 'An official announcement that the V menace weapon to Southern England has ceased may come at any moment. The battle of the V sites is moving rapidly to its end. It may be over already. Canadian troops are overrunning flying bomb and rocket sites used by the Germans against rear areas, but they are so bent on chasing the Germans northwards to Emden and the sea that they are not even bothering to take note of the sites. No more V 2's are being moved into Holland. If no more V 1's or V 2's fall in the rear areas or Southern England in the next seven days it will be safe to say it is all over.'

4 April 1945, Ian Gall, *Courier-Mail* (Brisbane, Australia)

VIENNESE WALTZ

According to the *Newcastle Journal*: 'Vienna, capital of Austria the first European capital overrun by the Nazis, in March 1938 — fell to the Russians yesterday. It was captured by Marshal Tolbukhin's troops after a battle which lasted less than a week. After driving clean through the city to the banks of the Danube Canal the Russians finally flung the Germans out of their last remaining strongholds on the east side of the canal. The capture is the climax to a campaign which began just west of Budapest and swept forward more than 100 miles in three weeks.'

11 April 1945, Cyril Price 'Kim', *Daily Sketch*

THE GRAVE-DIGGER

According to the *Newcastle Journal*: 'The battle for Central Germany is speeding towards its end with Allied troops within 48 miles of Berlin — possibly less and seven of Leipzig. "Collapse of the entire Central German position seems imminent and the entry into Berlin cannot be delayed more than a matter of days at the very longest," a *Reuters* correspondent at SHAEF cabled last night.'

13 April 1945, William Furnival, *Lancashire Daily Post*

From the Normandy Beaches to Victory in Berlin

HIS MEMORIAL STONE IS READY

Roosevelt suffered a massive stroke and died on 12 April. Just hours after his death, Vice President Harry S. Truman was sworn in as president. Roosevelt's death took the world by surprise. Although those close to him had feared that since his re-election campaign that his time was near, the public had not been aware of the seriousness of his condition even though photographs from Yalta showed his physical deterioration. In a speech he had given to Congress a month earlier, many had been shocked by his worn and frail appearance.

14 April 1945, George Middleton, *Birmingham Gazette*

FAMOUS LAST WORDS

According to the *Daily Express*: 'Goebbels has launched a full-dress werewolf campaign in the German Press. All newspapers publish appeals to men, women, and children to resist the Allies and exterminate Germans co-operating with the occupying troops. Deutsche Allgemeine Zeitung claims that werewolves are in action all over occupied Germany. It says that Allied soldiers have been killed at Heidelberg, Aschaffenburg, and Schweinheim. Press and radio tell the Germans, "the werewolf leaders are always in the thick of it and their orders must be obeyed blindly." A werewolf radio broadcast said: "Chalk up the wolf sign on every house and fence, on every enemy tank and vehicle. If they wipe it off put three other signs in its place. Mark the door of every traitor with it."'

15 April 1945, George Frederick Shilling, *The People*

GREETINGS

According to the *Evening Express*: 'Hitler is today spending his 56th, and most certainly last, birthday, at Berchtesgaden. Biographical notes in "Who's Who" will be transferred in 1946 to "Who Was Who." Latest reports reaching London state that Hitler is in fair health. Although he is war criminal No. 1, trial and sentence will be carried out in such a way as to obviate any possibility of becoming a legendary martyr in German history. He may, of course, save the Allies trouble by killing himself.'

20 April 1945, William Furnival, *Lancashire Daily Post*

THE JURY

According to the American cartoonist Daniel Fitzpatrick: 'Judgement day was drawing near for the Nazi operators of gas chambers, bake ovens, and other forms of mass civilian murder. When the swift American armoured units caught such places as Buchenwald unawares, unbelievable conditions were uncovered.'

21 April 1945, William Timyn 'Tim', *John Bull*

BERLIN BAROMETER

According to the *Daily Mail*: 'To defend Berlin means to wipe it from the face of the earth, said a Moscow broadcast to Berliners today. "The Nazis are prepared to do this," the radio said. "Their passion for destruction knows no bounds. Berlin's turn has now come after the Nazis have left behind them numerous towns in ruins. The only way to save your city, your home, wife and children, is to stop fighting at once. Turn your weapons against everyone who wishes to force a continuation of the Berlin battle."'

23 April 1945, William Furnival, *Lancashire Daily Post*

LEBENSRAUM

According to the *Nantwich Chronicle*: 'Marshal Stalin announced that the armies of Marshal's Zhukov and Koniev have joined north-west of Potsdam, thus surrounding Berlin. General Patton's forces driving deeper into Bavaria were closing on Regensburg and were thus on the fringe of the so-called Nazi redoubt. British forces in north Germany have launched an attack towards Bremen and were fighting inside the city boundary.'

24 April 1945, Thomas Arthur Challen 'Tac', *Daily Mirror* (Sydney, Australia)

From the Normandy Beaches to Victory in Berlin

The Nazis say Hitler is in Berlin directing the defence.

"I shall stimulate the Capital's defence with every means at my disposal." — Goebbels.

According to the *Daily Mail*: 'German Radio declared this afternoon that Hitler is still in Berlin, "We tell the whole world the Fuehrer has decided to stay in Berlin," Hamburg Radio said. It added: "The Fuehrer is directing the battle from the front line in Berlin, and he has thrown in all available forces to stem the Bolshevist onslaught." The report on Hitler was given immediately after a statement that many people were afraid that the German lines before Berlin would not hold against the Russian onslaught, but now it has been shown that these lines did hold fast after all."'

24 April 1945, Eric Clarke, *Daily Record*

GOEBBELS: "I WILL STAY WITH YOU"

According to the *Daily Dispatch*: 'Goebbels, Gauleiter of Berlin, in a speech, quoted by the German News Agency, said he, his wife and children, and his colleagues would remain in the capital. Berlin has become a front line city, Goebbels declared. Civilians must obey instructions without question. "Houses or apartments, which show white flags have no claim to protection or help by the community, and will be dealt with accordingly. In such cases the occupants will be held responsible. The local Party leader must keep watch with iron severity and must act accordingly. Such houses would become the disease carriers in the body of our city."'

24 April 1945, Thomas Arthur Challen 'Tac', *Daily Mirror* (Sydney, Australia)

OVER DEN LINDEN

According to the *Daily Mail*: 'After fresh penetrations into Berlin from the east, unofficial reports put Russian spearheads two miles from the capital's famous avenue, Unter Den Linden, which would mean an important breakthrough of the defence ring at one point. The capital is crumbling at the rate of several blocks an hour. The first Soviet flags are fluttering in the smoke-laden breeze from the biggest buildings captured inside the city boundaries. Other flags are waiting to be hoisted, including one of enormous size which a crack Soviet guards unit is carrying into the city with the intention of flying it over Hitler's Chancellery.'

24 April 1945, George Whitelaw, *Daily Herald*

Twilight Of The Goats

According to *Reuters*: 'A carefully coached former grocer who looks like Hitler's twin has been sent to the German capital "to die on the barricades" and to give the world the impression that the Fuehrer himself fell, according to the Free German Press Service in Stockholm. Hitlers "stand-in" was stated to be August Wilhelm Bartholdy. "Meanwhile," the agency added, "Hitler remains in Berchtesgaden awaiting the end of the war, while preparations are being made for him to disappear quietly."'

26 April 1945, Eric Clarke, *Daily Record*

THE GANG'S ALL HERE!

The German national redoubt had been envisaged by Himmler in 1943. The original plan was for the Nazi government and remaining armed forces to retreat to southern Bavaria. The scheme was never fully endorsed by Hitler, and no serious attempt was made to put it into operation, although the concept served as an effective tool of military deception carried out by Goebbels in the final stages of the war. After surrendering, the Wehrmacht General Kurt Dittmar revealed that the redoubt never existed.

26 April 1945, George Butterworth, *Daily Dispatch*

From the Normandy Beaches to Victory in Berlin

Hail, fellow, well met!

According to the *Daily Herald*: 'Two days of wild link-up rejoicing ended with an agreement between the Red and American Armies that henceforth trips east or west of the Elbe would be by invitation only, and that guests would be properly escorted while in each other's territory. The order came as a great disappointment to G.I.'s and Russians who had been ferrying back and forth as they liked. It was also a blow to war reporters, who were invited by Supreme Headquarters to travel many hundreds of miles to meet the Russians.'

28 April 1945, William Pidgeon 'Wep',
Daily Telegraph **(Sydney, Australia)**

REICHSTAG VISITOR: D'YOU MIND IF I LIGHT UP?

According to the *Bradford Observer*: 'Stalin in his Order of the Day, said: "Troops of the First White Russian Front, commanded by Marshal Zhukov, in co-operation with troops of the First Ukrainian Front, commanded by Marshal Koniev, after stubborn street battles, completed the rout of the Berlin garrison and captured the city of Berlin, the capital of Germany, the centre of German Imperialism and the hearth of German aggression."'

29 April 1945, J C Walker, *News of the World*

THE "DUD"

According to the *Manchester Evening News*: 'Himmler has offered unconditional surrender to Britain and the United States, but not to Russia, it was officially announced from San Francisco this afternoon. Later a statement from 10 Downing Street, said that Britain would not accept unconditional surrender except on behalf of all the Allies, including Russia.'

30 April 1945, William Furnival,
Lancashire Daily Post

WAStika

According to the *Daily Herald*: 'Hitler is believed to be dead. Mussolini is officially dead, very dead. Millions of people derive great satisfaction from the deaths, imminent or actual, of these two men and their accomplices. The satisfaction is natural. Hitler and Mussolini symbolise the horror that has gripped the world since 1939; the horror that, even before 1939, had throttled freedom in their own countries, and had tentacles to spare for the throats of Abyssinia and Albania, Spain and Czechoslovakia. Hitler and Mussolini were the leaders in a revolution against civilised standards of freedom, decency and law. As criminal tyrants they dwarfed the greatest outrages in the annals of despotism, and so they have richly earned their ignominious and exemplary fate.'

1 May 1945, George Whitelaw, *Daily Herald*

'The Paths of Glory Lead but to the Grave'

On 28 April, Mussolini and his mistress, Clara Petacci, were shot and killed by Italian partisans who had captured the couple as they attempted to flee to Switzerland. Their bodies were taken to Milan, where they were hung upside down and displayed publicly for revilement by the masses.

1 May 1945, Jim Berryman, *Washington Evening Star* (United States)

BUT NOT THIS WORLD

On 30 April, as Soviet troops entered Berlin, Hitler committed suicide by shooting himself in the head in his underground bunker. Eva Braun, whom he had just married, also took her own life. According to his wishes, both bodies were burned. According to *Reuters*: 'Rumours of Hitler's death continue to circulate in neutral capitals. His death is said to have occurred in the Nazis' great subterranean headquarters in the Tiergarten — Berlin's "Hyde Park" — Goebbels being present at the end.'

1 May 1945, George Butterworth, *Daily Dispatch*

THAT'S DOENITZ!

Job for the under-water expert.

According to the *Daily Herald*: 'Hitler is dead. Admiral Doenitz, 53-year-old Commander-in-Chief of the German Navy, is his successor. The new Fuehrer's first order to the beaten German nation is "Fight on!"' Hitler in his last political testament named Admiral Dönitz as his successor as president of the Third Reich, minister of war, and supreme commander of the armed forces. Hitler had named him his successor because he trusted him, and had fallen out with all other potential candidates. Assuming the reins of government on 2 May, Dönitz retained office for only a few days until he surrendered to British forces.

3 May 1945, George Middleton, *Birmingham Gazette*

"IT'S IN THE BAG!"

On 3 May, more than half a million German soldiers surrendered to Montgomery's army, followed by "far more than a million" (according to Churchill) the next day. With the total surrender of Germany imminent, Churchill was asked if he had any statement to make about the cessation of hostilities in Europe. He replied that he "had no special statement to make, except that it was definitely more satisfactory than it was this time five years ago".

4 May 1945, W. H. Woodburn 'Hengest', *Manchester Evening News*

TRIBUTE FROM A NEUTRAL

News Item: The Prime Minister of Eire, Mr. de Valera, called on the German Minister to offer condolences on the death of Hitler. "Don't take it so much to heart, Mr. de Valera — remember, they haven't found his body yet."

According to the *New York Times*: 'In making a personal call at the German Legation in Dublin it is possible that De Valera was merely following what he believed to be the protocol required of a neutral State. Considering the character and record of the man for whose death he was expressing grief there is obviously something wrong with the protocol of neutrality or with De Valera.'

5 May 1945, John Frith Sydney, *Morning Herald* (Australia)

HE TOLD US SO

From the balcony of the Ministry of Health, a triumphant Churchill gave his famous 'V for Victory' sign to crowds in Whitehall celebrating the end of the war. In May 1940 in his first speech as Prime Minister, Churchill had stated: "Victory at all costs, Victory in spite of all terror, Victory however long and hard the road may be. For without victory there is no survival."

8 May 1945, Sam Wells, *Herald* (Melbourne, Australia)

'Then I dived down to 300 feet and released 2,000 loaves of bread!'

According to the *Daily Herald*: 'A mercy fleet of 250 RAF Lancasters showered down sacks of food "like confetti" to the starving Dutch in occupied Holland. For an hour and a half the food went down in special slings more than 600 tons of it. In each of the slings were 71 sacks containing meat, flour, yeast, cheese, margarine, sugar, peas, dried milk, powdered eggs, potato mash powder, chocolate, tea and even pepper, salt and mustard. Some of the aircraft carried as much as 6.280lb. — enough to provide a balanced ration for over 3,000 people for a day.'

6 May 1945, Roland Davies, *Daily Sketch*

AIRBORNE AT LAST

At 3pm on 8 May, almost five years to the day since he became Prime Minister, Churchill broadcast to the nation that the war with Germany was over. The day was to be known as Victory in Europe day. Churchill appeared on the balcony at Buckingham Palace with the royal family before driving to Whitehall to address the crowd from the Ministry of Health balcony. To ecstatic crowds, he said: "God bless you all. This is your victory." To which the crowds shouted back: "No — it's yours."

8 May 1945, George Middleton, *Birmingham Gazette*

7
From Hot War to Cold War

Cartoonists Vicky, Whitelaw and the Australian Molnar treated the death or arrest of the Nazis leadership flippantly. Whilst these were characters they held in contempt, the cartoonists did feel the loss from material which had been the mainstay of their work throughout the war.

3 May 1945, Victor Weisz 'Vicky', *News Chronicle*

"And after all we've done for him, comrades, he tells us we're REDUNDANT!"

4 May 1945, George Whitelaw, *Daily Herald*

The purpose of our meeting gentlemen is to set out our claim for compensation

11 May 1945, George Molnar, *Daily Telegraph* (Sydney, Australia)

FINAL DEFLATION

According to the *Edinburgh Evening News*: 'Goering staged his surrender with typical cunning. For once it was not just vanity that made him give himself up in uniform. Members of the War Crimes Commission told me that they thought this was a ruse to get himself classed with the Wehrmacht captives and not with the Nazi leaders. That is in keeping with his story that he was on the run from Hitler. I learnt he surrendered, not as a member of the German Government, but as the former leader of the Luftwaffe. But if Goering thinks he can escape retribution by any such device, he is wrong. He is high on the list of war criminals and will be tried as such. An international lawyer said to me: "Legal machinery has been devised to put some prisoners of war among the war criminals. Goering has been indicted for his rapacious cruelty. and not even a plea of insanity should save him now."'

11 May 1945, George Whitelaw, *Daily Herald*

JURY

According to the *Belfast Newsletter*: 'Goering perspiring and uneasy before a number of war correspondents at Augsburg yesterday admitted that he had ordered the bombing of Coventry. He defended the saturation raid as legitimate "because of the concentration of aircraft and war industries there." "The order to bomb Canterbury," he said, "came from higher headquarters as a revenge for the British bombing of a German cathedral city. I don't remember which German city." The fat, shifty-eyed Field Marshal spoke bitterly of Hitler for refusing to take his advice in military matters.'

11 May 1945, W. H. Woodburn 'Hengest', *Manchester Evening News*

LET US LIFT UP OUR HEARTS!

According to the *News of the World*: 'The winning cartoon in the *"News of the World"* VE Competition, for which Mr. Arthur Clarke of Marlbrook House, Cottage-lane Marlbrook, Bromsgrove, Worcs, was rewarded the first prize of £500. A self-taught artist, married and in the middle forties, Mr. Clarke completed his training at the Bromsgrove Guild, the well-known Midlands art centre.'

13 May 1945, Arthur Clarke, *News of the World*

THEIR LOOPHOLE!

According to the *Daily Dispatch*: 'Doenitz and Goering, and other leading Nazis, are being held as prisoners of war and will stand trial as war criminals. Lt-Gen. Clay, Deputy Military Governor in Germany for Gen. Eisenhower, said today. "They are being removed to places of incarceration where there will be no luxuries. He said he hoped the first criminals would be tried "at an early date. Our first objective is to smash utterly whatever remaining power Germany may have with which to develop war potential and to drive the Nazis out of power and keep them out. War criminals will pay for their crimes with their lives, liberty, sweat and blood.'

15 May 1945, Thomas Arthur Challen 'Tac', *Daily Mirror* (Sydney, Australia)

THE MOVING FINGER

Amid all the revelry, Churchill reminded the nation that they remained at war with Japan. "We may allow ourselves a brief period of rejoicing," Churchill said during his VE Day broadcast, "but let us not forget for a moment the toil and the efforts that lie ahead. Japan, with all her treachery and greed, remains unsubdued. The injury she has inflicted on Great Britain, the United States, and other countries, and her detestable cruelties, call for justice and retribution. We must now devote all our strength and resources to the completion of our task both at home and abroad. Advance, Britannia!"

18 May 1945, William Furnival, *Lancashire Daily Post*

It'll Take Some Scrapping To Scrap It

To many in the United States, it seemed a foregone conclusion that Churchill would win the British general election. The Leader of the Opposition, Clement Attlee, was virtually unknown to most Americans.

23 May 1945, Reg Manning, *Arizona Republic* (United States)

TWO'S COMPANY

Churchill's popularity remained enormous, confirmed by the huge crowds that cheered him at every point on his election tour around the country. Even though opinion polls showed a significant swing towards Labour, it was widely anticipated by the media that the Conservatives would be returned to power. The Manchester Guardian went as far as to say that 'the chances of Labour sweeping the country and obtaining a clear majority . . . are pretty remote'. Churchill, however, was less convinced. In his broadcast on 30 June, he reminded the electorate that voting for Labour or the Liberal Party would mean 'at the same time voting for my dismissal from power'.

26 June 1945, George Butterworth, *Daily Dispatch*

"YES, YES, Mr. C., BUT PLEASE SIT DOWN"

The Conservatives still considered Churchill's popularity their trump card and, in the days before the election, billboards around the country carried huge photographs of the Prime Minister with the caption, 'Help him finish the job. Vote National.' Conservative Party organisers even thought it necessary to exhort their supporters not to stay away from the polling booths through overconfidence.

4 July 1945, W. H. Woodburn 'Hengest', *Manchester Evening News*

SUSPENSE

There was a sense of anti-climax following polling day on 5 July, as the country had to wait another three weeks for the results to be announced. The extra time was needed to allow for the collection and counting of the votes from servicemen and women still in Europe and the Far East.

9 July 1945, William Furnival, *Lancashire Daily Post*

Suit Yourself, Joe

According to the *Manchester Evening News*: 'President Truman is conferring separately with Mr. Churchill and Marshal Stalin today. This is the only concrete news yet to come through the veil of silence shrouding the Potsdam Conference. No indication is given of the subjects to be discussed but Washington is humming with rumours. One of these reports is that the "Big Three will consider either an unconditional surrender offer by Japan or a Soviet entry into the Far East war.'

16 July 1945, Reg Manning, *Arizona Republic* (United States)

Land of the SETTING sun

According to *The People*: 'The Japanese Government adopted a new line in their invasion warnings. Instead of emphasising the might of the Allied preparations and the imminence of attack, they boasted of the strength and security of the Jap defences. "Special attack units are already massed, backed by 100,000,000 people ready to sacrifice their lives for their homeland," said Tokyo Radio. These attack units are believed to have been built up on the same basis as the Jap suicide air corps, every man taking an oath to die for his homeland.'

13 July 1945, George Whitelaw, *Daily Herald*

THE KNOCK-OUT

According to the *Sunday Express*: 'Street lights in most parts of the country will be ready to turn on their full peace-time brilliance when Double Summer Time ends on 15 July. Electricians have been busy for weeks, and in nearly all the London boroughs a great effort is being made to get the lights cleaned and in working order for the big light-up said an official of St. Pancras Council: "London will be worth seeing that night."'

16 July 1945, William Furnival, *Lancashire Daily Post*

PATIENCE, PERSEVERANCE, PERSPICACITY, PERSPIRATION DOES IT

According to the *Western Daily Press*: 'Widespread reports that the "Big Three" are tackling their biggest immediate problem, the future of Germany, were given backing by Soviet appointments made in the past 72 hours to strengthen the provincial governments in Russian occupied Germany. This suggests that the Russians do not regard their point of view of the future of Germany as questionable in the "Big Three" discussions.'

17 July 1945, Dorman Smith, *Grand Island Independent* (Nebraska, United States)

"SAWING A WOMAN IN HALF."

"Isn't that too much left of centre, Winston? And isn't he being a lot too realistic?"

Stalin had promised at the Yalta Conference to allow free elections in those countries occupied by the Russians in Eastern Europe. However, by July, he had in fact started turning them all into a buffer zone between the Soviet Union and Western Europe. Stalin paranoia led him to fear that Eastern Europe could be the doorway for an attack on the Soviet Union by the Western powers.

18 July 1945, Norman Lindsay, *Sydney Bulletin* (Australia)

"Think Hon. Finest Hour is striking, Your Majesty."

According to *Reuters*: 'Allied naval forces have hit the Japanese homeland with approximately 100 tons of bombs and shells each hour since 10 July, when 1,000 to 1,500 carrier plane attacks began. Three warships' shelling's have been officially reported since 14 July. Air Marshal Sir Hugh Lloyd, commander of the British Air Forces in the Pacific, predicted that R.A.F Lancasters and the heavier Lincolns would soon be hitting Japan in round the-clock raids.'

20 July 1945, George Whitelaw, *Daily Herald*

What a pity I've only Seventy Million lives to lose

According to the *Daily Record*: 'Japanese-controlled Batavia radio said that all defence preparations have been completed in readiness for Allied landings on the Japanese mainland and in Malaya. "The fortress of Japan has completed its plans to meet almost all eventualities connected with the coming invasion," said the announcer. "The maximum of Japan's fighting power has been preserved to be deployed in the coming showdown battle on the mainland."'

20 July 1945, Victor Weisz 'Vicky', *News Chronicle*

"UNDER NEW MANAGEMENT"

At Potsdam, the Big Three confirmed plans to disarm and demilitarise Germany, which was to be divided into four Allied occupation zones controlled by the United States, Great Britain, France and the Soviet Union. They also planned to drastically remake German society, by repealing laws passed by the Nazi regime and removing Nazis from the German education and court systems, and to arrest and try Germans who had committed war crimes.

22 July 1945, R A Lewis, *Milwaukee Journal* **(United States)**

From Hot War to Cold War

'Bombed out? Of course we're bombed out'

According to the *Lancashire Daily Post*: 'Although Argentine newspapers are still theorising on the possibility of Hitler and Eva Braun seeking refuge in the Argentine, or an island in the southern hemisphere, Dr. Ameghino, Argentine Foreign Secretary, denied there was any truth in reports that they had landed on the Argentina coast from a U-boat. Hitler and Eva Braun could be hidden here and no one would ever hear of them. In 1939 many of the biggest estancias hundreds of square miles in area were owned by Germans and if Hitler is in Patagonia, and has ample funds, his helpers would not find it difficult to persuade Patagonians to keep their mouths shut.'

22 July 1945, Stephen Roth, *Sunday Pictorial*

"I didn't speak."

According to the *Sunday Sun*: 'The Japanese are now on the defensive. The presence of the Russian army, poised in a position to strike from the North, is tying down Japanese forces which the militarists dare not move. Whether Stalin intends to take a more active part in the war against Japan is still problematical to the outside world, but it is clear that the Japs are fully aware of the danger confronting them. In Washington there is a firm belief that Stalin is using the threat of his Eastern Army to help force the Japs to surrender.'

25 July 1945, George Whitelaw, *Daily Herald*

WOULD YOU GO BACK AS MY FRIEND & COUNSELLOR?

With the headline 'Getting Ready For The Count,' the *Western Daily Press* reported: 'The checking of votes cast by members of the Forces in all the war theatres will take place today. Tomorrow they will be added to the civilian votes for the "big" count. It is expected that most results will be known by 4 p.m. Recounts may cause delay in a few cases. Mr Churchill and Mr Attlee have arranged to be back in London from Potsdam to hear the results.'

25 July 1945, W. H. Woodburn 'Hengest', *Manchester Evening News*

NEXT OBJECTIVE

Our object all sublime, we shall achieve in time, to let the punishment fit the crime;

The punishment fit the crime" — "The Mikado." With apologies to W. S. Gilbert

According to the *Northern Whig*: 'Allied bombers hammered Japan again when up to 100 Super-Forts struck three oil refineries near Tokio after British and U.S. carrier planes had struck the naval bases of Kure and Kobe, where the remains of the jap fleet are believed to be lurking. General Kenney, commanding Allied Air Forces in the Pacific, has warned Japan to expect raids by 10,000 planes when "softening up" for the invasion begins. General Kenney promised that great air armadas will smash at every inch of Japan and Jap-held territory with at least 5,000 tons of bombs per mission, so that the Allies will be able to invade at any point without opposition."'

26 July 1945, Kimon Evan Marengo 'Kem', *John Bull*

ECLIPSE OF THE 'RISING SUN'

According to the *Gloucester Citizen*: 'Carrier-borne planes of the American-British fleet resumed their attacks in the Japanese inland sea region at dawn after two days' radio silence. Admiral Chester W. Nimitz at the same time announced that carrier borne onslaughts had damaged 25 Japanese warships — seven more than had been reported previously. Eleven Japanese cities have been warned in plane dropped-leaflets that they had been listed for destruction and that the 20th Air Force would raid four or more of them in the next few days it was announced earlier. The warnings were repeated in Japanese language broadcasts from American-held Saipan Island.'

28 July 1945, Kimon Evan Marengo 'Kem', *John Bull*

DROPPING THE PILOT

To Churchill's astonishment, Labour won a landslide victory, earning 393 parliamentary seats in one of the biggest electoral swings of the twentieth century. Attlee was able to form the Labour Party's first ever majority government. The title of this cartoon, 'Dropping the pilot', refers to Sir John Tenniel's famous cartoon of the same name. That cartoon, published in Punch in March 1890 following the resignation of Chancellor Otto von Bismarck, depicted the great statesman as a ship's captain forced to disembark his vessel by Kaiser Wilhelm II.

29 July 1945, J. C. Walker, *Western Mail*

CAGED

After the Allied liberation of France, Laval had fled to Germany. Upon their defeat in May, he escaped to Spain but was expelled and went into hiding in Austria, where he finally surrendered to American authorities in late July. Extradited to France, Laval was convicted of treason by the High Court of Justice. Condemned to death, he attempted suicide by poison but was nursed back to health in time for his execution, on 15 October 1945.

3 August 1945, William Furnival, *Lancashire Daily Post*

On 26 July the United States called on Japan to surrender, warning them of the 'varied and overwhelming character of the force we are about to bring upon the islands' and the 'inevitability and completeness' of the destruction that would follow if Japan did not surrender. After the Japanese had refused the ultimatum, the Americans, on 6 August, dropped an atomic bomb on the Japanese city of Hiroshima. Three days later, it exploded an another one over Nagasaki.

8 August 1945, Ian Gall, *Courier-Mail* (Brisbane, Australia)

REMOTE CONTROL

According to the *Press and Journal*: 'A frantic last-minute attempt seems to have been made by the Japanese war lords to induce their people to fight on. General Suki Anami, the Japanese War Minister, in a broadcast, objected to the surrender offer, and in the name of Emperor Hirohito commanded all Japanese armed forces and people to continue resistance. This bid to halt the inevitable trend of events was made three hours before the receipt of the Japanese Government's surrender offer. It remains to be seen whether the General will maintain his attitude in face of his own Government's declaration, which obviously could not have been forthcoming without the Emperor's concurrence.'

14 August 1945, John Santry, *Daily Telegraph* (Sydney, Australia)

ECLIPSE

On 10 August, Japan offered to surrender to the Allies, the only condition being that the emperor be allowed to remain the nominal head of state. The only question was if Japan's military leaders would allow the emperor to surrender. Loyalty to the emperor was an absolute in the Japanese military, but so was the refusal to surrender, and now that the two had come into conflict, open rebellion was a possible result. On 15 August, the emperor made a broadcast announcing Japan's surrender. As a result, everyone in Japan now knew that surrender was the emperor's personal will.

15 August 1945, John Santry, *Daily Telegraph* (Sydney, Australia)

From Hot War to Cold War

FINAL TRIBUTE

According to the *Yorkshire Observer*: 'This is a tribute to Mr. Churchill paid in the House of Commons by Mr. Attlee: "However much we may be divided politically in this House, I believe I shall be expressing the views of the whole House in making acknowledgment of the great services rendered by Mr. Churchill to this country and to the Commonwealth and Empire and to the world during his tenure of office. During those years he was leader of the country in war we have seen in Fascist countries a detestable cult of leadership which has only been a cover for dictatorship, but here there was true expression by one man of the soul of the nation and the translation of its common will into action."'

16 August 1945, George Middleton, *Birmingham Gazette*

The man who asked for a double scotch and a packet of cigs. on V-J Day

According to the *Staffordshire Advertiser*: 'Sir Ben Smith, at his first Press conference as Minister of Food, declared: "There is no prospect of any improvement in the rations. The restoration of recent cuts is at the moment something for the future. "It is too early to say what benefits we shall derive from the end of the Pacific war. Ultimately, if the shipping is available, the position should improve.'

19 August 1945, George Frederick Shilling, *The People*

SAVING FACE

According to the *Daily Mirror*: 'Earlier yesterday the Japanese News Agency reported that the Japanese surrender mission had received full powers from the Emperor to make arrangements for the Allied landings. But fears were expressed that armed action might be necessary to "establish" the Allied occupation forces in Japan, as the Japanese Army still considered itself "undefeated".'

22 August 1945, George Whitelaw, *Daily Herald*

THE ONLY HOPE

According to the *Liverpool Evening Express*: '"Today and forever into the future our world lives under the sword of Damocles," declared Mr. John G. Winant, the American Ambassador. "The moral problem which was posed in that garden where the world began, when man first tasted the tree of knowledge, must now be settled once and for all. We have uncovered the last secret of nature and our power for destruction has become absolute. We must learn one more secret — a moral secret this time — before we can use this dynamic power for good."'

24 August 1945, William Furnival, *Lancashire Daily Post*

From Hot War to Cold War

Santa Claus Starts Homeward

According to the *Banbridge Chronicle*: 'The announcement of the termination of our Lease-Lend arrangements with the United States was a nasty jolt to almost all sections of the people of the United Kingdom. We knew, of course, that it had to come some time, that in the end we would have to stand on our own feet once more, but there may have been some excuse for the rather wishful thinking that in this case it might have been later rather than sooner. Once again, our people have been brought face to face with stern reality. The truth is plain if not palatable. We shall have to cut down our imports where they involve the payment of dollars, for the simple reason that we have no longer the money with which to pay for them.'

28 August 1945, Cy Hungerford, *Pittsburgh Post-Gazette* (Philadelphia, United States)

LET THERE BE PEACE

According to the *Scotsman*: 'The first sea-borne troops of the American occupation forces are due to land in Japan. General MacArthur seems to have decided upon the following procedure: First, he himself would land in Japan on Thursday next; Secondly, on Sunday next the instrument of surrender would be signed. Thirdly, the Emperor would. then issue a rescript to his armies overseas, ordering them to lay down their arms; Finally, on receipt of this rescript, the various Japanese theatre commanders would surrender their forces to their Allied opposite numbers.'

29 August 1945m W. H. Woodburn 'Hengest', *Manchester Evening News*

"MIND IF WE LOQK OVER YOUR SHOULDER, GENERAL?"

According to the *Halifax Evening Courier*: 'General Jonathan Wainwright, "defender of Corregidor," who arrived in Chungking yesterday, will be a privileged spectator at the special invitation of General MacArthur. General Wainwright expressed the hope that General Homma, the Japanese commander to whom he capitulated after the Bataan campaign, will also be present when the Japanese sign the instrument of surrender. General Wainwright will afterwards be allowed to supervise the surrender of Marshal Yamashita, the Japanese commander in the Philippines, when the latter gives up in Northern Luzon.'

30 August 1945, Dorman Smith, *Grand Island Independent* (Nebraska, United States)

THE LIST

According to the *Lancashire Daily Post*: 'The first list of notorious Germans to be tried as major war criminals, "whose offences have no particular geographical location," is a colourful and variegated assembly. It Includes several names of prominent members of the Nazi hierarchy and the German High Command against whom public opinion has often spoken in condemnatory terms. It is expected that the trials will commence in Nuremberg, before the first International Criminal Court in history, near the end of October.'

31 August 1945, William Furnival, *Lancashire Daily Post*

From Hot War to Cold War

"COMING, SIIR!"

According to the *Nottingham Journal*: 'General MacArthur was still silent about the visit of Emperor Hirohito yesterday. In Tokio the general opinion was that the Emperor had "lost face" by his visit to the Supreme Commander. Recognising him as undisputed conqueror, the Japanese people felt he was entitled to receive the "Divine Emperor." MacArthur's personal Signal Corps photographer has given the only description of the meeting: "Hirohito! wearing top hat and morning dress, was met by the General in plain khaki uniform and open shirt without decorations. The Emperor bowed and shook hands with the General, who extended his hand to greet him. As they shook hands General MacArthur spoke a few words then he asked Hirohito if he would pose for a picture. Hirohito agreed and I took three shots."'

31 August 1945, John Frith, *The Sydney Morning Herald* **(Australia)**

THE ROAD BACK

Franco's tacit support for the Axis powers during the war left Spain in the immediate aftermath both isolated and marginalised. One result of this was Spain forced withdrawal from Tangier in Morocco, which it had seized control of from after France's defeat in June 1940. The withdrawal was the result of the Paris Conference on Tangier in August, where the United Kingdom, France, the United States, and the Soviet Union demanded Spain's departure.

7 September 1945, William Furnival, *Lancashire Daily Post*

SO SORRY

According to the *Liverpool Echo*: 'The Allied occupation of Japan is going smoothly, and all demands are being met. The Japanese appear to be revelling in defeat, and are now making a virtue of necessity. The Japanese have proved themselves barbaric people who have treated their prisoners with fiendish cruelty. Ghastly accounts of the conditions under which Allied prisoners lived and died are coming to light. We are trying Germans for their war crimes, and Japanese criminals must not be allowed to escape. Great Britain will support any measures to bring guilty Japanese to justice.'

10 September 1945, Victor Weisz, 'Vicky' *News Chronicle*

PLUMS

According to the *Birmingham Gazette*: 'The Foreign Ministers took up the question whether peace should be signed with the Balkan satellites. M. Molotov will have to satisfy at least the British and American delegates that elections about to be held in Rumania and Bulgaria would be likely to produce Governments satisfactory to the people and conforming to democratic practice. Some Western statesmen regard the Balkan administrations as little better than police government, maintaining their positions by intimidation. They were in the first instance hastily assembled when the Red Army entered without any reference to their representative character. M. Molotov, however, says that they have a good record in re-establishing order and fulfilling the armistice terms faithfully, and can now be recognised as democratic.'

24 September 1945, William Furnival, *Lancashire Daily Post*

LAST NUREMBERG RALLY.

According to *John Bull*: 'Let us be quite clear about the War Trials which are opening soon. They are not a mere act of revenge, but something much bigger. They represent the first real effort in history to outlaw war — to make mass-murder as punishable an offence as individual killings. They are an essential step to World Peace.'

3 November 1945, William Timyn, 'Tim', *John Bull*

From Hot War to Cold War

WHY NOT TRY THE BIG ONE?

According to the *Dundee Courier*: 'How will Russia take the declaration from Washington of the policy of the American, British, and Canadian Government heads on the atomic bomb secret? The possession of the knowledge of how to produce this revolutionary instrument of destruction by these three Governments alone has caused great unsettlement in the relations of the Western Allies with the Soviet Union. Moscow resents their monopoly, feeling that something is being held back from her by her great war-time partners — something that might be used to give them the whip-hand over her in diplomatic negotiations. It is not a good basis for that mutual trust which, as we are constantly and rightly reminded, is the only hope of stable future peace.'

17 November 1945, William Timyn, 'Tim', *John Bull*

HE CAN'T REMEMBER — THEY CAN'T FORGET

(Hess is suffering from loss of memory).

According to the *Yorkshire Post*: 'Rudolf Hess is mentally incapable of defending himself, but was sane and competent at the time of the crimes alleged against him in the Nuremberg indictment, states the British psychiatric commission's report to the Allied Military Tribunal. A British spokesman states: "There was a time in Britain when Hess was completely insane, but his basic personality is purely hysterical and he has a true amnesia. He is crafty and in some respects very sharp, but remembers nothing of the past. When accused of a crime, he doesn't know what his accusers are talking about. He is incapable of defending himself."'

20 November 1945, George Whitelaw, *Daily Herald*

Twenty Million Voices Say: "AND SO WERE WE"

According to the *Civil and Military Gazette*: 'The United States opened its case against the 20 accused Nazi war criminals in a tense courtroom after the accused had dramatically entered pleas of not guilty and had made a futile challenge of the Allied nations' right to bring them to trial. The overlords of Nazism, on trial for their lives on three counts of high international crime, unanimously entered pleas of not guilty, a number of them employing oratorical flourishes. Hermann Goering was the first to plead. He stepped to the microphone and said: "I declare myself in a sense wholly not guilty." The other defendants, following in order one by one, also entered pleas of innocence, some of them pausing before the microphone to deliver brief statements that their consciences were clear.'

25 November 1945, Stephen Roth, *Sunday Pictorial*

According to the *Daily Dispatch*: 'In the Nuremberg Courthouse today we listened with attention to the opening of the British case for the prosecution by Sir Hartley Shawcross, K.C., the Attorney-General. Sir Hartley, who is only 43, castigated the wretched men in the dock, whose crime of fraud, he said, had put them in position to murder and rob. Goering and his gang heard from this polished orator the story of "their lust and sadism, their deliberate slaughter and degradation of so many millions of their fellow creatures that the imagination reels incomprehensively" of their "diplomacy founded on cunning, hypocrisy, and bad faith," and why it is they have been brought before this tribunal of the Powers. Sir Hartley's main argument was that war of aggression has been a clear and positive crime against international law since the Kellogg Pact of 1928, and that Germany and her leaders could be held personally responsible.'

5 December 1945, George Whitelaw, *Daily Herald*

From Hot War to Cold War

"You need not be at all anxious that any particular part of society will be protected if their guilt is established." — Mr. Hector McNeil yesterday

M.P.'s who asked about British subjects associated with the Nazi movement before the war were given an assurance by Hector McNeill an Under-Secretary at the Foreign Office. He said that staff examining German documents had so far concentrated on evidence for the Nuremberg trials. He then suggested that the Foreign Secretary would consider what use might be made of documents revealing the names and activities of British subjects.

11 December 1945, Victor Weisz 'Vicky', *News Chronicle*

"AMNESIA IS EASIER"

(Ribbentrop now claims to be suffering, like Hess, from amnesia-loss of memory.)

According to the *Lancashire Evening Post*: 'Ribbentrop's counsel said he had been having sleeping draughts for the last four years and these had affected his memory. Ribbentrop asked that the former Foreign Minister's ex-secretary, Margareta Blank, should help prepare his defence. He also asked permission for about six of his former Foreign Office assistants to be brought to Nuremberg to assist him. Lord Justice Lawrence said the request would be considered.'

27 December 1945, George Whitelaw, *Daily Herald*

Lighting the Fuse

Invited by President Truman to give a lecture at Westminster College in Fulton, Missouri, on 5 March, Churchill had used his speech to warn of Soviet duplicity: "From Stettin in the Baltic to Trieste in the Adriatic, an iron curtain has descended across the Continent." He claimed that this territory was subject to an "increasing measure of control from Moscow". This was "certainly not the liberated Europe we fought to build up. Nor is it one which contains the essentials of permanent peace."

7 March 1946, Fred Ellis, *Daily Worker* (United States)

RINGSIDE SEATS

In reaction to Churchill's 'Iron Curtain' speech, Stalin gave an interview to *Pravda* in which he labelled Churchill a 'warmonger'. The speech was, according to Stalin, 'a dangerous act, calculated to sow the seeds of discord among the allied states. In essence Mr Churchill and his friends in England and the USA have presented the non-English-speaking nations with something like an ultimatum: recognise our dominance voluntarily and then all will be in order; in the contrary case, war is inevitable.' The battle lines of the Cold War were already being drawn.'

11 March 1946, W. H. Woodburn 'Hengest', *Manchester Evening News*

THE FIRE HE STARTED

According to *Reuters*: 'Brought from a prison cell to give evidence for Goering, Field Marshal Kesselring, Hitler's commander in Italy, said the bombing of Rotterdam in May 1940, after the armistice negotiations, was a mistake owing to lack of radio communication with the planes. "Our photographs showed the bombing of Coventry was perfect." Kesselring said. He then astounded the Court with the statement. "I was happy that Coventry was selected as a target as it was an important military objective and was not to be hit by a terror attack. I myself examined the preparations. It was very simple. The night was clear and flying was easy. You could see what you hit. Missing the target was practically impossible."'

13 March 1946, George Whitelaw, *Daily Herald*

NURSERY RHYME

With the headline 'Hermann Goering Confesses,' the *Lancashire Daily Post* reported: '"As supreme commander of the German Air Force, I had to break the enemy's air strength," Goering told the Nuremberg War Crimes Tribunal. "Although the Führer wanted London attacked, I chose Coventry as the target because of my information that in and around Coventry the main part of Britain's aircraft industry was located." "We attacked London as a form of political pressure," he continued. "I did not consider it an attainable goal. I knew from the first world war that the people of London could take it, and that we could not break their military resistance that way."'

15 March 1946, William Furnival, *Lancashire Daily Post*

A REFRESHER COURSE

During the Nuremberg trials, the Nazis leaders in the dock were shown The Nazi Plan, a film compiled by US military personnel as evidence of their crimes. The film played an important role in making their incredibly horrendous crimes appear believable. The graphic footage of the Nazi concentration camps shocked both the defendants and the judges, who felt the need to temporary adjourn the trial.

18 May 1946, John Frith, *The Sydney Morning Herald* **(Australia)**

FOR WHOM THE BELL TOLLS

According to the Sunday Times: 'The British hangman, Albert Pierrepoint, has arrived at Nuremberg to carry out the executions of the condemned Nazis. Two American sergeants will assist him.' Pierrepoint was given the order to execute 13 Nazi war criminals in one day. Along with the commander of Bergen-Belsen concentration camp, he would also execute the "young 21-year-old blonde who used to carry a riding crop to beat inmates to death, as well as the doctor who decided who would go to the gas chambers and who be put to work.

29 September 1946, George Aria, *Sunday Sun* **(Sydney, Australia)**

Schacht to Papen: "Now, let's form a German democratic party"

At the Nuremberg trials, Schacht and Von Papen were found not guilty of all charges against them and acquitted. Both men were then tried at a German denazification court where they were sentenced to time in a labour camp. However, Von Papen was released immediately following appeals.

2 October 1946, Victor Weisz 'Vicky', *News Chronicle*

LIFE SENTENCE AFTER ALL

According to the *Gloucester Citizen*: 'The Soviet member of the Tribunal has put on record his dissent against the acquittal of Schacht, von Papen and Fritsche. The Russian Judge also dissented from the sentence on Hess. In the Soviet Judge's opinion Hess should have been sentenced to death and not life imprisonment. There was a possibility that Schacht, von Papen and Fritsche, to be discharged when the Tribunal finally adjourns, would be arrested by German authorities on their release to be tried before denazification courts.'

4 October 1946, George Whitelaw, *Daily Herald*

From Hot War to Cold War

COLD COMFORT

According to the *Belfast Newsletter*: 'Captain Noel Baker, who recently visited Spain, declared in the House of Commons there was real danger for Britain in his Majesty's Government's inactivity and apparent indifference towards the Spanish situation. Spain was in the grip of a tyrannical degenerate fascist administration and the longer Franco's dictatorship lasted, the greater the probability that it would end in bloodshed. It was not too late to save democracy in Spain but Britain must make her position clear. There must lie a threat of action and, if this failed, then action itself to convince Spain that this time Franco must go. The simplest method would be economic sanctions.'

On the day this cartoon was published, Hans Frank, Wilhelm Frick, Alfred Jodl, Ernst Kaltenbrunner, Wilhelm Keitel, Joachim von Ribbentrop, Alfred Rosenberg, Fritz Sauckel, Arthur Seyss-Inquart, and Julius Streicher were executed by hanging in the gymnasium of Nuremberg Prison.

16 October 1946, George Middleton, *Birmingham Gazette*

WOE AND ALAS

According to the *Daily Mail*: 'Marshal Stalin in answer to a series of questions put by an American news agency, has denied Mr Churchill's suggestion that Russia has 200 divisions on a war footing in occupied countries, and has put his former colleague of the Big Three conferences in the category of a "warmonger." To a question which asked what he thought was the most serious threat to world peace at present, Stalin is reported to have replied: "The warmongers, first among them Churchill and all those in Britain and the USA who think like him." The Russian leader said that he had only 60 divisions in Europe, the majority of which were not up to full strength. In two months' time they would be reduced to 40 divisions.'

29 October 1946, W. H. Woodburn 'Hengest', *Manchester Evening News*